Participating Witness

Princeton Theological Monograph Series

K. C. Hanson, Charles M. Collier, D. Christopher Spinks,
and Robin Parry, Series Editors

Recent volumes in the series:

Peter D. Neumann
Pentecostal Experience: An Ecumenical Encounter

Ashish J. Naidu
Transformed in Christ:
Christology and the Christian Life in John Chrysostom

Jamey Heit
Liturgical Liaisons
The Textual Body, Irony, and Betrayal in John Donne and Emily Dickinson

Gerry Schoberg
Perspectives of Jesus in the Writings of Paul
A Historical Examination of Shared Core Commitments with a View to
Determining the Extent of Paul's Dependence on Jesus

Larry D. Harwood
Denuded Devotion to Christ
The Ascetic Piety of Protestant True Religion in the Reformation

Jennifer Moberly
The Virtue of Bonhoeffer's Ethics
A Study of Dietrich Bonhoeffer's Ethics *in Relation to Virtue Ethics*

Anette I. Hagan
Eternal Blessedness for All?
A Historical-Systematic Examination of Schleiermacher's Understanding of
Predestination

Stephen M. Garrett
God's Beauty-in-Act
Participating in God's Suffering Glory

Participating Witness
*An Anabaptist Theology of Baptism
and the Sacramental Character of the Church*

ANTHONY G. SIEGRIST

☙PICKWICK *Publications* · Eugene, Oregon

PARTICIPATING WITNESS
An Anabaptist Theology of Baptism and the Sacramental Character of the Church

Princeton Theological Monograph Series 199

Copyright © 2013 Anthony G. Siegrist. All rights reserved. Except for brief quotations in critical publications or reviews, no part of this book may be reproduced in any manner without prior written permission from the publisher. Write: Permissions, Wipf and Stock Publishers, 199 W. 8th Ave., Suite 3, Eugene, OR 97401.

Pickwick Publications
An Imprint of Wipf and Stock Publishers
199 W. 8th Ave., Suite 3
Eugene, OR 97401

www.wipfandstock.com

ISBN 13: 978-71-62032-488-2

Cataloguing-in-Publication data:

Siegrist, Anthony G., 1979–

Participating witness : an anabaptist theology of baptism and the sacramental character of the church / Anthony G. Siegrist.

xxiv + 198 pp. ; 23 cm. Includes bibliographical references.

Princeton Theological Monograph Series 199

ISBN 13: 978-71-62032-488-2

1. Baptism—Anabaptists. 2. Anabaptists. 3. Anabaptists—Doctrines. I. Series. II. Title.

BV811.3 .S54 2013

Manufactured in the U.S.A.

Contents

Acknowledgments vii

Introduction ix

1. The Undoing of Baptism 1
2. In Favor of Ecclesial Mediation 27
3. On the Ecclesial Character of Divine Presence 62
4. The Spirit and the Problem of Fratricide 104
5. Baptism: A Theological and Liturgical Proposal 150

Bibliography 187

Acknowledgments

It is difficult to remember every person and institution that deserves thanks for assistance in the completion of this project. Even though I probably will not name everyone I should, I would like to express my gratitude to those who have been my companions through the various stages that led to the publication of this book. The roots of this project rest most evidently in my doctoral studies at Wycliffe College in the University of Toronto. I chose to study there because of the strong reputation of these institutions and in an effort to step outside the stultifying polarities that fracture so much of the theological landscape in the United States. I was not disappointed on either of these accounts. The fruitfulness of the ecumenical environment of the Toronto School of Theology and the hospitality of Wycliffe College is evident in the pages that follow. In Toronto I also benefited from the collegiality of the Toronto Mennonite Theological Centre, which was then under the leadership of Jim Reimer and Jeremy Bergen.

Beyond the institutions mentioned above, a variety of others have also supported me during my advanced theological studies. These include the Young Center for Anabaptist and Pietist Studies at Elizabethtown College, Eastern Mennonite Seminary, Prairie Bible College, and Lancaster Mennonite Conference. I spent the summer of 2007 as a fellow at the Young Center. There, Donald Kraybill prompted me to think more seriously about the role Amish initiation practices might play in this project. I am also thankful to Eastern Mennonite Seminary and the faculty there that encouraged me to consider advanced studies, specifically Professors Nate Yoder and Mark Thiessen Nation. Without their influence I would probably not be writing from within the Anabaptist tradition. I trust that the quality of my work gives them little cause for regret, though I am sure that both will take issue with some of the specifics of my argument. I am appreciatively teaching at Prairie because of the flexibility of several administrators willing to accommodate my doctoral studies and ongoing scholarship. The staff of the T. S. Rendell Library has been most helpful in chasing down resources. Many students have asked me good questions and inquired about what it is I'm working on

Acknowledgments

when my office door is closed. Being pressed to describe my work has helped me pursue clarity, whether or not I have been successful is another matter.

I intend this exercise in theological reflection to be grounded in the actual practice of Christian community. While my approach may not quite be characterized by the traditional phrase *lex orandi, lex credendi*, it shares that sentiment. The book as a whole is a statement of intellectual deference to those communities of faith and worship in which I have participated. I am particularly grateful for the uncommon fidelity of River Corner Mennonite and St. Barnabas Anglican. Life in these communities has not been perfect, but I remain thankful for their lived witness to the gospel. If there are points in this project where the ideas I attempt to synthesize seem impossibly disparate, it is because I am grappling with the breadth of the Christian tradition symbolized by these two congregations, which are separated by an international border, several time zones, and a chasm of tradition. There are other churches that have been formative in my life. I think specifically of those I participated in as a student. Their hospitality sustained my faith. It is also the reason I tell my students that the study of Christian theology is only half-hearted if it is not pursued beyond the classroom and the library: shared meals and worship are also occasions for learning to talk rightly about God.

Participating Witness began as a doctoral dissertation written under the supervision of Professor Joseph Mangina. His advice had the uncommon quality of being both patient and incisive. Along with Jim Reimer and George Sumner, Joe helped me clarify what it was that I was trying to say. That fact that two of my committee members were Anglicans pushed me to understand my own tradition more clearly. The attention of a number of other readers has helped me avoid needless errors. David Nadeau, Karl Koop, Reid Locklin, William Kervin, David Siegrist, Jeremy Bergen, and Ruth Sesink Bott have each read the manuscript at one point or another. I am thankful for their feedback. I am also thankful for the publishing expertise of the folks at Wipf & Stock. The errors that remain are my own.

This project could not have been completed without the ongoing encouragement of friends, family, colleagues, and students. Yet I am indebted to Sarah most of all. There is nothing I can write to adequately express my thanks for her companionship. Thanks also to Amos and Elias for being part of our family. They both add so much.

Introduction

THE VAST MAJORITY OF Christian communities began baptizing infants at some point during the four centuries after the faith transcended the boundaries of its Jewish origins. In the West, pockets of dissent existed throughout the Medieval era, but it was the Radical Reformation of the sixteenth century that forcefully reopened the question. In the wake of works critical of received sacramental theology such as Martin Luther's *The Babylonian Captivity of the Church*, Anabaptists of that period searched the Scriptures with newly critical eyes.[1] Following the models of Luther and Ulrich Zwingli they arrived at a position more discontinuous from the received tradition than did any of the Magisterial Reformers. Debate and contradictory practice persists within Christianity to our own time. A variety of strong biblical and theological arguments have been advanced on both sides. The exchange between Oscar Cullman and Karl Barth is a classic example.[2] The clash of theological giants, to say nothing of the endless debates in the pew and on the web, has failed to settle the issue. And even though some representatives of both sides have lately exhibited remarkable flexibility, the disagreement remains intractable.

The *Baptism, Eucharist and Ministry* document, produced by the World Council of Churches in 1982 and still one of the most important contemporary statements on baptism, engages this obvious ecumenical problem. It affirms the goal of mutual recognition of baptism across lines of church division and advocates that, where it is possible, "mutual recognition should be expressed explicitly by the churches."[3] Toward this end it advises,

> In order to overcome their differences, believer baptists and those who practice infant baptism should reconsider certain aspects of their practices. The first may seek to express more visibly the fact that children are placed under the protection of God's

1. Luther, *Babylonian Captivity*.
2. Cullman, *Baptism in the New Testament*; Barth, *Regarding Baptism*.
3. *Baptism, Eucharist and Ministry*, 6.

Introduction

grace. The latter must guard themselves against the practice of apparently indiscriminate baptism and take more seriously their responsibility for the nurture of baptized children to mature commitment to Christ.[4]

This is valuable counsel expressed in an important forum, yet it is also demonstration of the fact that despite important commonalities, the deep differences over baptism are not going to be resolved in the near future. It is now time to forgo attempts to prove one traditional form of the practice right or wrong and to pursue instead how baptism might aid us in the task of being faithful Christian communities in an era marked by fracture. Even though sociological and political tectonics may yet destabilize the divide, the working assumption of this book is that the gift of unity on this issue has not yet been granted to the church. Each way of understanding and practicing baptism possesses an internal theological coherence, but neither can be rightly elucidated according to the assumptions of the opposing view. This is evidenced by the protraction of the debate and the ancient legacy of each tradition. Therefore, even though the divisive practice of baptism presents the issue with which this book wrestles, my argument will be developed in such a way as to avoid both tired polemics and undue ecumenical optimism.

Tradition is better understood as a vine than as a tree. At least that is what one inheritor of the Radical Reformation legacy, Mennonite theologian John Howard Yoder, has suggested. His point is that a productive vine's health is not maintained through untended organic growth. It requires careful pruning.[5] This is the type of work I intend to take up here. Even though the major division over baptism is not one that can be "fixed," attentive pruning of each branch is needed. In the context of North American Anabaptism, developments related to the practice of baptism require just such attention. This is because the working theology of baptism suffers from a deficient account of divine action, especially as mediated through the church. This project's goal is to develop resources to mend this weakness, and in so doing to strengthen the key Anabaptist distinctive of believers' baptism. Toward this end I will draw not only on the Anabaptist tradition, but also on a range of theological resources related to the sacraments and ecclesiology. This project probes the integrity of the current practice and theological construal of believers' baptism within the wider web of Ana-

---

4. *Baptism, Eucharist and Ministry*, 6.
5. Yoder, *Priestly Kingdom*, 69.

Introduction

baptist life and thought. In response to problematic developments I will attempt to ground baptism in a doctrine of God and an ecclesiology that is practical and Trinitarian, concrete and Anabaptist. The jumble of genealogies and contemporary alliances that make up Christianity is so deep and impenetrable that to speak of any substantial theological project as merely Christian is simply unworkable; therefore, readers should know that this book's argument is intentionally developed within the Anabaptist tradition. Yet I do hope this volume contributes to the ecumenical conversation on baptism, and throughout it I will offer hints about ways my analysis might apply beyond its intended focus on the beliefs and practices of North American Anabaptist communities.

ASSUMPTIONS

This book is an exercise in constructive theological reflection. I could elaborate on this in various ways, but Thomas Aquinas captures many of the implications near the beginning of his *Summa Theologica* when he writes, "As other sciences do not argue in proof of their principles, but argue from their principles to demonstrate other truths in these sciences: so this doctrine does not argue in proof of its principles, which are the articles of faith, but from them it goes on to prove something else."[6] It seems to me that Thomas worked under the assumption that the creator of the universe is indeed self-revealing and has commissioned human creatures to reflect on this fact. Working within such a frame allows the theologian to move with all due humility beyond description of historical or social phenomena toward constructive and normative applications. In recent Anabaptist scholarship the church's practices have often been analyzed from historical or sociological perspectives. In this project I intend a deeper, dogmatic treatment. This means that my analysis and constructive proposal will not shy away from the center of Christian theology—the doctrine of God. This does not mean that the themes opened up here are hopelessly abstract. This book is after all intended for the betterment of concrete worshiping communities and the ways they respond to the One without whom nothing would be.

Several other assumptions support the argument of this book. One stems from the observation that the communities I seek to address are still trying to find ways to adjust to their post-Christendom context. Gone are

---

6. Aquinas, *Summa Theologica*, I.q1.a8 (5). Numbers in parentheses refer to the page number(s) of the ET.

Introduction

the days when churches could pretend to control the society in which they found themselves. A related observation is that this project is being undertaken in an age of dying denominationalism. This is one of the reasons for my deliberate ecumenical tone. I assume that even though theology rightly acquires local inflection, listening to the voices of the broader tradition, past and present, is an essential part of the theologian's task. As we attend to voices less like our own, our most pressing concerns are given new texture. It is precisely such cross-tradition pollination that holds the promise of a Christianity capable of bearing faithful witness to Christ in this new and relatively uncharted age after the death of Christendom.[7] Specifically in this case, if it was not for the witness of pedobaptist traditions the critique that follows might never have been conceived. One final assumption is worth naming directly: initiatives of repentance and reconciliation between denominations that at one time denounced or even fought one another represent new conversations and point to avenues of learning and unity that did not exist a mere fifty years ago.[8] The appreciation given to believers' baptism by the *Baptism, Eucharist and Ministry* document, as well as the impact of the Rite of Christian Initiation of Adults developed by the Roman Catholic Church demonstrate parallel liturgical developments. It is with these factors in mind that this project's focus on contemporary Anabaptism will be deliberately interwoven with ecumenical threads that were simply not available to a previous generation of scholars.

THEMES

This book is about the church's practice of baptism. In various ways the argument that follows will position itself conceptually with reference to two traditional ways of understanding the practices of the church. I will refer to these as the "testimonial" and "sacramental" approaches. In the former, the ordinances are understood to point to the work of Christ and involve Christians subjectively. In the latter, God is understood to make direct use of these rites to affect Christians more objectively. Both reject an approach

---

7. On this point George Lindbeck's work is especially helpful. See especially "Ecumenism and the Future of Belief."

8. Here I am thinking of both official acts of reconciliation and ongoing unofficial dialogues between various Anabaptist groups and the Roman Catholic, Swiss Reformed, and Lutheran churches. For one concrete example see G. Schlabach, ed., *On Baptism*. Also see Enns, "Believers Church Ecclesiology," 107–24.

Introduction

that might be called "spiritualist." In the spiritualist perspective, all rituals and practices are viewed with suspicion. Rites such as baptism are considered unnecessary or virtually so because the core of the Christian faith is believed to be interior, to be occupied with analyzing the invisible soul's posture before the invisible God. The conceptual fulcrum that activates spiritualist approaches to traditional church practices is the assumption that the eternal/temporal and holy/profane dichotomies are equivalent to a spiritual/physical dichotomy. The spiritualist approach was embraced by some early Anabaptists and forms of it are still upheld among branches of the Religious Society of Friends, the Salvation Army, and some Evangelical and Anabaptist groups. Spiritualism in its various forms holds that physical acts like rituals are at best a distant outworking of the more meaningful and determinative inner life, which is thought to have access to God that is direct and unmediated.

Most streams of Christianity have rejected the spiritualist approach. One reason for this is that it does not seem to take seriously enough the Eucharistic command of Jesus to "Do this in remembrance of me."[9] More generally, spiritualism appears insensitive to God's approval of the material world and the embodied character of human creatures. Despite the fundamental nature of these critiques, the place of formal practices in many Anabaptist congregations remains tenuous. Irma Fast Dueck, writing from her vantage point as a faculty member at a Mennonite university, has noticed among her students what she calls an ongoing "lack of ritual sensibility." She suggests, "There may be an implicit assumption that somehow the rites and rituals of the church belong to less mature stages of human development, destined for obsolescence by the triumph of reason. Or perhaps there is a suspicion of rituals and the rites of the church as somewhat pagan, magical, or idolatrous. Or, quite possibly, the way we engage in the ritual fails to capture the theological imagination of those observing the practice." She concludes, "No matter what the reason, many of those in the Believers Church tradition are left to sustain meaningful baptismal practices against this lack of ritual sensibility."[10] This project will endeavor to overturn such minimizations of baptism, seeking to cultivate what Fast Dueck calls a "baptismal ecology." This means that I will attend most closely to the dynamics of the two central Christian construals of baptism, the testimonial and sacramental approaches.

---

9. Luke 22:19. Unless otherwise noted, biblical quotations are taken from the NRSV.
10. Fast Dueck, "(Re)learning to Swim in Baptismal Waters," 240.

Introduction

The disparity between these two ways of construing Christianity's central rites marks the divide of vast ecclesial watersheds. Each encompasses both great rivers of tradition and numerous lesser streams of practical and ideological variance. There are also commonalities. In the first place, both affirm that baptism is a sign. Its function is not limited to the physical dirt or germs that water might remove. In other words, both affirm in some way the twin Augustinian descriptions of a sacrament as a "visible sign of an invisible grace" and as a "visible word."[11] Second, each affirms, though in significantly different ways, that baptism involves the coming together of the actions of God and those of human creatures. Neither position denies the importance of human dependence on God or God's empowering recognition of human activity. Third, both affirm the public nature of baptism. Baptism is understood to be public in that it is never practiced by a lone individual and always invokes the historical and concrete nature of the church. Fourth, both acknowledge the importance of a relative similarity in form. For most Christian communities, regardless of whether they involve infants or not, baptism involves a ritual washing in the name of the Father, the Son, and the Spirit. The fifth and final basic commonality is the assumption that baptism is carried out in obedience to the command of Jesus. The divisive question is what this means. Thus in a parallel debate about communion, Jesus' words in the Gospel of Luke are much debated: "This is my body, which is given for you. Do this in remembrance of me."[12] The tension lies between the words "is" and "remembrance." Despite the significant commonalities, the testimonial and sacramental approaches diverge.

Sacramental theology, to even the initiated, can appear to be more than a neatly defined watershed; including the Reformed, Lutheran, Anglican, and Catholic traditions, it seems to be a whole world unto itself.[13] One access point into the jumbled folds of this landscape can be found in Robert Jenson's claim: "The word in which God communicates himself must be an embodied word, a word 'with' some visible reality, a grant of divine objectivity. We must be able to see and touch what we are to apprehend from god; religion cannot do without sacrament."[14] The Anglican *Book of Common Prayer* provides another point of entry through its com-

---

11. Migliore, *Faith Seeking Understanding*, 279.

12. Luke 22:19; Matt 26:26–28; Mark 14:22–24; 1 Cor 11:24–25.

13. A helpful overview of the history and lines of tension in the sacramental tradition can be found in Fahey, "Sacraments."

14. Jenson, *Visible Words*, 28.

Introduction

monly affirmed definition that sacraments are "outward and visible signs of inward and spiritual grace, given by Christ as sure and certain means by which we receive that grace."[15] In a sacramental understanding of baptism the individual is acted upon; she receives a gift.

The etymological background of the term "sacrament" is slippery. Though it seems to originally have been used to refer to the oath of allegiance given by a soldier to his commander, its common usage in the Christian tradition, with the exception of Tertullian's early employment of the term, bears little resemblance. The language is conflicted significantly because of the Vulgate's use of "sacrament" in instances when a more apt translation might be something like "mystery." Most scholars agree that although the notion of a sacrament is older than Augustine's use of it, his rather fluid theology of the sacraments is the baseline for subsequent development in the West. The Augustinian view is that a sacrament is a visible sign of an invisible grace, and each one pertains to the *magnum sacramentum mysterium*, Christ and the church. In the twelfth century Hugh of St. Victor added nuance to the traditional Augustinian description by providing, according to Leonard Vander Zee, "a distinction between what might be called a general sign, one thing merely pointing to another, and a sacramental sign, which also confers the reality to which the sign points."[16] Seven sacraments were then thought to fall under the standard medieval definition of a "sign which brings about what it signifies." This was made more pointed through the traditional phrase *efficient significando*, which presses sacraments "bring about what they signify *precisely by signifying it*."[17]

The nature of the sacraments was furiously debated during the Protestant Reformation, both in the parting of ways between the reformers and medieval sacramental theology and between the Protestant leaders themselves. Most famous is the contentious debate, only distantly related to this project, about the doctrine of the real presence of Christ in the Eucharist. Though Luther rejected descriptions dependent on Aristotelian metaphysics, he opposed Zwingli's more radical approach. For Luther the concept of promise was central to his understanding of the sacraments. In *The Babylonian Captivity* he argues that even though all of Scripture can be described as either a command or a promise, "[I]t has seemed proper to restrict the

---

15. *Book of Common Prayer*, 857.
16. Vander Zee, *Recovering the Sacraments for Evangelical Worship*, 29.
17. Yeago, "Apostolic Faith," 2:177.

name of sacrament to those promises which have signs attached to them."[18] Ultimately, this means that there are only two sacraments. In this same text Luther rejects the traditional sacramental assumption that the sacraments are effective in themselves, *ex opera operato*, or "by the work performed," because he believes that a sacrament is only effective if it is received in faith.[19] Despite these and other ways in which Luther revised sacramental theology, for contemporary Lutherans it remains of paramount importance that God acts "in, with, and under" these rites. David Yeago further explains this axiom: "On the one hand, the reality of the sacraments cannot be accounted for simply in terms of their efficacy as human communal acts of verbal and more-than-verbal communication; in the sacrament, we encounter the present saving action of *God*. On the other hand, this action of God is not *separable* from the ceremonial action of the community; it is indeed *through* the public significance of what the church does that the action of God becomes concretely identifiable and *experienceable,* and so draws us into lived communion with God."[20] The agency of the church and the agency of God are inseparable since the church makes the sign apparent and God grants that which is signified.

The emphasis is slightly different in Reformed theology where the terminology of "sign" and "seal" dominates.[21] In his *Institutes* Calvin describes a sacrament as "an outward sign by which the Lord seals on our consciences the promises of his good will toward us in order to sustain the weakness of our faith; and we in turn attest our piety toward him in the presence of the Lord and of his angels before men."[22] Thus, in this view, a sacrament is a sign or pledge of inclusion in the grace of the new covenant.

From the view of the church as the enactor of these signs it can be said that through the power of the Spirit the sacraments are a means of participating in the work of Christ. In the sacraments God's promise of his presence in the midst of the church is taken to apply in a particular way to practices ordained by Jesus.[23] For the basic purpose of this typology the determinative characteristic that I wish to carry forward is that *through the grace of God a sacramental sign effects what it signifies.* Thus, an eccle-

---

18. Luther, *Babylonian Captivity,* 124.
19. Ibid., 67.
20. Yeago, "Apostolic Faith," 177.
21. As derived from Rom 4:11.
22. Calvin, *Institutes,* 1277.
23. See for example Matt 18:20 and John 14:17.

Introduction

sial practice such as baptism can be understood to be regenerative when rightly practiced precisely because God works in, with, and under what the church does. A sacramental understanding of baptism places emphasis on the objective nature of the event—something happens *to* the candidate. This is made most poignant in Protestant sacramental thought, which emphasizes the objectivity of grace by describing sacraments as effective signs. In contrast to the rather vague implications of the Augustinian visible sign, the Protestant description identifies them as events in which God's grace is assuredly encountered precisely because it is made visible and audible. Though Protestant theology holds that faithful reception is necessary for these rituals to be effective, the origin of their efficacy lies beyond the persons involved. Therefore, as a sacrament, baptism is to be received as a gift. This is most obvious in the case of infants, but in a sacramental view all persons are to come to Jesus precisely as children.

The testimonial approach to baptism is more popular in Anabaptist, charismatic, Baptist, and independent evangelical communities. It is often signaled by describing baptism as an ordinance instead of as a sacrament. It is regularly paired with the celebration of "communion," instead of the sacrament of the Eucharist. The popularity of this approach among Anabaptists and related groups is due in part to the influence of the sixteenth-century reformer Ulrich Zwingli. Zwingli's view of the sacraments differed from Luther's in that he was generally much more skeptical about the value of outward signs. Though his position on the sacraments is somewhat fluid, the central feature of his view is that the sign cannot participate in what it signifies. Thus a sacrament is something like a pledge or a badge of allegiance sown on a soldier's garment. Zwingli writes: "a sacrament is nothing else than an initiatory ceremony or a pledging. For just as those who were about to enter upon litigation deposited a certain amount of money, which could not be taken away except by the winner, so those who are initiated by sacraments bind and pledge themselves, and, as it were, seal a contract not to draw back."[24] A testimonial approach to baptism parallels a memorialist approach to communion, or the Lord's Supper, as a response to sacerdotalism. In a testimonial construal baptism is taken to be a communicative act, a public statement, on the part of the baptizand in response to the prior saving work of God. As a "testimony" to this work, its effectiveness depends upon the disposition of the one being baptized. In this vein, Baptist theologians Brad Harper and Paul Louis Metzger write: "On

---

24. As quoted in Stephens, *Huldrych Zwingli*, 183.

Introduction

our view, water baptism does not regenerate anyone. However, baptism by water serves as a participatory sign in salvation history, functioning as a creaturely pointer to God's saving actions in our lives."[25] It is important to realize, that although in the testimonial view baptism is understood to be a more subjective practice than it is in a sacramental view, on account of its ordination by Jesus it is still believed to be indispensable for the church.

According to the testimonial view nothing happens to the baptismal candidates in the ceremonial washing; however, their proclamation is a necessary response to what God has already done in their lives. By undergoing baptism they proclaim they have been called, forgiven, and cleansed by God, and they pledge to live in ways congruent with this. Here the notion of "pledge" functions opposite to the way it does in the Reformed view. For the Baptist theologian Stanley Grenz thinking of ordinances as "acts of commitment" actually affirms the original meaning of the term sacrament.[26] In a sweeping way the testimonial approach can be distinguished from the sacramental in that, while it assumes that God has acted redemptively in Jesus and that God continues to call people to a saving relationship with himself, baptism itself is a human act alone. Instead of participating in what God does, *an ordinance such as baptism is a response to God's prior gift of faith*. In this view even though baptism is generally undertaken in an ecclesial context, it is an individual response that follows a personal faith commitment.

If we shift our focus from this historical topography and consider more specifically how contemporary theologies of believers' baptism might be mapped, we can observe the timeworn divide from a different aspect. Millard Erickson, a Baptist, describes baptism as "an act of faith and a testimony that one has been united with Christ in his death and resurrection, that one has experienced spiritual circumcision. It is a public indication of one's commitment to Christ."[27] Meanwhile Joe Jones, from the Disciples of Christ tradition, writes: "As an act of the church [as opposed to the baptizee], the act of baptizing is a legitimate means of grace inasmuch as it leads to the life of appropriating God's grace in sanctification and emancipation in the life of the nurturing church."[28] In these two examples we see the disparity within the Believers Church family at its widest.

---

25. Harper and Metzger, *Exploring Ecclesiology*, 141.
26. Grenz, *Theology for the Community*, 516.
27. Erickson, *Christian Theology*, 1110.
28. Jones, *A Grammar of Christian Faith*, 2:667.

Introduction

There are those who take mediating positions. Grenz, though a Baptist like Erickson, demonstrates a bit keener attention to the power of symbols. Grenz treats baptism under the heading of "Acts of Commitment." He understands these acts, baptism and the Lord's Supper particularly, as oaths of allegiance. These are "enacted pictures or symbols of God's grace given in Christ," and through them Christians "act out [their] faith."[29] A third Baptist theologian, Jim McClendon, leans toward the sacramental view when he construes baptism as a "performative sign."[30]

Two prominent Mennonite theologians also stand between the far poles marked by Erickson and Jones. In his short book *Body Politics* John Howard Yoder emphasizes the socio-political function of baptism. He treats four other ecclesial practices similarly. He believes that all are "actions of God, in and with, through, and under what men and women do." Yoder writes, "Where they are happening, the people of God is real in the world."[31] Yoder's approach is an attempt to mitigate against a deep leaning within Anabaptist theology toward "rationalism," a word I use here nontechnically, that runs the whole way back to the early Swiss Anabaptists' affinity with the Zwinglian movement. This sort of rationalism denies out of hand, in ways that go beyond Zwingli, the possibility of Christ's presence in and through the practices of the church. As I will argue later, this hems in the witness of Scripture and screws down tightly the lid on what we think is possible. A more recent Mennonite treatment of the subject can be found in Thomas Finger's *A Contemporary Anabaptist Theology*. In this book he covers baptism under the heading, "The Communal Dimension." Here Finger follows the early Anabaptist leader Pilgrim Marpeck in seeking to articulate an understanding of the sacrament that links the inner baptism of the Spirit with the outer baptism of water. He pairs this approach with contemporary ecumenical developments to describe the possibilities of a growing convergence between historically divided Christian communities.[32] Finger raises concerns about the risks of a traditional Anabaptist emphasis on the voluntary individual. His concern is one that this project will attempt to take seriously. It echoes that of the systematic theologian Robert Jenson, who writes, "baptism, first, lets the gospel be *unconditional* and, second,

---

29. Grenz, *Theology for the Community*, 516.

30. McClendon, "Baptism as a Performative Sign," 403–16; also see his *Doctrine*, 2:386–406.

31. Yoder, *Body Politics*, 72–73.

32. Finger, *Contemporary Anabaptist Theology*, 158–83.

Introduction

prevents the separation of faith from *community*."[33] Both Yoder and Finger are willing to use sacramental terminology.[34] Their work, along with that of a few others, hints at another of this book's themes, which is that Anabaptist theology invites an approach that is not easily captured by either of the pure traditional types. The description of baptism toward which the following chapters move will be attentive to the gifts that various approaches bring to the contemporary church. It will gather momentum by striving to resist the temptation to consider baptism abstracted from the actual existence of the church or detached from its proper dogmatic location.

To take up the theological task is to work within the medium of words. This can only be done with a combination of boldness and humility, endeavoring to point toward a God who is not embarrassed to be described with such tools but whose being such tools are incapable of spanning. In preparing this manuscript I have often been reminded of these limitations. In spite of this, I seek to use certain terms in deliberate ways. For example, the terms "Jesus" and "Christ" will be used interchangeably to communicate the assumption that the Jesus of history is not separable from the Christ of faith. The term "church" will be used at times to indicate the community catholic and at others to describe local congregations. I am unconvinced that a neat separation of the two is relevant to the ontology of Christ's body. When I speak of the church in a nonspecific way I usually intend the reference to be broadly understood, not merely referring to what occurs under the official auspices of specific denominations. The term "practice" will be often used to describe baptism in a generic sense. The terms "sacrament" and "ordinance" will be used with the specificity described earlier: the term "sacrament" applied to the practice in question to indicate that it effects what it signifies and the term "ordinance" when it functions only as a testimony to the work of Christ. If the terms "sign" or "symbol" are used in technical ways this will be noted. Beyond these specific terms I will employ some variety in references to baptism (i.e. "rite," "ritual," "ceremony") to avoid a false confidence in the categorical distinctions of pure types. It seems to me that behind official denominational statements and confessional clarity churns the instability of congregational life in which the church's practices are understood in numerous ways and with little consistency. I hope the raggedness of terminology at times communicates this.

---

33. Jenson, *Visible Words*, 147.

34. Yoder, *Body Politics*, 72–73, 44–46; and Finger, *Christian Theology*, 2:331–51, as well as *Contemporary Anabaptist Theology*, 158–83.

Introduction

At other points in this book the inconsistency of language is more regrettable. For example, while inclusive language will be used with respect to humanity, masculine pronouns are sometimes used with respect to God as this seems to be the only way to maintain the personhood and relationality of the Trinity. My assumption, though, is that such terms function analogically to describe the relationships of the triune God. They say little if anything about God's gender or disposition. Lastly, at various times the focal community and thematic anchor of this study will be described as Christian, Believers Church, Anabaptist, or Mennonite. Some readers might even find evidence of my roots in the Swiss Mennonite tradition. These communities and the terms employed to name them are used to narrow or broaden the field of discourse at important points. The narrowing is not intended to be exclusive, but rather to clarify the participants in the conversation and the dynamics under analysis. It is impossible to fully represent the diversity of views held by those within any of these groups, and therefore it should be recognized that ultimately the argument presented here is my own.

SEQUENCE

This project will proceed in three stages. The first, consisting of the first two chapters, is descriptive and analytical. Here I make the case that believers' baptism must be reconceived. The first chapter focuses on the problematic phenomenon of young children being baptized in Anabaptist contexts and explores the theological assumptions that enable it. The second chapter furthers the analysis of the first by critiquing two alternatives to ecclesial mediation, which is the conceptual correction I propose. It also presents an outline of this concept in dialogue with the work of Karl Barth and John Howard Yoder. Though the analysis of denominational statements and confessions at various points in these first two chapters risks being tedious, it is essential to my approach that this book grapple with the practices and beliefs of actual communities instead of merely batting about the views of one theologian or another.

The second stage of the project will pick up where the constructive gestures in the first leave off and work toward an understanding of baptism through the larger topic of the relationship of the church to the second and third persons of the Trinity. The third chapter considers the work of Pilgram Marpeck alongside that of Dietrich Bonhoeffer to explore how

Introduction

Anabaptist communities might affirm that the church's life is in some sense sacramental, that it constitutes God's effective presence in the world. Here I propose that baptism be understood as a participating witness, a revision of Marpeck's view. The next chapter opens with a description of a highly formative Anabaptist text, the *Martyrs Mirror,* and argues that God's work through the church cannot be divorced from questions of the Spirit's presence in this conflicted body across time. I suggest that even though this issue has been particularly challenging for Anabaptists, addressing it is crucial for a coherent construal of baptismal practice. Both of these chapters attempt to anchor believers' baptism in the doctrine of God.

The third stage of this project moves from the theology proper discussed in the previous two chapters to a set of concrete recommendations. In this fifth and final chapter, I expand my description of baptism as a participating witness and, in conversation with ancient sources, propose a way of practicing baptism that can better serve the church and its new members.

My aim in this book is to make a contribution to the practical and intellectual life of the church. While the Anabaptist tradition claims roots in the Radical wing of the Protestant Reformation, it tacitly claims historical affinity with various movements and groups reaching back to the first century. Despite this long legacy of lived Christianity, Anabaptists have produced little critical theological reflection. I hope to contribute here to the newly blossoming body of literature written by those reflecting on Christian belief and practice from an Anabaptist perspective. A logical implication of this project for the Anabaptist community would be the conviction that our politics and ethics should be formed, and indeed could be greatly enriched by, bringing to bear a broader set of doctrines and practices than the more traditional, and I think highly reductive, methodological axioms of biblicism or non-violence. The ethical undissmissablity of non-violence will not be challenged here; however, it has become clear that this ethic alone is inadequate for developing a positive account of the life of Christian communities. The fruitfulness of the memory inherited in the full range of practices that make up Anabaptist life must be re-investigated to resource Christian faithfulness in our emerging post-Christendom context. Furthermore, since a broad group of Christians share the practice of believers' baptism with Anabaptists, I intend this work to participate in conversations ranging across traditional lines of division because such networks are increasingly needed to sustain the performance of the Christian life.

Introduction

The current disinclination of younger people toward denominational loyalty and the ongoing decline of previously dominant denominations make the future shape of the church in North America difficult to discern. However, cross-pollination between traditions and an ongoing transience among members likely means that old boundaries between communities will become fuzzier. As the rigidity and independence of traditional theological streams fragments, an opportunity will exist for Anabaptist theology to have a significant voice in describing how local church communities can maintain integrity in a disestablished context. In this spirit, this project hopes to bend itself toward anticipating the needs of Anabaptist-like communities that are at the forefront of a re-formation of the Christian tradition. In addition, I hope that this book will contribute to a growing body of scholarship related to Christian liturgy and practices not confined to communities that practice believers' baptism. Specifically, I hope to further the possibility of a form of ecumenical engagement that moves beyond, while not dismissing, the traditional contentious, polemical debates. Finally, my hope is that this work of Anabaptist theology will contribute to a renewed practice of believers' baptism and a greater understanding of the significance of related practices. In such a spirit this project inquires after the apostle Paul's unitary vision, in which baptism plays a crucial role: "For just as the body is one and has many members, and all the members of the body, though many, are one body, so it is with Christ. For in the one Spirit we were all baptized into one body—Jews or Greeks, slaves or free—and we were all made to drink of one Spirit."[35]

---

35. 1 Cor 12:12–13.

1

The Undoing of Baptism

> Jesus said, "Let the little children come to me, and do not stop them; for it is to such as these that the kingdom of heaven belongs." And he laid his hands on them and went on his way.
>
> (MATT 19:14)

FLANNERY O'CONNOR WAS A Catholic Christian and one of the most distinguished twentieth-century American writers of fiction. One of her short stories, "The River," provides a provocative and disturbing picture of the baptism of a child. O'Connor's story functions like a parable, drawing our attention to the issues raised by the baptism of children. I recount it here not as the basis for an argument, but as a heuristic for investigating what is at stake in this book's thesis.[1]

"The River" takes place, as many of O'Connor's stories do, in the religiously flamboyant American South. It begins with a young boy, a child of dissolute parents, being taken by his sitter to a "healing," an informal revival service featuring a charismatic traveling preacher. On the way there the sitter told the boy that he had been made by a carpenter named Jesus. This was a surprise, as the boy had always assumed it had been a fat doctor

---

1. The following summary is taken from O'Connor's short story, "The River," 157–74. O'Connor engages similar themes in a more extended format in her book, *The Violent Bear It Away*. Fredrick C. Bauerschmidt reflects briefly on O'Connor's "The River" in the context of baptism in "Baptism in the Diaspora," 16–61. In "The River" the child's name and subsequent re-naming is given theological significance. Since I cannot explore this here, I simply avoid mentioning the child's name at all.

Participating Witness

with a moustache. He thought that maybe his parents were joking about the doctor. O'Connor tells us, "They joked a lot where he lived. If he had thought about it before, he would have thought Jesus Christ was a word like 'oh' or 'damn' or 'God,' or maybe somebody who had cheated them out of something sometime."[2] The preacher's rhetorical gifts and rumours of his healing powers had begun to attract a following. A crowd of curious onlookers gathered at the side of a river to observe this spectacle. The banks of the river served as a sort of outdoor amphitheatre accentuating the dynamism of his words; the river itself became a metaphor for the preacher's pronouncements. He spoke to the gathering crowd: "There ain't but one river and that's the River of Life, made out of Jesus' Blood. That's the river you have to lay your pain in, in the River of Faith, in the River of Life, in the River of Love, in the rich red river of Jesus' Blood . . . !"[3] He told the people that the river was the one that healed the leprous, gave sight to the blind, and even brought the dead to life. "This old red river is good to Baptize in, good to lay your faith in, good to lay your pain in," he told them.[4]

As the singing and preaching reached a natural pause, the sitter called out to the preacher, telling him that the child with her was in need of his help. In trying to figure out what exactly the boy needed, the preacher asked him if he'd ever been baptized. The child, lacking any real religious schooling, didn't know the meaning of the word. "'If I Baptize you,' the preacher pronounced, 'you'll be able to go to the Kingdom of Christ. You'll be washed in the river of suffering, son, and you'll go by the deep river of life. Do you want that'?"[5] The child said, "Yes." He didn't want to go back to his parents' apartment; he wanted to go under the water. Events unfolded quickly: "Suddenly the preacher said, 'All right, I'm going to Baptize you now', and without more warning, he tightened his hold and swung him upside down and plunged his head into the water. He held him under while he said the words of Baptism and then he jerked him up again and looked sternly at the gasping child . . . 'You count now', the preacher said. 'You didn't even count before.'"[6]

The next morning the boy woke up back in his apartment. His parents were still asleep, paying for a late night of inebriated socializing. The child scrounged a breakfast, using whatever his short body could reach in

2. O'Connor, "The River," 163.
3. Ibid., 165.
4. Ibid., 166.
5. Ibid., 168.
6. Ibid.

the kitchen. As he waited alone for his parents, the child realized what he wanted to do. He stole a streetcar token and a half packet of lifesavers from his mother's purse and made the journey back to the exact spot beside the river where the previous day's events had unfolded. As O'Connor says, "He intended not to fool with preachers any more but to Baptize himself and to keep on going this time until he found the Kingdom of Christ in the river. He didn't mean to waste any more time. He put his head under the water at once and pushed forward."[7] He gasped for air and sputtered. Pushing his head back under the water he tried again:

> He stopped and thought suddenly: it's another joke, it's just another joke! He thought how far he had come for nothing and he began to hit and splash and kick the filthy river. His feet were already treading on nothing. He gave a low cry of pain and indignation . . . . He plunged under once and this time, the waiting current caught him like a long gentle hand and pulled him swiftly forward and down. For an instant he was overcome with surprise: then since he was moving quickly and knew that he was getting somewhere, all the fury and fear left him.[8]

Despite the well-intended efforts of a passerby the boy never surfaced—the river swept him away.

BAPTISM AMONG ANABAPTISTS

In O'Connor's story the child's belief in the efficacy of baptism stands sharply contrasted to contemporary nonchalance. For the early Anabaptists, as is still the case for some around the globe today, baptism was an act of obedience to Jesus that could cost one's life, yet in North America this same rite is easily carried out. If baptism was once a matter of life and death, here and now it seems to be no longer the case. The story of the drowned child is striking because we find it unbelievable that baptism would be taken so seriously.

An Evolving Practice

One of the most vivid moments in the origin of the modern practice of believers' baptism occurred in Zurich in 1525. In the growing momentum

---

7. Ibid., 173.
8. Ibid., 173–74.

of the Protestant Reformation a number of young radicals gathered there under the teaching of Ulrich Zwingli. Following the spirit and perhaps even the logic of Zwingli's reforms, they began to question the validity of the sacrament of baptism. Some took the drastic step of refusing to submit their children to the rite. Highly controversial, this was viewed by authorities as a threat to civil order. In January of that year the city of Zurich held a public disputation on the matter. Conrad Grebel and Felix Manz represented the position of those who would eventually be called the Swiss Brethren against Zwingli, who argued for the more widely accepted and traditional approach of baptizing infants. Zwingli was pronounced the winner of the debate and believers' baptism was forbidden. Manz, Grebel, and their community were, however, not persuaded. Within a week they had met together, performed new baptisms, and taken communion. Both Manz and Grebel were later imprisoned on several occasions. After finally fleeing the city, it appears that Grebel contracted the plague and died in 1526. Manz was eventually re-arrested and drowned in Lake Zurich in 1527. This series of events represents some of the founding moments of the Anabaptist movement. It is with good reason that the story is often recounted.

Just as most children in North American Anabaptist communities are not baptized by traveling preachers with healing gifts, most are not baptized in opposition to civil laws as were their spiritual forebearers. There are many variances in the way believers' baptism is practiced. The one essential commonality among communities that practice believers' baptism is that the process of initiation begins with a confession of faith and a request to receive baptism. The oldest prominent Anabaptist confession, the Schleitheim Confession of 1527, describes this assumption:

> Baptism shall be given to all those who have been taught repentance and the amendment of life and [who] believe truly that their sins are taken away through Christ, and to all those who desire to walk in the resurrection of Jesus Christ and be buried with Him in death, so that they might rise with Him; to all those who with such an understanding themselves desire and request it from us; hereby is excluded all infant baptism.[9]

---

9. This statement is also known as the "Schleitheim Brotherly Union." *Global Anabaptist Mennonite Encyclopedia Online*, s.v. "Schleitheim Confession (Anabaptist, 1527)." http://www.gameo.org. Hereafter all references to this online encyclopedia will be abbreviated *GAMEO*.

Likewise, the 1632 Dordrecht Confession of Faith, widely used in North America until the twentieth century, states: "All penitent believers, who, through faith, regeneration, and the renewing of the Holy Ghost, are made one with God, and are written in heaven, must, upon such Scriptural confession of faith, and renewing of life, be baptized with water."[10]

The story of Manz and Grebel and the confessions of Schleitheim and Dordrecht leave an important issue untouched. They do not provide precedent for the crucial question of how *children* of Anabaptists are to be incorporated into the church. If baptism based on an adult conversion is to be the norm for a missionary church, this policy leaves the children of those converts in uncharted waters. No one is made a Christian biologically; nevertheless, the experience of joining a church in which one has been nurtured since childhood is different than that of being an adult convert. The change in Anabaptist communities over the last four centuries is testament to this ambiguity. The social historian Leland Harder describes the age of baptismal candidates in the sixteenth century like this: "The estimated average age of baptism for ten representative Anabaptist men and women, 1525–1536, was 36.4, with none under the age of 20, two between the ages of 20 and 29, four between 30 and 39, and four between 40 and 49."[11] These were first-generation Anabaptists. Yet, since they assumed the propriety of marriage and having children, the scenario of adult conversion could not remain static. Thus, over time, Anabaptist groups have developed various ways of incorporating children. Some have been more successful than others. One method has been a simple adaptation: baptize children—instead of just adults—still assuming of course that these children make a confession of faith. In contrast to the representative sample from the sixteenth century, a 1973 study by Leland Harder and J. Howard Kauffman of four Mennonite denominations and the Brethren in Christ Church showed a downward trend in the age of baptism running through the twentieth century. At the time of that study the median age was just under fifteen.[12] Similar observations have been made at the beginning of the twenty-first century.[13] And this trend seems to have resonance beyond

10. *GAMEO*, s.v. "Dordrecht Confession of Faith (Mennonite, 1632)."

11. Leland D. Harder, *GAMEO*, s.v. "Age at Baptism."

12. The reference is to the article cited above, but the data Harder is referring to here is from the 1973 study of the Mennonite Church, General Conference Mennonite Church, Mennonite Brethren, Evangelical Mennonite Church, and the Brethren in Christ Church published as Kauffman and Harder, *Four Centuries Later*.

13. This is demonstrated by a study done by Donald Kraybill, Conrad Kanagy, and

immediate members of the Anabaptist family. The Baptist theologian James Leo Garrett, for instance, has observed that in some Baptist churches children as young as six are baptized.[14] Another Baptist leader, Brian Haymes, attests to something similar. Haymes is from the United Kingdom, and he recounts a visit to the United States, relating that upon meeting other Baptists there he initially was appreciative of their passion for believers' baptism, but then was "stunned as they [told] me they baptize children of six or seven years of age."[15] Haymes goes on to tell of one of his students who was baffled by similar observations.

Heirs of the Radical Reformation are now regularly baptizing *children*, pre- and early-adolescent persons. Certainly there is always a variety of trends at work across the spectrum of Anabaptist groups in North America. My point is not that every group and every individual fits this trend. This sociological snippet demonstrates that the practice is fluid. However, even if only one pre-adolescent child is baptized as a believer, that event would beg for an explanation. The fact that these aberrations seem to have become more common suggests a broad shift pointing to a widespread theological change. The assumption behind incorporating children through believers' baptism is that the practice still upholds the central Anabaptist affirmation that individuals should be baptized only after making a confession of faith and a genuine decision to begin a disciple's form of life. It might appear as though this attempt to secure the outcome of our children's faith development were the only real option for Anabaptist communities today. However, the example of one Anabaptist group stands in contradistinction to this trend—the Old Order Amish (Amish). Their practice shows that, even in the twenty-first century, Anabaptist communities do not *need* to baptize children.

Ronald Burwell. These sociologists have published various aspects of their study in diverse venues; however, data related to baptism was shared with me in private correspondence, June–July, 2008. Some of the data from this survey was published by Kanagy in *Road Signs for the Journey*.

14. Garrett, "Baptists Concerning Baptism," 65. Also see George, "Southern Baptists," 47.

15. Haymes, "Baptism," 125.

Anabaptist Practice of a Different Order

The contemporary Amish draw their name from the seventeenth-century rigorist Jacob Amman who led his followers to separate from the larger Anabaptist movement over a number of issues, notably a more demanding application of the Dordrecht Confession. The followers of Amman later immigrated to North America and today the Amish have settlements in over twenty-five states and one Canadian province. They are known for their close-knit communities and their particularly leery approach to technology. For instance, many Amish communities loath the interruption to family life caused by telephones, and as a result some relegate them to small sheds located at the far end of their laneways. Where Christians in the revivalist tradition focus on an individualized and experiential appropriation of faith, the Amish take an approach that, though not entirely unemotional, is highly rational and irreducibly communal. The Amish understand themselves to be mutually accountable for matters of faith and practice. For them baptism is not only an event testifying to the relationship of the individual to God, but just as prominently it marks a change in the relationship of the baptismal candidate to the church community.[16] In fact it is difficult to say that Amish theology could speak at all of a relationship with God without the community of the church.

An important aspect of the coherence of the Amish approach can be observed by attending to the dynamics of the period of young adulthood that some communities call *rumspringe*, or a time of "running around." This important exception to the generally highly disciplined and communal character of Amish life constantly catches the attention of outsiders. Non-Amish find this apparent anomaly particularly intriguing since its occasional manifestation as "worldly living" contrasts so clearly to the subdued reputation of Amish adults. One example is the fact that most Amish communities forbid the owning and operating of cars by their members on the grounds that these vehicles scatter families and easily become opportunities to display pride and competitiveness. Yet non-Amish neighbors know that some young Amish, usually males, do own and operate cars. Occasionally these Amish-owned vehicles are even equipped with after-market sound systems. On the surface this double standard seems hypocritical. However, what outsiders often fail to realize is that, even though the Amish do encourage their children to consider the possibility of being baptized in the future and seek to raise them

---

16. Nolt, *History of the Amish*, 87–88.

in light of the community's understanding of the gospel, those who are not baptized—even the children of Amish parents—are not required to live according to the discipline or rule of the church. The adolescent freedom of *rumspringe* endows the act of joining the church with greater meaning. John Hostetler, a prominent scholar of Amish life, tells us that in Amish communities, young people are reminded that it is better not to make a vow, such as baptism, than to go back on one once made. Because of the seriousness of this event it is often delayed until early adulthood, near the time when Amish young people commonly get married.[17]

Amish children are taught how to live according to the gospel and are nurtured in a spirituality that stresses the virtues of forgiveness and humility. The direct preparation for baptism, though, is a discrete sequence that usually takes six to eight weeks. Particularly important for young men to consider at this point is the assumption that in choosing to become a baptized member of the community they publicly state their willingness to serve as the community's minister, should they be asked.[18] A contemporary Amish-oriented publication illustrates the larger point well. It has the rather flat title, *1001 Questions and Answers on the Christian Life,* and is an Amish reworking of an older question-and-answer-ordered Mennonite text. The following two questions are most relevant:

> Q: Should there be an age limit in the baptism of children?
>
> The New Testament gives none, but it does teach us the seriousness of baptism and of becoming a member of the Bride of Christ, His Church (Eph 5:27; Matt 18:15–18; 1 Cor 12:12–27). This decision to serve God is the most important event in one's life. It is not for children but only for those who have reached the age of understanding and maturity. The new birth comes to a thinking, surrendered believer, not to an immature child who is easily influenced and hardly able to comprehend the gravity of the matter.
>
> Q: How then can we know if a person is old enough for baptism?
>
> We believe a person is old enough when he is mature enough (1) to recognize he is lost without a Savior, (2) to understand the conditions of salvation, (3) to renounce the world and its sins and his own flesh and blood, (4) to accept the blood of Jesus as the atonement for his sins, and (5) to solemnly promise before God to help labor and counsel in the church, and to not depart from the faith, whether it means life or death. According to article twenty-one of

---

17. Hostetler, *Amish Society*, 77–78, 365–66.
18. Ibid.

the Thirty-Three Articles of Faith, Christian baptism can "be given to none but those who are regenerated by faith, dead to sin, desire the same, rise from the death of sin, and walk in newness of life, observing whatsoever Christ has commanded them."[19]

Baptism, in the Amish view, implies saying "Yes" to Christ and "No" to the world. It commits one to the community of faith and grants access to the resources of grace that lie within it. It makes individual pride and desires secondary to the discernment of the community.

Amish baptismal services communicate even more of the community's understanding of the centrality of baptism to the life of the Christian. These services can be long affairs, sometimes stretching to four hours. The liturgy drives home the point that with God's help, the candidates, or *tauflingen*, are expected to cultivate lives characterized by humble piety and discipleship.[20] The *tauflingen* are baptized by the bishop, but not in the grandeur of a cathedral or even a local church, for they find these buildings prideful and contrary to the witness of Scripture.[21] Amish Anabaptists hold their meetings, even the vital baptismal services, in homes or barns.

Despite the obvious social distinction of Amish communities, their attempt to remain faithful to the biblical description of baptism and their interpretation of the Anabaptist tradition leads them to preserve the ordinance as a rite of paramount importance for the definition of their life together. Baptism is not just an individualized expression or a happenstance marker of spirituality. Even so, Amish do not feel the need to buttress the practice with an elaborate sacramental theology. To the extent that baptism participates in salvation, it does so through the life of community. This means that Amish practice represents a coherent form of Christian initiation that skirts wide the temptation to use baptism to incorporate children into the community's life. Their children learn and worship as members of

---

19. *1001 Questions and Answers*, 43–44. This text appears to be an anonymously redacted version of one written by Daniel Kauffman in 1907 entitled, *1000 Questions and Answers on Points of Christian Doctrine*, which seems to have been later published by Mennonite Publishing House of Scottdale, PA in 1933. The "Thirty-Three Articles of Faith" is a reference to "The Confession of Faith" published in Winchester, Virginia in 1837. This was an English translation of the much older *Belydenisse near Godts heylig woort*, which appeared in the Hoorn Martyr Book (*Historie der warachtighe getuygen*) in 1617. It was published most influentially in the *Martyr's Mirror* in 1660. The confession itself is believed to be an edited compilation of sentences from Menno Simons. For more information and an English translation, see *GAMEO*, s.v. "Confession of Faith (1617)."

20. Miller, *Our Heritage*, 148–69.

21. Hostetler, *Amish Society*, 79–81.

their families before they make the decision to officially join the community as adults, which the vast majority does.[22] Furthermore, the prominence of children in these communities demonstrates to other Anabaptists that children can be included and nurtured spiritually without being baptized. The continuity of the way Amish Anabaptists carry this out is an ongoing counter-witness to the child baptism of more acculturated Anabaptists.

Some readers may object at this point, saying that the Amish cannot serve as examples for other contemporary Christians since they, horse-drawn carriages and all, live an eighteenth-century sort of life. This sort of objection, however, misses the obvious: the Amish do live in the twenty-first century. They have not arrived here by time machine and they do not reject culture as such—that would be impossible. In one way or another they face all the same challenges that other members of society face. They simply make intentional choices as a church community, sometimes quite baffling to outsiders, about their use of technology and their participation in various cultural trends and institutions. This intentionality enables their ongoing intelligible practice of believers' baptism. Near the conclusion of his influential book, *After Virtue*, Alasdair MacIntyre somewhat hesitantly compares the current state of affairs in the West to the decline of the Roman empire—the beginning of the "Dark Ages." MacIntyre writes, "What matters at this stage is the construction of local forms of community within which civility and the intellectual and moral life can be sustained through the new dark ages which are already upon us."[23] My suggestion is that Anabaptists have examples of just such "forms of local community" closer at hand than we might think. The Amish posture toward modernity is certainly not perfect. However, if we cease to gawk and romanticize, if we cease to be embarrassed by these Christian sisters and brothers, we might see within this remnant of an old monasticism something instructive for the new.

BAPTISM IN DOCTRINAL CONTEXT

In the story with which this chapter opened, voluntary baptism is displayed in revivalist mode, yet both the preacher and the child in O'Connor's story

---

22. Kraybill reports that the Amish have a retention rate above 90 percent (*Amish Culture*, 186). Other sources describe a range between 65 and 95 percent, depending on the community.

23. MacIntyre, *After Virtue*, 263.

betray sacramental expectations in that they assume something will happen when one is dunked in the river. In O'Connor's fictional world this expectation has devastating consequences. In the world of contemporary theology this sacramental earnestness troubles the ecclesial divide over these traditional rites. A child, barely old enough to comprehend what is going on, is "voluntarily" baptized without catechetical training, and this baptism is terribly effective. This image raises the question of precisely what it means to be voluntarily baptized, and whether or not this is equivalent to the Anabaptist practice of *believers'* baptism. Pursuing these questions will begin to expose shortcomings of some versions of current baptismal practice. To do so requires us to first consider some points of relationship between Anabaptism and the revivalist movement in North America.

Symptoms of Theological Confusion

The relationship of Anabaptism and revivalism is important for at least two reasons: First, the very existence of some Anabaptist denominations—the Mennonite Brethren are one example—is due to a convergence of traditional Anabaptism with one stream or another of revivalist pietism. Second, in North America the infusion of revivalist thinking and methodologies into the Anabaptist world in the late nineteenth and early twentieth centuries parallels the declining age of baptism.

Like the beginnings of the Mennonite Brethren in nineteenth-century Russia, early encounters between Mennonites and revivalists in North America led to the creation of several new associations. The life of Martin Boehm, an eighteenth-century Mennonite preacher from Lancaster, Pennsylvania, is a good example. Boehm took up preaching at mass meetings and was summarily censured by the established Mennonite structure. Upon departure from the Mennonite community in 1800 Boehm went on to become one of the founders of the Church of the United Brethren in Christ. This denomination had so many ex-Mennonites that they were sometimes referred to as the "New Mennonites."[24] The influence of revivalism was challenged by the more staid Mennonite leadership both because its ecclesiological assumptions upset long standing forms of church order and because its piety was more emotional than many were used to. The antipathy, however, did not last. According to Harold Bender it was the direct influence of Dwight Moody upon John F. Funk that led

24. T. Schlabach, "Mennonites, Revivalism, Modernity," 398–415.

to the first North American Mennonite Church revival meeting in 1872. Working with Funk was another prominent Mennonite revivalist, Daniel Brenneman. Brenneman's "progressive" evangelical ideas led him to the same fate as Boehm's—expulsion from the Mennonite Church. In contrast, Funk remained a member of the Mennonite Church and went on to run a highly influential publishing house whose reach spanned the continent. These two figures show the changing dynamics of the late nineteenth century that marked a shift in which revivalist methods found increasing acceptance. Mennonite revivalism reached its pinnacle in the 1950s under the leadership of well-known preachers such as George B. Brunk II, Howard Hammer, Myron Augsburger, and Andrew Jantzi. During this period mass revival meetings were held by Mennonites and other Anabaptists in tents and halls across the United States and Canada. The movement exerted significant influence. At one revival campaign put on by the Brunk brothers in Lancaster, Pennsylvania 15,000 people were reported to have attended the final meeting.[25]

Though it was widely recognized and appreciated that these crusades sparked renewal and signaled a new emphasis on evangelism in Mennonite communities, not everyone was supportive. Several revivalist themes were believed to be at odds with traditional Anabaptist Christianity: the focus on the individual, the prominence of the themes of evil and God's wrath, as well as conversions that were not linked to church membership. According to Beulah Stauffer Hostetler, the primary concern was the way these meetings encouraged the baptism of young children. In fact the Mennonite Church began a formal inquiry into the issue in 1953 and adopted an official statement in 1955.[26] The 1955 statement titled "The Nurture and Evangelism of Children" recommends that baptism be reserved for those who have reached the age of accountability, which it describes as "about twelve years of age or above."[27] The document recognizes the religious experience of younger children and their place in the church, but it denies that they are in need of conversion or are appropriate candidates for baptism. It is evident that Mennonite leaders in the twentieth century were aware of and concerned about the shifting baptismal practice. In the same spirit, Marlin Miller, writing nearer the end of the twentieth century, reflects on the ambiguous legacy of revivalism: "Revivalism's emphasis on conversion and a

---

25. Juhnke, "Review of *Mennonite Tent Revivals*, 484–85.
26. *GAMEO*, s.v. "Revivalism."
27. Mennonite General Conference, "Nurture and Evangelism of Children."

voluntary response to the Gospel renewed the view that baptism as a public sign should be preceded by a voluntary and personal faith. Revivalism's preoccupation with an individual's crisis conversion has, however, diminished both the direct relation between baptism and church membership and the understanding of faith as a commitment to Christian discipleship in all areas of life, both personal and social."[28] The revivalist obsession with crises conversion as the basis for the Christian life, what we might call 'conversionism', is now woven through the fabric of North American Christianity. This has found resonance with the larger social trends of individualism and religious consumerism, thereby amplifying its impact. In a society where it is assumed that faith is a matter of individual voluntary choice and where spiritual experience has been commodified, it is not surprising that Anabaptist communities have been affected by revivalism's emotional appeal and individualized focus. The crucial questions are whether or not the revivalist influence on Anabaptist baptismal practice has transformed it into something else altogether and whether or not this new phenomena can be coherently integrated into the larger form of Anabaptist life.

The child in O'Connor's story is baptized under his own volition. However, we must ask if this sort of minimalized qualifier is capable of making sense of the seriousness of the Apostle Paul's words when he asks, "Do you not know that all of us who have been baptized into Christ Jesus were baptized into his death?" Or if it can be congruent with his continuation, "Therefore we have been buried with him by baptism into death, so that, just as Christ was raised from the dead by the glory of the Father, so we too might walk in newness of life."[29] The gravity of being joined to Jesus is not a marginal theme in the NT. The words of Paul evoke those of Jesus in Mark's gospel: "If any want to become my followers, let them deny themselves and take up their cross and follow me. For those who want to save their life will lose it, and those who lose their life for my sake, and for the sake of the gospel, will save it."[30] It is by no means self-evident that being voluntary is sufficient to render a ritual washing as the practice that initiates persons into this sort of a life. The fact that Anabaptist communities have adopted revivalist approaches to baptism, chiefly the assumption that children are eligible candidates, is one indication that the theology of baptism needs to be revisited.

28. Miller, "Mennonites," 23.
29. Rom 6:3–4.
30. Mark 8:34–35.

To avoid being too dismissive, let us consider this issue further. We must first ask what it could possibly mean for a child to confess faith, in a revivalist context or any other. In Matthew 19 Jesus forbids his disciples to banish children from his company, saying, "it is to such as these [children] that the kingdom of heaven belongs."[31] Clearly the community of Jesus' followers should have a ready place for children; however, Jesus' words maintain the categorical distinction between children and disciples. Though Jesus *blesses* children he *instructs* disciples. Does discipleship then demand an end of childhood? For Anabaptists to undergo baptism is in the words of Mark's Jesus to take up one's cross. In the gospel of Matthew the risen Jesus tells his disciples to "Go therefore and make disciples of all nations, baptizing them in the name of the Father and of the Son and of the Holy Spirit, and teaching them to obey everything that I have commanded you."[32] Here discipleship, baptism, and teaching are tied together. Anabaptists have long denied that this can be applied to babies. Yet the prevalence of child-baptism in the twentieth-century runs headlong against this.

The case that the baptism of children represents a theological problem can be further supported by observing the incongruity of several of the assumptions that support it. First, this practice assumes that what is being done is actually a coherent form of baptism. To receive any benefit of doubt it must make sense within one of the traditional approaches to baptism. Though some elements of folk-revivalism might, like the fictional story "The River," hold to a sacramental understanding, this is not generally the case in Anabaptist circles. And though Anabaptists likely have absorbed many spiritualist assumptions through the pietism implicit in revivalism, the fact that baptism is still practiced mitigates against this being the operative approach. More likely these communities ostensibly hold to some form of the testimonial approach.

If the baptism of children is understood as a testimonial form of the practice it must be assumed that these children are capable of making the sort of statement that this theology of baptism requires. However, might it not be the case that the same sort of plausibility structure and related social pressure that convinced parents in Christendom to baptize their infants now pressures children to request baptism? Might it not be the case that a child's request for baptism, as well intentioned as it likely is, is not the sort of statement demanded by believers' baptism? This is not to question

31. Matt 19:14.
32. Matt 28:19–20.

whether children want to identify with Jesus in some way or whether they might want at some level to have their sins "forgiven." The crux of the matter is just that it is difficult to understand how a child is capable of making a non-coerced confession of faith. This means that the semiotic character of baptism is blurred; intentional discipleship cannot be differentiated from socialization or the desire of a religious community to secure its future. Modern society realizes this: we do not allow children to fight in our wars or to marry even if they volunteer to do so. For children to join the church through baptism is to reduce the practice to a gate-keeping ceremony that initiates children into the next developmental stage of their lives. It reduces baptism to the weak formality of connecting to a community without risk or distinctive ethical commitments.

A second operative assumption in child baptism is the conversionist belief that children are in danger of divine judgment—that a nine-year-old needs to repent of his life of sin. The assumption that children are objects of God's wrath did not begin with modern revivalism. It has a long history going back at least to Augustine, who avers in his *Confessions*, "The harmlessness of babes is in their body's effect, not their mind's intent."[33] For many groups that practice believers' baptism the doctrine of the age of accountability is used to make some sense of this pre-pubescent predicament. In the Assemblies of God context a document endorsed by the Commission on Doctrinal Purity and the Executive Presbytery exemplifies this approach clearly: "The Assemblies of God believes that children are loved by God, and until they come to an age of understanding (some call it 'the age of accountability'), they have a place in the kingdom of God."[34] The underlying assumption is that after reaching this age the child is left vulnerable before God. The doctrine is traditionally grounded in biblical references such as 2 Sam 12:23, in which David states that his son will not return to him, but rather that David will "go to" his son (thereby affirming the son's innocence), or Deut 1:37–40 in which the children of the rebellious Israelites are not subjected to judgment because they "do not yet know right from wrong."[35]

---

33. Augustine, *Confessions*, 10. Though the Wills translation is not an academic one, I appreciate the candor with which he renders Augustine's reflections.

34. This document can be found under the "Beliefs" heading on the Assemblies of God website, http://www.ag.org/top/Beliefs/gendoct_11_accountability.cfm.

35. Similar passages include 1 Sam 3:7; Jer 1:4–7; and Luke 2:52.

The age of accountability is an attempt to reign in runaway repercussions of the doctrine of original sin. However, it is precisely in its tentative formalization that it creates irresolvable pastoral dilemmas. One cannot help but wonder at precisely what age one is actually accountable before God. Would it not be fairer if accountability was linked to developmental progress instead of age? Might there then be a quantitative test to determine when a child qualifies as one accountable before God for her sin? The doctrine of the age of accountability is at best built on marginal biblical references. Furthermore, it fails to provide the clarification it suggests. In Anabaptist circles it is further undermined by the implications of the term "accountability," which implies a specifically forensic understanding of the atonement. According to Thomas Finger's analysis of the roots of Anabaptism this was not the dominant view. Finger claims that the primary soteriological model for early Anabaptists was more akin to divinization, involving a gradual ontological transformation intrinsically patterned by the life, death, and resurrection of Christ.[36] This does not dismiss the need for the process of conversion, but it does downplay any sort of legal necessity for quickly baptizing children out of fear for their eternal destiny. It undercuts the assumption that children must be baptized as soon as possible to avoid divine judgment.

In his book *Believers Baptism for Children of the Church* Marlin Jeschke argues convincingly that significant confusion around the status of children has arisen from the assumption of a false dichotomy, that all of humanity falls into one of two neat categories: they are either saved or reprobate. As a result child evangelism has taken the place of Christian nurture. Jeschke's recommendation is that Anabaptists recover an understanding of the innocence of childhood.[37] This does not avoid the difficulty of giving definition to the process of nurture but it does, in the face of revivalist assumptions, begin to put the discussion of the initiation of the children of Christians on the right field. It also gestures toward a way of understanding the life of the church that can take into account those with developmental or cognitive impediments. Space does not permit the development of an alternative to the notion of the age of accountability and the false dichotomy Jeschke names; nevertheless, it is definitely the case that we can question the assumption that children are objects of divine judgment in need of conversion. The baptism of children has been challenged before

---

36. Finger, *Contemporary Anabaptist Theology*, 131.
37. Jeschke, *Believers Baptism for Children*, 103–24.

in Anabaptist circles, and my argument is that because of its theological incoherence it should continue to be critiqued. It should not be allowed to become normative, for in doing so I fear it would reshape Anabaptist theology in destructive ways.

Locating the Problem in Denominational Theologies

In O'Connor's presentation of baptism the passion of the central characters—the young boy, the sitter, and the preacher—is juxtaposed to a detached, empty cosmopolitanism represented by the boy's parents and their friends. This aspect of the story calls into question the sentimentality and triumphalism inherent in many religious practices. A well-known anecdote about O'Connor makes her view clear. The story is told that once at a dinner party in which a writer-sophisticate proclaimed that the sacraments were still useful—as literary symbols—O'Connor is said to have bluntly responded: "Well, if it's a symbol, to hell with it."[38] For O'Connor a sacrament implies much more than symbolism. Likewise, the central characters in her story are more than merely open to the possibility of God acting in their world. They expect it. If the Christian faith is to have any of the serious sort of impact to which baptism portends we should wonder how the life of the church could be characterized in any other way. Indeed, this question arises from the very history of Anabaptism itself. Arnold Snyder has stated that the closest analogue early Anabaptists had to the medieval eucharistic sacrament and its concept of the real presence of Jesus was the life of the church itself.[39] Nevertheless, for many contemporary Anabaptists the rite of initiation does not participate in the divine nearness of sacramentality. To both support this claim and to explain more clearly how believers' baptism is understood today it will be helpful to look to the way some Anabaptist denominations present their beliefs and practices.

The category is hard to define, but conservative estimates are that more than 1.6 million people participate in Anabaptist-affiliated congregations in the world. Only slightly more than 0.5 million of those reside in the United States and Canada.[40] These congregations, though, make

---

38. As quoted in Wood, *Flannery*, 23.
39. Snyder, *Following in the Footsteps*, 109–10.
40. See the MWC map on the Mennonite World Conference website: http://www.mwc-cmm.org/en15/index.php?option=com_content&view=article&id=14&Itemid=17&lang=en.

up more than fifty denominations or independently affiliated Anabaptist groups.[41] They range from very acculturated denominations with high levels of education and professional training to culturally distinct groups who see little use for formal education. They include highly mobile individuals as well as those who have decided not to ride in airplanes or even drive cars.[42] Giving a theologically significant and succinct description of the beliefs that these groups hold to be true about baptism is challenging. It is a job that threatens to slowly and laboriously swamp this project with detail. Rowing through extended quotations varying only slightly one from the other would tire even the most committed reader. Nevertheless, a sketch of how some prominent self-identifying Anabaptist groups describe the practice will provide helpful context for the discussion that follows. It will also advance the thesis of this project by displaying the theology of baptism and opening it for critique. I will describe key features of the current statements of five Anabaptist denominations: (1) The Conservative Mennonite Conference (Conservative Conference), which includes about 110 congregations in North America. The Conservative Conference is rooted in the Amish Mennonite expression of Anabaptism. With its denominational origins traceable to 1910, this group formed from congregations that sought a middle ground between more assimilated Amish Mennonites and the traditional and distinct Old Order Amish. (2) The Canadian Conference of Mennonite Brethren (Mennonite Brethren), which includes some 250 congregations in Canada. The Mennonite Brethren trace their origin to revival movements among Russian Mennonite settlements in the 1860s. Today the Mennonite Brethren describe themselves as both Anabaptist and Evangelical. (3) The Brethren in Christ of North America (Brethren in Christ), which includes about 295 congregations in both the United States and Canada. The Brethren in Christ count both Pietism and Wesleyanism as formative theological traditions alongside their older Anabaptist roots. The final two denominations under examination currently use the same confession of faith, the "Confession of Faith in a Mennonite Perspective" ("Confession of Faith"), affirmed in 1995. These two denominations are (4) Mennonite Church USA, which includes roughly 940 congregations in the

---

41. See the NA Anabaptist map available on the Mennonite World Review website: http://media.mennoweekly.org/ static/images/anabaptist_map.pdf.

42. A variety of reference works can provide details. For example, see Kraybill, *Concise Encyclopaedia*. The variety of Anabaptist groups is not merely geographical. Kraybill reports that in 2001 there were more than thirty Anabaptist groups and 370 congregations in Lancaster County, Pennsylvania alone (*Amish Culture*, 15).

US, and (5) Mennonite Church Canada, which includes close to 230 congregations in Canada. These two denominations are the result of the recent merger of the General Conference Mennonite Church and the Mennonite Church and include some of the oldest Anabaptist conferences, groups of mutually accountable congregations, in North America.

The statements described below are the way in which these groups publicly articulate their beliefs in the form of a confession of faith or a doctrinal statement. These denominations have each taken a variety of steps in formulating these documents, which themselves hold differing levels of confessional and teaching authority within each denomination and its affiliated organizations. Formal statements of belief and practice are not new in the Anabaptist tradition even though the proper status of central Christian statements like the Apostles Creed and the Nicean Creed is debated.[43] Classic statements such as the sixteenth-century Schleitheim Articles and the seventeenth-century Dordrecht Confession have served as gathering points for Anabaptists throughout history. In what follows I will first consider the doctrine of baptism and then provide a further description of the ways in which it is dogmatically related to the doctrines of God and the church.

Every denominational document surveyed here describes baptism in testimonial terms. Some denominations like the Conservative Conference list water baptism alongside communion, washing of feet, anointing the sick, laying on of hands, and marriage as "ceremonies and symbols of the Christian faith."[44] The specific language that the Conservative Conference uses to describe baptism depicts it as an "external symbol of internal spiritual baptism." It symbolizes being buried with Christ and joined in his resurrection, being cleansed by God from sin and guilt. In addition, the Conservative Conference describes baptism as a "public confession of faith," and it is linked to membership in a local congregation.

The testimonial understanding of baptism is also clearly evident in the Mennonite Brethren statement. It says, "We believe that when people

43. Koop provides a helpful introduction to the status of confessions of faith in Anabaptist studies as well as an analysis of key seventeenth-century confessions in his *Anabaptist-Mennonite Confessions*.

44. This and following references to the Conservative Conference view of baptism are drawn from the CMC "Statement of Theology" and the "Statement of Practice." These can be found at http://cmcrosedale.org/index.shtml. For each denominational description discussed I choose to reference official documents posted on the web since this is the most public and accessible venue in which these views are expressed. However, this means that quotations will not be cited with page numbers. Instead, in the text I will try to make clear to which section of the document I refer.

receive God's gift of salvation, they are to be baptized in the name of the Father, Son, and Holy Spirit. Baptism is a sign of having been cleansed from sin. It is a covenant with the church to walk in the way of Christ through the power of the Holy Spirit."[45] The Mennonite Brethren statement also reads: "Baptism is a sign of the believer's incorporation into the body of Christ as expressed in the local church. Baptism is also a pledge to serve Christ according to the gifts given to each person." This shares the perspective of many early Anabaptists, which inverts Calvin's view of how baptism functions as a pledge. For the Mennonite Brethren the one who makes a promise in baptism is not God but the individual. Of the denominations surveyed here, the Mennonite Brethren state most directly their belief that infant baptism is invalid, saying, "Persons who claim baptism as infants and wish to become members of a Mennonite Brethren congregation are to receive baptism on their confession of faith."

In their "Articles of Faith and Doctrine" the Brethren in Christ describe baptism and communion as "ordinances."[46] They also recognize "practices" such as footwashing, marriage, and the dedication of children as important to the life of the church. The Brethren in Christ say that baptism is a "public witness" that "symbolizes the believer's submission to Jesus Christ and identification with His death and resurrection." The Brethren in Christ expect baptized believers to "commit themselves to the membership covenant," which is a way of affirming their loyalty to the church as a local body of disciples and a global unified body of Christ. Of the denominations surveyed here the Brethren in Christ most clearly affirm a particular mode of baptism, which in their case is immersion.

In the confession of faith upheld by both Mennonite Church Canada and Mennonite Church USA baptism is described most prominently as a "sign," "testimony," and "pledge."[47] It is a sign of cleansing, repentance, forgiveness, renunciation of evil, as well as death to sin. It is a testimony of

---

45. This and following references to the Mennonite Brethren view of baptism are drawn from the "detailed version" of the CCMB "Confession of Faith": http://www.mbconf.ca/home/products_and_services/resources/theology/confession_of_faith/detailed_version/.

46. This and following references to the Brethren in Christ view of baptism are drawn from the "Articles of Faith and Doctrine" of the BCNA: http://www.bic-church.org/about/ articlesoffaith.asp.

47. This and following references to the "Confession of Faith in Mennonite Perspective" can be located at http://www.mcusa-archives.org/library/resolutions/1995/index.html.

God's gift of the Spirit, which enables new life. It is a pledge to "serve Christ and to minister as a member of his body." Baptism, the confession says, is "done in obedience to Jesus' command." Baptism's relationship to Jesus means that "Those who accept water baptism commit themselves to follow Jesus in giving their lives for others, in loving their enemies, and in renouncing violence, even when it means their own suffering or death." With these goals in view it is not surprising that this document claims directly that baptism is only for those who "are of the age of accountability and who freely request baptism on the basis of their response to Jesus Christ in faith."

To strengthen the analysis of the theology of baptism presented in these documents it is important to consider the practice within a broader dogmatic context. For this we must pay special attention to the doctrines of God and the church. I am particularly interested in how these texts describe the church's relationship to God and how they describe the present work of Jesus. We begin with the Conservative Conference's doctrinal description of the church, which outlines several common Anabaptist themes:

> The church of Jesus Christ is the universal body of redeemed believers committed to Jesus Christ as Lord, and finds expression in the local church in worship, fellowship, holiness, discipline, teaching and preaching the Word, prayer, spiritual gifts, and the New Testament ordinances. The church is called out from and is separate from the world, but reaches out to the world with the Gospel and the "cup of cold water". The church, as the body of Christ, is the visible representation of God on earth and is ready to suffer and serve as required by Christ and His Word.

A key feature of this statement, which it shares with most other contemporary Anabaptist doctrinal statements, is the theological distance it maintains between the church and God. The language used here of "representation" is the closest most Anabaptist statements come to equating the presence or work of the church with that of God. The way in which the body of Christ motif is understood in representational terms is evidence of this. The Conservative Conference's "Statement of Theology" explains that Jesus' present work is that of intercession. Representation and intercession imply absence and distance.

The Mennonite Brethren describe the church as "the people called by God through Jesus Christ." The church "makes Christ visible in the world." Like the Conservative Conference, the Mennonite Brethren describe the ongoing work of Christ as "intercession" and "advocacy." In addition, they say that Jesus also "calls [believers] to be his witnesses." At this point we can begin to observe a formal parallel in the way that the church represents God just as baptism represents God's work. Though the Spirit is said to unite the church and is described as the presence of God, the Mennonite Brethren statement does not elucidate how the Spirit's presence or work actually involve the church.

In describing new life in Christ the Brethren in Christ believe "Persons thus justified by grace through faith enjoy peace with God, are adopted into God's family, become part of the church, and receive the assurance of eternal life. We become new creatures in Christ, regenerated by the Holy Spirit." Notice that in this statement becoming part of the church happens alongside enjoying peace with God, being adopted into God's family, and receiving the assurance of eternal life. These are all listed as effects of justification by grace through faith, yet there is no clear role for the church in bringing about these realities. The "Articles of Faith and Doctrine" of the Brethren in Christ describe Jesus as the head of the church and the one who established it. The Lordship of Jesus is deemed a current reality; though, like other Anabaptist statements, Jesus' primary ongoing role is said to be intercession. Nevertheless, the body of Christ motif has a prominent role in the Brethren in Christ description of the church. Its invocation, though, is highly metaphorical.

The "Confession of Faith" used by the two relatively large denominations in the United States and Canada describes the church as "the assembly of those who have accepted God's offer of salvation through faith in Jesus Christ." It is "the assembly of those who voluntarily commit themselves to follow Christ." Recognizing the popularity of the body of Christ motif among Anabaptists, this confession stresses it as well: "We believe that the church as the body of Christ is the visible manifestation of Jesus Christ. The church is called to live and minister as Christ lived and ministered in the world." In the present tense this document describes Jesus as "the model human being" and "the image of the invisible God." Jesus is further affirmed as "our Lord and the not-yet-recognized Lord of the world."

The "Confession of Faith" of these Mennonite denominations is theologically ambiguous at two key points. In various ways the other documents share these features as well. The first point of ambiguity can be seen in this statement: "Baptism by water is a sign that a person has repented, received forgiveness, renounced evil, and died to sin, through the grace of God in Christ Jesus. Thus cleansed, believers are incorporated into Christ's body on earth, the church." While reference to the church being Christ's body is noticeably less abstract than in some of the other statements, the relationship of the sign of water baptism to either cleansing or incorporation is not clear. It is unclear what "thus cleansed" refers to. Does baptism participate in this? Does baptism have anything to do with the subsequent incorporation in Christ's body? The "Confession of Faith" is imprecise. The second point of ambiguity has even wider ramifications. In the portions of the confession that deal most directly with Jesus and the Spirit, the ongoing relationship of these two members of the Trinity to the church is indistinct. The "Confession of Faith" tells us the Spirit calls people to repentance, convicts of sin, and leads in the way of righteousness. The Spirit teaches, guides in truth, and empowers individuals. It says the Spirit empowers the church to preach, teach, testify, heal, suffer, and so on. A similar point is made regarding Jesus: "We recognize Jesus Christ as the head of the church, his body. As members of his body, we are in Christ, and Christ dwells in us. Empowered by this intimate relationship with Christ, the church continues his ministry of mercy, justice, and peace in a broken world." The belief that Jesus' ministry is continued in the church is clear. It is important to notice though that the theological structure of this ongoing ministry is vicarious. The continuity of the work of Jesus with that of the church comes through its attribution not through agential constancy. The Spirit works directly in the lives of individuals, but does not work in the world through the corporate church; rather, the church's work is "empowered" by the Spirit.

Each of these denominational statements has two broad features in common. First, baptism, a practice central to the Anabaptist tradition, is presented as theologically non-essential to the Christian life. It is carried out as an act of obedience. Baptism is described as a statement, a testimony, or a sign about that life, but not necessary for it. The doctrinal statements do not present a construal of baptism that would provide rationale for why a ritual washing is more effective than a verbal testimony. If we were to compare the Christian life to a journey, say hiking the Appalachian Trail, baptism would not be a form of preparation or a natural and necessary way of beginning. It would be more like a moment in which the hiker, following the instructions of some ancient backpacking authority, held up a sign telling others that he or she had decided to tackle the challenging trail. Obedience is an admirable reason for continuing to baptize. However, its nonessential characterization contradicts Anabaptism's history and the ancient Christian practice. It fails to account for passages such as 1 Pet 3:21, which places some constitutive element of baptism in a causal relationship with salvation. This nonessential description leaves Anabaptist communities open to short-sighted redefinitions of the practice, manifested in the last century by the declining age of baptismal candidates.

The second common feature is that the visible church, another central aspect of the Anabaptist tradition, exists in a sort of second class relationship to the individual believer's relationship with God. At a conceptual level, and in colloquial terms, the church is a bit like a third wheel in an individual's personal relationship with God. Though the Spirit is said to do many things in the lives of believers and is also described as the Spirit of the church, the Anabaptist documents are careful to avoid stating that the Spirit works in the world *through* the church. Though the church is affirmed as the body of Christ, the most straightforward way of receiving this proposition—that Jesus remains present to humanity through the church—is mostly dismissed. Instead, the church is said to be the visible *representation* of Jesus, as though a body were a representation of a mind or a soul. In these documents the presence of the church does not constitute the presence of God in the world. Not only is this logically strained—for how can the Spirit of God be in the church and the church not constitute God's presence in the world—but this ecclesial marginalization allows for the continuation of a revivalist practice of baptism that loses discipleship in its search for conversion.

Throughout the rest of this volume my evaluation of these contemporary documents will be both affirming and critical. I will affirm the importance of Anabaptist communities continuing to describe baptism as an individual's pledge to live according to the pattern of the life of the first-century Jew, Jesus of Nazareth. This view correlates with the discipleship emphasis of Matt 28:19–20 and the widely held assumption that baptism is done in part as an act of imitation of Jesus' own baptism. I will be critical of the fact that the practices and the body ordained by God are not affirmed as ways of mediating divine presence. The work of God in the world is seen to circumvent Christ's body and to proceed directly to the hearts of individuals. These assumptions are debilitating because they enable a form of discipleship that can ignore God, for if the work and presence of God are both invisible and exclusively personal then they are rightly held in suspicion or even dismissed. If God's presence is unnameable and his work beyond apprehension, then individuals are ultimately alone in their quests to follow the example of Jesus. If God's presence and work cannot be understood—even using theological categories—then this God is unpredictable and unreliable, maybe even unidentifiable.

The critical elements of this analysis will make some nervous. I can imagine a critic pointing to 1 Tim 2:5, which reads: "For there is one God; there is also one mediator between God and humankind, Christ Jesus, himself human, who gave himself a ransom for all . . ." The critic might argue that my thesis could lead to the denial of the universal accessibility of God through Jesus. I believe such fears are misguided since the sort of divine mediation lacking in the Anabaptist statements is not that which would create a barrier between individuals and God, what seems to be Paul's worry. It is not of the sort that would nullify the life and work of Jesus. The mediation of God's presence and action that would fill the lacuna in these Anabaptist construals of baptism is that which the writer of this letter to Timothy participated in and the type that the church which produced the Bible remains. These were real, flawed people enabled to undertake the work of God in the world. In them God made his presence and will accessible to others. The form of ecclesial mediation I will argue for is one that upholds the necessity of the church as the body through which God chooses to be present in the world. It is a form that upholds God's choice to act through the church in baptism both to cleanse and to welcome new members of Christ's body. It is a form of ecclesial mediation in which God chooses to be present to humanity in much the same way as ancient Israel. At its best Israel was not a barrier between God and the rest of the nations. Israel was the people in which God's presence was manifest and where God's will for human sociality could be recognized. Of course Israel was not always at its best, and it was at these times that God's grace was most evident. God's non-rejection of Israel despite its unfaithfulness is pre-figured by God's non-rejection of humanity despite the fall. Jesus himself is the mediator that the writer of 1 Timothy speaks about, and Jesus is God's gracious faithfulness in making Israel a blessing. In this volume I am arguing that baptism must be understood to participate in Jesus' continued bodily mediation through the church.[48]

I refer to the lack of appropriate ecclesial mediation in these Anabaptist documents as a lacuna. Just as nature is said to abhor a vacuum, so does a community's theology. What these contemporary Anabaptist documents assert in place of an appropriate form of ecclesial mediation is the voluntary power of the individual. Instead of God acting through

---

48. Miroslav Volf has developed an argument from a Free Church perspective toward similar ends (*After Our Likeness*, 160–68).

the church in baptism, the individual makes a proclamation of her own. For children to be baptized as "believers" is to have the very concept of belief, which in this case is meant to denote a response to the call to follow Jesus in the community of other disciples, reduced to a very basic mode of self-assertion—the ability to speak. The story that this chapter opened with invites us to challenge the logic that equates voluntariety and speech with belief and discipleship. It also points to the poverty of a cosmopolitan reduction of spiritual life and maybe even the dryness or one-dimensionality of non-sacramental construals of ecclesial practices. As an alternative to this rationalist flattening out of life, revivalism presents the experience(s) of conversion. Contemporary Anabaptism, to speak very generally, vacillates between these two modern postures. And yet as revealing as O'Connor's story of a child's baptism might be, it is ultimately a parable of deconstruction. It tugs at the loose threads of our assumptions but knits no new garments. In a parallel way I am suggesting that the baptism of children is a crucial distortion in the implementation of believers' baptism. It is one that Amish Anabaptists demonstrate is not inevitable. Even though the trend of child baptism can be correlated with the influence of revivalism, Anabaptist theologies of baptism bear responsibility for its perpetuation. Or at the very least they show how much Anabaptists have internalized this theological ambiguity. Lacking a clear affirmation of concrete media through which God is present to the world or acts in it, these communities have made themselves vulnerable to continually marginalizing practices such as baptism—even the church.

2

In Favor of Ecclesial Mediation

> It was the duty of the trumpeters and singers to make themselves heard in unison in praise and thanksgiving to the LORD, and when the song was raised ... the house, the house of the LORD, was filled with a cloud, so that the priests could not stand to minister because of the cloud; for the glory of the LORD filled the house of God.
>
> (2 Chr 5:13–14)

Could a Mennonite be an atheist and still be a Mennonite? On the face of it, the question deals with boundaries and culture, orthodoxy and tradition. Oddly enough, it is also related to the line of thought being explored here. It is a question that arises when one functional alternative to my proposal is pushed to its logical end. My thesis is that Anabaptist communities need to express more clearly how the church mediates the presence and work of God. Extending the analysis begun in the last chapter will show that there is actually some precedent for this in Anabaptist thought. Nevertheless, some readers might wonder about other options. This chapter explores two alternatives, one related to the puzzling possibility of Mennonite atheism. After evaluating these, I turn in a more positive direction. Acknowledging that certain developments and applications of ecclesial mediation do not fit the larger body of Anabaptist theology, the second part of the chapter charts the conceptual outlines of an appropriate form of this concept.

ANABAPTISM AND THE CHURCH'S MEDIATING ROLE

The unwillingness of Anabaptists to see baptism as a practice that mediates God's work in their midst is of a piece with the ambiguity that surrounds their views of the function of the church in the Christian life more generally. The Anabaptist view is best described as "ambiguous" because, despite what is said about the church and about baptism, there actually are points at which Anabaptist belief and practice are amenable to a notion of ecclesial mediation. This is true even though the concept is usually not employed directly. The more common stance of Anabaptist ecclesiology is such that the presence of the church and its work are clearly distinguished from God's in favor of a more individualized, divine personalism.

Discipline, Discipleship, and Ecclesial Ambiguity

In a further analysis of Anabaptist confessions it is evident that the process of church discipline, or formalized structures of discipleship, is often described differently than baptism. Church discipline can be seen as an instance of ecclesial mediation. This is not new. The sixteenth-century Schleitheim agreement shows its origins. It states: "[E]verything which has not been united with our God in Christ is nothing but an abomination which we should shun."[1] The abominations these Anabaptists intended to avoid included "winehouses"; the "works and idolatry, gatherings, church attendance" of Protestants and Catholics; as well as the use of "diabolical weapons of violence." The goal of this "shunning" is for true Christians to be prepared for "the service of God and the Spirit." The initial result would be the perceptibility of the true body of believers. Not only is this body apparent, but it plays an important role in calling members to ongoing obedience to Jesus. This is most evident through the description of the ban: "The ban shall be employed with all those who have given themselves over to the Lord, to walk after [Him] in His commandments; those who have been baptized into the one body of Christ, and let themselves be called brothers or sisters, and still somehow slip and fall into error and sin, being inadvertently overtaken." According to Schleitheim, the ban was to be carried out "according to the ordering of the Spirit of God before the breaking of bread," in order that the unity of the Spirit in charity would be preserved.

---

1. This and the following references to this confession refer to a translation found online at the *GAMEO*, s.v. "Schleitheim Confession (Anabaptist, 1527)."

About a century after the Schleitheim agreement was produced, a second prominent statement known as the Dordrecht Confession made similar claims about the availability of the true church to human perception:

> We believe in, and confess a visible church of God, namely, those who, as has been said before, truly repent and believe, and are rightly baptized; who are one with God in heaven, and rightly incorporated into the communion of the saints here on earth. These we confess to be the chosen generation, the royal priesthood, the holy nation, who are declared to be the bride and wife of Christ, yea, children and heirs of everlasting life, a tent, tabernacle, and habitation of God in the Spirit . . .[2]

Here we notice that the ambiguity of the relationship of actions such as true repentance, right baptism, unity with God, and communion with the saints—the same sort of ambiguity that was observed in contemporary Anabaptist documents in the last chapter—is present in this much older confession. Nevertheless, the Dordrecht Confession calls this body "the habitation of God in the Spirit." Among several identifying markers of Christ's church are "the fruitful observance, practice, and maintenance of the true ordinances of Christ." Like Schleitheim, Dordrecht claims the necessity of the ban to maintain the true practice of the ordinances:

> Concerning the withdrawing from, or shunning the separated, we believe and confess, that if anyone, either through his wicked life or perverted doctrine, has so far fallen that he is separated from God, and, consequently, also separated and punished by the church, the same must, according to the doctrine of Christ and His apostles, be shunned . . . and no company be had with him that they may not become contaminated by intercourse with him, nor made partakers of his sins; but that the sinner may be made ashamed, pricked in his heart, and convicted in his conscience, unto his reformation.

The purpose of the ban seen in this last clause is consonant with the Spirit's work. The confession further clarifies that the goal of this harsh practice is not that the individual be condemned but that he repent and reform. This should not be carried out, the same document tells us, as if these persons are enemies but precisely because they are siblings, in hope that they might

---

2. This and following references to this confession refer to a translation that can be found online at *GAMEO*, s.v. "Dordrecht Confession of Faith (Mennonite, 1632)." For additional background and analysis see Koop, *Anabaptist-Mennonite Confessions*, 55–82.

know and turn from their sins, "so that they may become reconciled to God, and consequently be received again into the church."

Without whitewashing the hazard of perfectionism and the inherent potential for abuse, we must acknowledge that the ban functions as an example of a point at which these historic Anabaptist confessions describe the interweaving of the actions of the church and the actions of God.[3] God works through the discipline of the church; likewise, as the "habitation of God in Spirit," the Christian community is the place where God is present. Obviously, the concept of ecclesial mediation is not entirely foreign to the Anabaptist tradition. This is quite remarkable since many of these early Anabaptists would have been keenly aware of the violent and stifling potential of this assumption.[4]

The view of church discipline in the contemporary Anabaptist denominational documents introduced in the last chapter resonates with the theology of these two historic statements. These resonances occur under a variety of topical headings including, "Discipline within the Church," "Discipleship," or "Mutual Accountability." The strictures have softened since the seventeenth century, but theological similarities remain. The Conservative Conference's statement of practice is one example:

> We believe Jesus Christ has given authority to His church to exercise corrective discipline within the community of believers. This discipline is intended to bring those who are in error to repentance, helping them to receive the forgiveness, grace, and love that are available in Jesus ... At any point if the erring one hears the admonitions brought and repents, he/she is restored to full fellowship with Christ and His church. The purposes of discipline include maintaining the integrity and witness of the church, restoring to fellowship those who are in error, building faithfulness in the believers, and strengthening godly teaching and conduct.[5]

Similarly, the "Confession of Faith" used by the Mennonite Church in Canada and the United States reads:

---

3. For the biblical grounding for Dordrecht's defence of the ban see Jer 59:2; 1Cor 5:5, 13; 1 Tim 5:20; 1 Cor 5:6; 2 Cor 10:8; 1 Cor 13:10; Jas 5:19; Titus 3:10; and 1 Cor 5:13; and regarding shunning see 1 Cor 5:9–11; 2 Thess 3:14,15.

4. The difficult workings of ecclesial discipline in Anabaptist communities are perhaps best described in works of fiction. See Toews, *Complicated Kindness*.

5. The CMC "Statement of Practice" can be found at http://cmcrosedale.org/about/practice.shtml.

> We believe that the practice of discipline in the church is a sign of God's offer of forgiveness and transforming grace to believers who are moving away from faithful discipleship or who have been overtaken by sin. Discipline is intended to liberate erring brothers and sisters from sin, to enable them to return to a right relationship with God, and to restore them to fellowship in the church. It also gives integrity to the church's witness and contributes to the credibility of the gospel message in the world.[6]

In this statement the meaning of the word "sign" is clarified by the fact that discipline is said to "liberate," "enable," and "restore." In this context, the ecclesial practice of discipline is more than a testimony or a memorial: it effects what it signifies. Anabaptists believe that the discipline of the church is a sacrament.

Both historic and contemporary Anabaptism contains elements of theology and practice in which it is recognized that God's sanctifying task is furthered by the church community. This is the high ecclesiology by which some Anabaptist groups are recognized to be more Catholic than Protestant. The extract above from the "Confession of Faith" is an example of the church's concrete involvement in liberating individuals from bondage to sin. In this practice, Anabaptist groups approach a clear naming of the church community as a body through which God acts. It might seem as if we need only to apply the theology of church discipline to Christian initiation to recover the objective elements of baptism. In a limited sense this is true, but it is also simplistic.

These contemporary documents do not offer many general statements about the function of the church in the divine economy. At one point the "Confession of Faith" used by Mennonite denominations in the United States and Canada comes close. Under the heading "Discipleship and the Christian Life," it says, "The experience of God through the Holy Spirit, prayer, Scripture, and the church empowers us and teaches us how to follow Christ." Despite being one of the strongest statements in this regard, it is important to notice what it does not say: it does not say that we experience the Spirit through the fellowship of the congregation; it does not say that we learn to pray in the congregation; it does not say that we learn to rightly read Scripture by participating in congregational life. This confession does not say these things because it seems not to assume that Christians learn

---

6. The "Confession of Faith in a Mennonite Perspective" can be found at http://www.mcusa-archives.org/library/resolutions/1995/1995-14.html.

to follow Jesus in the presence of others. In fact, the statement that directly precedes the one just quoted reads: "We believe that Jesus Christ calls us to take up our cross and follow him. Through the gift of God's saving grace, we are empowered to be disciples of Jesus, filled with his Spirit, following his teachings and his path through suffering to new life. As by faith we walk in Christ's way, we are being transformed into his image. We become conformed to Christ, faithful to the will of God, and separated from the evil in the world." This is the lead paragraph in this confession describing "Discipleship and the Christian Life." It is only in the context of an individualized, spiritual encounter with Jesus that the church is named as a way in which people "experience God." The nature of response to the call of Jesus as stated here almost disregards the church.

The Brethren in Christ, like other Anabaptists, affirm the church's role as a disciplining body. Under the heading "Nature of the Church" their denominational statement says, "The objective of church discipline is to restore the erring church member and to maintain the integrity and purity of the church's fellowship and witness."[7] In contrast to this, the view propounded under the heading "Coming to Faith" describes initiation in faith as an individual process involving personal encounter with God. The Spirit is invoked as the causal bridge between the unseen realm of divine activity and the gritty physical world of repentance and obedience, the church—the visible community of Christ's followers—fades from view. In a relevant part of the "Coming to Faith" section we read:

> The salvation graciously provided by the death and resurrection of Jesus Christ becomes effective in our lives by the ministry of the Holy Spirit. It is the Spirit who prepares us for faith in Jesus Christ. He awakens us to our need, enables us to acknowledge our guilt, and calls us to respond to God in faith and obedience. The response of faith is a personal reliance on God's grace and a turning from sin to righteousness . . . [Repentance] is expressed in genuine sorrow, forsaking sin, and a change in attitude toward God, preparing for the continuing ministry of the Holy Spirit. Repentance includes a willingness for reconciliation and restitution.

As in the "Mennonite Confession" this portion of the Brethren in Christ "Articles of Faith and Doctrine" fails to parallel what is said about church discipline.

---

7. The BCNA "Articles of Faith and Doctrine" can be found at http://www.bic-church.org/about/articlesoffaith.asp.

The confession used by the Mennonite Brethren is another example. It declares, "By calling his followers to take up the cross, Christ invites them to reject the godless values of the world and offer themselves to God in a life of service. The Holy Spirit, who lives in every Christian, empowers believers to overcome the acts and attitudes of the sinful nature."[8] Again the place of the church's mediation of God is filled by an individualistic and incomprehensible spiritual encounter. By describing this as "incomprehensible" I aim to point out the vagaries of the language of the Spirit's empowerment. It has no specified location, characteristic features, or physical signals. It is not clear when, how, or where the individual meets this empowerment. In other contemporary Anabaptist documents the church's mediating role is taken not by this sort of encounter with the Spirit, but more brutishly by a sort of individual voluntariety. This language shows up quite clearly in the Brethren in Christ statement when it says, "The response of faith is a personal reliance on God's grace and a turning from sin to righteousness." The "Confession of Faith" of the Mennonite denominations includes a statement comparable in tone that demonstrates similar reliance upon the individual's will: "Conformity to Christ necessarily implies nonconformity to the world. True faith in Christ means willingness to do the will of God, rather than willful pursuit of individual happiness."

Several important observations can be made at this point. To begin with, though the concept of ecclesial mediation is not foreign to Anabaptism, as the affirmations about the ban and church discipline demonstrate, it is employed inconsistently. Though the church can excommunicate members in the name of God, it does not welcome them or nurture them in that same name. Instead, when Anabaptist churches address these more obviously positive aspects of the Christian life they do not speak of God acting through his people but of either the power of an individual's will or the mysterious, invisible workings of the Spirit. The question is whether or not this footing provides enough traction to support the rigors of the sort of life intended.

Miroslav Volf notes the ramifications of this challenge in *After Our Likeness*. He observes, "Because human beings appropriate salvific grace in faith, the understanding of salvation (and thus also of the church) is shaped in an essential fashion by the way the faith is mediated. Hence, an

---

8. The "detailed version" of the CCMB "Confession of Faith" can be found at http://www.mbconf.ca/home/products_and_services/resources/theology/confession_of_faith/detailed_version/#8.

individualistic understanding of the mediation of faith is at once also an individualistic view of salvation, and a communal understanding of the mediation of faith is also a communal view of salvation."[9] Though Volf's categories of faith and salvation are not the operative ones in our present discussion, his insight about the link between the mediation of faith and the subsequent view of salvation is critical. If Anabaptists understand the process of initiation into the community to be one of personal and entirely spiritual encounter with God, the view of the subsequent life of that community must either uphold this initial encounter or exist awkwardly in dissonance with it. If the church is not a necessary medium through which God initiates new believers, the subsequent life of the believer will remain at odds with the claims the community makes about its role in something like redemptive discipline. The conceptual link with baptism is the belief that it functions in part as a pledge indicating of the candidate's voluntary submission to the church's power of the keys. The early Anabaptist leader Balthasar Hubmaier explains: "[W]hen he receives the baptism of water the one who is baptized testifies publicly that he has pledged himself henceforth to live according to the Rule of Christ. By virtue of this pledge he has submitted himself to sisters, brothers, and to the church so that when he transgresses they now have the authority to admonish, punish, ban, and reaccept him."[10] It is crucial to remember that this act of submission is granted to a body in which the candidate has voice. In the Anabaptist tradition it is not an alien clerical structure that claims divine power.

Yet the double standard remains: Anabaptist churches are willing to claim the role of divine mediator in discipline but not in welcome. They are willing to serve as the film critic but not its producer. Before turning more directly to a description of ecclesial mediation it will be useful to consider in a more formal way the two most prominent alternatives to affirming the church's mediatorial role. I have alluded to these in various ways, yet considering representatives of these two alternatives will strengthen my case that a more directly affirmed concept of ecclesial mediation is necessary to rightly practice believers' baptism.

---

9. Volf, *After Our Likeness*, 160.
10. Hubmaier, *Theologian of Anabaptism*, 127.

In Favor of Ecclesial Mediation

Alternative One: Human Agency in Place of Divine

Stated rather crudely, one alternative to ecclesial mediation is to deny that individuals need the assistance of God to live righteously. "Righteous character" is how Thomas Finger describes the goal of salvation in the view of most early Anabaptists. He suggests they, like many Catholics, were more concerned with the goal of salvation than with the process through which it was achieved.[11] This first alternative to ecclesial mediation extends, even caricatures this by denying that divine assistance is needed to achieve this goal. Here the powers of reason and the will form the gravitational field within which the human creature subdues unrighteousness. Nothing more than a clear-eyed, rational view of ethics is needed to produce the cruciform life. This alternative is ready at hand for Anabaptists because of the tradition's humanist roots.

Balthasar Hubmaier's emphasis on commitment is one example of a theology of baptism shaded this way. In his 1525 treatise, *On the Christian Baptism of Believers,* he describes the rite as "an outward confession or testimony through which visible brothers and sisters can know each other . . ."[12] Summarizing Hubmaier's view, Wayne Pipkin writes, "In the act of baptism one commits oneself to be a follower of Christ—if necessary, to the point of martyrdom."[13] The relevant idea here is that as a product of the will, commitment represents a cognitivist understanding of discipleship that privileges the role of reason. This strips baptism of any objective, effective, or performative power. It is only semiotic. For people like Hubmaier, who retained much of his Catholic training, this was tempered by a high ecclesiology so that baptism was not distanced from Christian formation. However, the same assumption cannot be made of contemporary Anabaptism where this medieval ecclesiology has been replaced by a revivalist ecclesial minimalism. The denominational statements surveyed earlier demonstrate the results of this quite clearly. This rationalist emphasis loses sight of the goodness of creation and the ability—even the preference—of God to make use of common elements and practices such as those by which the church is constituted.

A more current example of this thinking comes in the form of an essay titled "Can a Mennonite be an Atheist?" written by a prominent Mennonite

---

11. Finger, *Contemporary Anabaptist Theology,* 131.
12. Hubmaier, *Theologian of Anabaptism,* 127.
13. Pipkin, "Baptismal Theology of Balthasar Hubmaier," 53.

professor of English.[14] Though the title of the essay betrays its extreme character, it is a logical extension of the rationalism noted above. At the essay's crux is a familiar observation regarding the common parentage of Anabaptism and humanism and the fact that both endeavored to shake themselves loose from ecclesial strictures. The suggestion is that being a Mennonite might not, after all, necessitate being part of a tradition constituted by a particular response to God's redemptive work in Jesus. Rather, it might be understood as essentially the avowal of a humanist ethic that at one time made use of religious language but needs to do so no longer. Being a Mennonite is to do the right sort of things, and the essayist assumes our late modern sensitivities reveal that reason can guide us to the right sort of behavior. God, or belief in God, is unnecessary either to determine what these actions are or to carry them out. In this view the remedy for an evil as complex and ingrained as racism is entirely within the salvific capability of reason. After all, the author claims, racism is simply "the absence of reason."[15] In addition to dispensing with the need for God, this perspective holds that the Bible is similarly archaic and outmoded. Subsequently it is unnecessary. It follows then that in a moment of reflection on the maturation of his own thinking, the writer says, "I think now that the Bible was written for another time."[16] And he later concludes, "We don't have to have an anointed one, as Messiah, walking on this earth and telling us that he is the Son of God. We have our minds, as fallible as they are, that can tell us that we must care for the poor, not commit murder, not destroy our environment, love our neighbours, respect our parents, not kill the dark-skinned poor in other lands."[17]

Though this monistic lionization of reason cannot be fully evaluated here, a basic line of critique might proceed in this way. We might start by observing that embedded within this response to the question of the sufficiency of reason and individual will is a failure to recognize the troubling possibility that given a certain set of presuppositions and a particular social narrative, evils such as racism might appear eminently "reasonable." The idea that the Bible is written for a different time ignores the basic human

---

14. Wiebe, "Can a Mennonite be an Atheist?," 122–32. Wiebe introduces his essay as a thought experiment, but with the inclusions of his own biography it is unclear where the experiment starts or ends.

15. Ibid., 129.

16. Ibid.

17. Ibid.

need to learn to tell time within a tradition or a community.[18] Telling time and judging what seems reasonable are no different. The premise that the Bible was written for a different time disavows an important theological aspect of the incarnation—its apocalyptic nature—which affirms that the Christian Scriptures are clearly written for a time other than our own. Its time is that which turns on the apocalyptic chronology of God's self-revelation. Yet if Scripture was written for this other time, it would not necessarily follow that human reason ought to stand in judgment of Scripture, but rather that the event of Christ makes a time possible that destabilizes both reason and chronology. By overlooking the apocalyptic nature of the incarnation, the rationalist perspective supposes that the actions of humanity are prior to God's. Though the idea of a rationalist Mennonite atheism appears to be little more than a boundary case, the central assumption is not. At its core what this view holds is that modern liberal ideals such as peace, justice, tolerance, and the concept of universal rights are capable of standing in for the biblical vision of *shalom* and the redemptive work of God.

In his short book *Why I Am Not a Secularist*, the American political philosopher William Connolly cautions readers against relying on such generic conceptual tools, the very reliance that underwrites secularism.[19] He observes that in the struggle to mitigate the powers of exclusion and to lessen the suffering of those whose very identities render them marginalized our society places the burden of realizing the good upon the ideal of justice. Yet Connolly points out that justice in itself is unable to move us beyond the reality that some modes of suffering go unnoticed because their very nature disqualifies the sufferer from the basic sanctity of personhood. If one does not deem a slave to be fully human, justice loses its leverage.

Justice is not as powerful as we might wish it were, for it is only after a movement crosses the "threshold of cultural attentiveness" that the mode of suffering it names fits into the categories in which justice can be efficacious. Connolly argues that "Failure by many secular theorists to acknowledge this fundamental ambiguity at the center of justice disable them from registering the importance of an ethos of responsiveness to justice itself."[20] In Connolly's view then it is not surprising that Western society has been forced to supplement justice with a value like tolerance—but even tolerance remains insufficient. For Connolly, tolerance "implies benevolence toward

---

18. I have in mind MacIntyre, *After Virtue*; and *Whose Justice?*
19. Connolly, *Why I Am Not a Secularist*, 27–41.
20. Ibid., 63.

others amid stability of ourselves..."²¹ And this stability always comes at others' expense or exclusion. Here it is worth quoting Connolly at length:

> It is extremely probable that all of us today are unattuned to some modes of suffering and exclusion that will have become ethically important tomorrow as a political movement carries them across the threshold of cultural attentiveness and institutional redefinition. This is so because each effective movement of difference toward a new, legitimate cultural identity breaks a constituent in its previous composition that located it below the operational reach of personhood and justice by rendering it immoral, inferior, hysterical, sinful, incapacitated, unnatural, abnormal, irresponsible, monomaniacal, narcissistic, nihilistic, or sick.²²

In the face of the view that reason itself can provide a foundation for the righteous society, Connolly exposes genuine limitations.

The question is what sorts of sources are capable of facilitating an "ethos of responsiveness," which Connolly sees as a necessary correlate to a value such as justice. Connolly does not see these sources readily available within secularism. Why then would Anabaptists abandon biblical assumptions about the necessity of divine redemption and constitutive practices of biblical communities for the generic reasoning of modern cosmopolitanism? Might this not be an abandonment of the very material that forms an ethos capable of giving content and precision to values like justice and tolerance? Though these ideals and the dispositions they invoke are useful, their ability to form persons capable of reasoning morally or possessing judgment sensitive enough to see beyond the limits of the assumed horizon of justice is doubtful.

Connolly's critique of secularism undercuts the optimistic foundation that holds up the view that the voluntary individual is capable of producing the life to which the Anabaptist moral imagination is drawn. Though this analysis is too cursory to *prove* this alternative to ecclesial mediation incoherent, it does at least cast doubt on the idea that ecclesial practices such as baptism and the divine activity they assume should be easily dismissed as outmoded.

---

21. Ibid., 62.
22. Ibid., 68–69.

Alternative Two: Spiritualizing Divine Action

It is almost twenty years since Stephen Dintaman wrote the manifesto, "The Spiritual Poverty of the Anabaptist Vision." The attention that the essay received shows that it succinctly articulated something many Anabaptists already sensed.[23] Dintaman argued that the contemporary Anabaptist approach to the Christian life lacks sufficient practical and spiritual theology to undergird its demanding ethics.[24] This line of thinking represents an alternative to ecclesial mediation in which the view of human potential is decidedly more pessimistic.

In Dintaman's view the contemporary Anabaptist ethic has become overly focused on activism and is essentially behavioral. He declares that Anabaptists have tended to "keep the language of behavioral discipleship fresh and green and growing, while little passion or creativity was invested in positive instruction about sin, the work of Christ, and the existential reality of the Spirit."[25] This development of the Anabaptist vision is, in his view, impoverished in three important ways: (1) Contemporary understandings of human behavior are not brought to bear and it is thereby assumed that behavioral changes are the result of simple willful decisions.[26] (2) It fails to maintain an awareness of *God's* liberating work. Human-powered processes such as social activism and conflict mediation have taken the place of faith and have marginalized the essence of the gospel.[27] (3) This version

---

23. Dintaman, "The Spiritual Poverty," 205–8; also published in the more popular *The Gospel Herald*, 23 February 1993, 1–3.

24. Dintaman borrows the phrase "Anabaptist Vision" from the seminal neo-Anabaptist historian and church leader Harold Bender. See his *The Anabaptist Vision*. Before being published in the pamphlet form cited here, *The Anabaptist Vision* was presented by Bender as his presidential address to the American Society of Church History in 1943. In this pamphlet Bender takes up the thesis that Anabaptism is best understood as the culmination of the Reformation—a hyper-Protestantism. In his view the early Anabaptists held onto the original vision of Luther and Zwingli and "enlarged it, gave it body and form, and set out to achieve it in actual experience." Bender's essay is available online at *GAMEO*, s.v. "Anabaptist Vision (Text, 1944)."

25. Dintaman, "Spiritual Poverty," 207.

26. Ibid., 206.

27. Dintaman writes: "The good news is not that Jesus has given us peace ideals and we are called to implement them non-violently. That would make God passive and make us the central actors in the drama of redemption" (ibid., 207).

of the Christian faith amounts to a pre-Pentecost form of discipleship that does not recognize the empowering presence and work of the Holy Spirit.[28]

The solution to the problem, Dintaman believes, is a renewed spirituality more obviously dependent upon what we receive in Christ: "What I covet for myself and anyone else who has been spiritually impoverished by adherence to the Anabaptist vision, is a fresh realization that to be a disciple is not simply to do but to be in a new way." He hopes for a renewed awareness of the "spiritual presence and power of the risen Christ."[29] Put another way, he thinks Anabaptists need to experience "what it means to have a vital and life-changing personal friendship with the crucified and risen Jesus."[30]

The "Spiritual Poverty of the Anabaptist Vision" was first published in *The Conrad Grebel Review* in 1992. In 1995 the entire winter edition of the same journal was dedicated to engaging Dintaman's essay. In the context of the argument being laid out in this book, Dintaman's article can be seen to parallel my critique of optimistic humanist versions of Anabaptism. This is particularly true when he writes, "Peace and justice social activism and engagement in conflict mediation can be authentic expressions of faith in Jesus Christ, but I believe that for many it has become more of a *substitute* for faith."[31] Dintaman points Anabaptist theology in a positive direction, toward the doctrine of God. If we recall the ecclesiological disparity noted at the beginning of this chapter it seems plausible that its origin is related to a poorly conceived doctrine of God and that a recovery of this doctrine is necessary for Anabaptist life and witness to remain intelligible as Christian life and witness.

The fact that many Anabaptists found Dintaman's argument either compelling or inflammatory is not surprising. One of the points of greatest internal tension for early Anabaptists was the extent to which their movement overlapped with the radical spiritualists. As the pietism of the Dintaman article demonstrates, this differentiation remains difficult. It is hard on a practical level to parse between radical spiritualism, which denies the importance of the physical, and the important role of the Spirit in any genuinely Christian movement. The controversial early Anabaptist leader and schoolteacher Hans Denck embodies this tension well. In Anabaptist circles Denck is best known for his oft-quoted line, "No one may

28. Ibid.
29. Ibid.
30. Ibid., 205.
31. Ibid., 206.

In Favor of Ecclesial Mediation

truly know Christ except he follows him in life." Born before the Protestant Reformation, Denck's theology was influenced by medieval mysticism as well as Thomas Müntzer. But Denck was an Anabaptist, at least for a time. Sources say that he was baptized by Balthasar Hubmaier and briefly led the Anabaptist community in Augsburg. Denck was skilled in several languages and became a prolific writer, earning in the minds of some of his ironical detractors the title of Anabaptist "pope." Denck believed that baptism had both an inner and an outer form. It was the former which he deemed most important and eventually he denied that physical baptism was necessary at all. Consistent with this development he embraced Casper Schwenckfeld's brand of radical spiritualism. Denck's spiritual journey was not a long one—he died of the plague at twenty-seven years of age.[32] Part of his legacy is the challenging overlap between the Anabaptist movement and sixteenth-century spiritualism. In a way it parallels Dintaman's pietist response to contemporary challenges.

Against the rationalist rejection of the Divine other, "The Spiritual Poverty of the Anabaptist Vision" points readers in the right direction. Yet the precise solution Dintaman offers is ultimately disappointing because it actually reinforces the ambiguity of contemporary denominational statements in which God is encountered only in the abstract. Dintaman believes what Anabaptists need is what pietists already have—a personal, spiritual friendship with Jesus. If the language he uses about "relationship" with Jesus, the "empowerment" and "renewing work" of the Spirit, and God's work of "redemption" were not so familiar, his Anabaptist readers would be struck by the obvious: they are not told how or where these spiritual encounters with God should occur. Though Dintaman's worry about the practical atheism of Anabaptist activism is insightful, his solution gathers little momentum because, like spiritualist movements across the centuries, it lacks ecclesial enmeshment. Divine action is cut free of Christ's body. The alternative to ecclesial mediation represented by "The Spiritual Poverty of the Anabaptist Vision," though it rightly names and rejects the problems of individualistic voluntarism, does not represent a useful course forward.

Both the spiritual-pietist approach and the rational-humanist approach lack a concrete account of God's ongoing activity and presence in the world. The assumptions that one can remain agnostic about God's self-revelation, in an effort to affirm human potential, or that one can speak about a relationship with Jesus as an abstract notion both avoid elements of

---

32. Finger, *Contemporary Anabaptist Theology*, 27–29.

God's willingness to relate to humanity through the media of creation. The rational-humanist alternative to ecclesial mediation dismisses the incarnation, and the spiritual-pietist alternative dismisses its ecclesial echoes. The inadequacy of these two representative alternatives pushes us once more toward the necessity of ecclesial mediation.

CONCEPTUAL CONTOURS

In light of the insufficiency of these two alternatives, the goal of the second part of this chapter is to work toward a clearer conception of how baptism might be both an act of discipleship and a redeeming act of God. This requires a description of ecclesial mediation congenial to Anabaptist belief and practice. Toward this end I will present two differing views on the matter: the first comes from Karl Barth, the second from one of his students, John Howard Yoder. Through the consideration of these two views I will begin to address the crucial problem of baptismal agency. To whom do we attribute the efficacy of baptism? Is it to God, the baptizand, the church, or some combination of these? Orienting this initial foray around the work of Barth and Yoder moves the argument forward by critically delimiting the concept. Though the part of Barth's work surveyed here does not present us with a clear doctrine of ecclesial mediation, it will help develop a dogmatic framework within which the role of the church can be more carefully understood. If Barth's description of human action, or ethics, can be said to be primarily from above, the part of Yoder's work under scrutiny here presents a view of the same topic from below. Both descriptions require the other. As I will show, however, an aspect of Yoder's presentation is problematic and stands in the way of an appropriate employment of ecclesial mediation as a theological concept.

Karl Barth on Baptism

Karl Barth confounded many of his admirers in the latter part of his career when, breaking with his own Reformed tradition, he made public his stance against infant baptism. His position on baptism does not make him an Anabaptist theologian but it does mean his work is uniquely situated for involvement in the present discussion.[33] Barth's provocative view was

---

33. For instance, Barth affirms neither the humanist synergism of Hubmaier, nor the anthropology upon which it is based.

In Favor of Ecclesial Mediation

unveiled in two key stages. The first was in his 1943 lecture "The Teaching of the Church regarding Baptism." Here Barth called infant baptism into question while at the same time maintaining a fairly strong view of the role of the church and the propriety of its sacraments. The second stage was in the late 1960s, which saw the development of volume 4 of his extensive *Church Dogmatics*. In the part-volume 4/4 Barth treats baptism as a discrete topic. Here he draws a sharp distinction between the work of God and the response of humanity and rejects the doctrine of the sacraments—save the one true sacrament, Jesus Christ.[34] Various explanations have been given for the disparity between his position in 4/4 and his prior work. One is that the shift amounts only to a change in terminology behind which still stands theological continuity. Another is that his later position is a necessary corrective to his earlier work. Finally, it is also charged that 4/4 is simply a mistake, an inconsistency that amounts to gnostic dualism.[35] Yet, in both iterations Barth's theology of (adult) baptism provides us with a construal of the practice that upholds the centrality of God's revelation in Christ, unequivocally requires individual response, and manages to retain the priority of divine initiative in the process of redemption. I view this combination as both amenable to Anabaptist assumptions and as foundational for this reconsideration of believers' baptism. The following summary of Barth's position is taken from *CD* 4/4.

We begin by noting that for Barth, baptism is a transitional event marking the first step of a life lived in Christ and serves to set its trajectory. Baptism with water follows baptism in the Spirit as a distinct event, a response to the work of God in the awakening of conversion. Baptism with water is a response to God's action in which Christians declare that their lives are bound up in the task of God's graced people to bless the world: "[One] becomes in baptism an active member of the holy people of Israel which according to Is. 42:6 is set as 'a mediator of the covenant among the nations.'"[36] The responsive character of baptism is found in its relationship to the command of God, which has reconciliation in Jesus Christ through the Holy Spirit as its goal.[37] In Barth's view baptism is a part of the larger

---

34. Yocum, *Ecclesial Mediation*, 142. An alternative ecclesiology that upholds both the role of Christ as the "primordial sacrament" and the ongoing necessity of the sacraments can be found in Schillebeeckx, *Christ the Sacrament*.

35. Yocum, *Ecclesial Mediation*, xi–xiv.

36. Barth, *CD* 4/4:201.

37. Ibid., 72.

biblical drama in which God through Christ moves toward humanity and involves human creatures in God's triune history. Paul's words in Romans 6 are paradigmatic: "For if we have been united with him in a death like his, we will certainly be united with him in a resurrection like his. We know that our old self was crucified with him so that the body of sin might be destroyed, and we might no longer be enslaved to sin . . . The death he died, he died to sin, once for all; but the life he lives, he lives to God. So you also must consider yourselves dead to sin and alive to God in Christ Jesus."[38] For Paul, and Barth in his wake, baptism is inseparable from God's action in Christ and God's ongoing faithfulness to humanity. Baptism is not a rite of passage into freedom, liberty, equality, or the *good* as such. For Barth, baptism into anything other than the work of Christ is not Christian baptism.[39]

For all that Barth affirms about divine priority it may strike some readers as strange to look to him to clarify the work of God in the practices of the church since in 4/4 he so clearly rejects a sacramental understanding of baptism. However, it is important to clarify what Barth means when he disavows the sacramental quality of baptism and splits the baptism of the Spirit from the baptism of water. Barth writes, "Baptism responds to a mystery, the sacrament of the history of Jesus Christ, of His resurrection, of the outpouring of the Holy Spirit but is not itself, however, a mystery or sacrament."[40] Instead of being a sacrament, baptism is human action embodying an acknowledgment of the work of God in Christ—the one true sacrament—and it must continue, in Barth's words, to "bear witness to it, to confess it, to respond to it, to honor, praise, and magnify it."[41] Again, this must not be misinterpreted. Barth is rejecting the traditional Catholic, Lutheran, and Reformed theologies of the sacraments, but this does not mean he sees no place for creaturely elements in God's work.[42] In 4/2 of Barth's *Dogmatics* he discusses conversion and writes: "We are thus forced to say that this awakening is both wholly creaturely and wholly divine . . . . [T]here can be no question of co-ordination between two comparable elements, but only of the absolute primacy of the divine over the creaturely. The creaturely is made serviceable to the divine and does actually serve it.

---

38. Rom 6:5–11.
39. Barth, *CD* 4/4:92.
40. Ibid., 102.
41. Ibid., 72.
42. Ibid., 102–7.

It is used by God as His organ or instrument."[43] Furthermore in 4/4, though Barth affirms the sufficiency and priority of God's work in the baptism of the Spirit, he acknowledges that "[T]he witnessing ministry of the community of Jesus Christ, in the form of the human life, speech, and action of some of the Christians who are its members is not without share, but has a very important share, in this event."[44] Barth does not reject in total the creaturely or the role of the church; but rather, he firmly locates the valid role of both within the prior determinative agency of God.

In spite of his non-sacramental position, Barth's description of baptism does not reduce it to a human project. It depends entirely on the movement of God, and only within this is it a free human act. As a human response to God's grace revealed in Jesus Christ, baptism can, and for Barth *must*, be understood as a free act. Since baptism is the beginning of a life of faithfulness to God it cannot be cloaked in coercion, for that in Barth's view, would undercut the act of obedience: "Obedience to God can only be free obedience."[45] The freedom of the act of baptism parallels the sanctifying and redeeming work of Jesus Christ and the Holy Spirit, and it supports the charge that the baptism of children is both misguided and surreptitiously coercive. Of course for Barth the other side of the dialectic remains in place; while baptism is an act of obedience, it is not independent of the work of God. This retains an account of the frailty of the human creature that voluntarist visions lack. Barth is aware that as a human action baptism is inherently tenuous, possibly even presumptuous. Who can know what such a commitment may eventually demand? Who can presume the ability to be faithful? Thus Barth is careful to affirm that God underwrites the ordinance. It is God's faithfulness and goodness that assures the propriety of baptism. And yet, for Barth, human action is not overwhelmed by God but is taken seriously.[46] Therefore, even though Barth insists that baptism cannot be compulsory and that it must be an act chosen by the candidate and the church community, his thinking does not imply an exclusion of God's activity.[47] It is not even in tension with it. Believers' baptism rightly carried out affirms the compatibility of Divine grace and human agency.

---

43. Barth, *CD* 4/2:557.
44. Barth, *CD* 4/4:32.
45. Ibid., 132.
46. Ibid., 163.
47. Ibid., 131–32.

James Buckley describes Barth's understanding of the relationship of human and divine action in baptism as "differentiated unity."[48] Admittedly, this phrase implies a more optimistic analysis than some would be comfortable with, yet it begins to describe a relationship between the acting agents that is neither mutually exclusive nor reductionist. This is in contrast to the way some less reflective versions of the sacramental and testimonial views contribute to the antagonistic divide between the two theological emphases.

Baptism, for Barth, is a way of stepping into God's promise of which the enabling presence of the Spirit is a foretaste—a foretaste of the coming full reign of Jesus Christ.[49] This enables them to welcome the past, where, to use Barth's scheme, the *sacrament* of Jesus Christ took place in history, as well as the future where the eschatological ramifications of that same event reach full consummation.[50] This confident Christian hope in Christ is as distinct from modern optimism about reason and justice as it is from the pessimistic postmodern reverence encountered in the work of someone like William Connolly. Through death and new life in Christ—the reality enacted in baptism—Christians confess that their individual and collective identity rests in something beyond the contingencies of human knowledge and will. In this ritual the inherently marginalizing concept of selfhood as self-centered, which engenders postmodern skepticism, is replaced by the eccentric self, a way of being that depends on the particular universality of Christ. For Anabaptists a key consequence of this construal is that the eccentric self baptismally realized in the triumphant and slain Lamb can more readily avoid the temptation of violent self-defense. Baptism that recognizes the concreteness of Divine action enables Christians to live peaceably and to truly welcome others into the community of the worship of God.

Though Barth's view of baptism functions as a corrective to Anabaptist thought, it is not always corrective enough. In fact it shares the common flaw of dichotomizing the one event into two by distancing God's act in the baptism of the Spirit from the church's act in the baptism of water.[51] Yet for Anabaptist readers Barth still provides the doctrine of believers' baptism with missing theological depth. What emerges from reading Barth in this context is the conclusion that believers' baptism need not be allergic to a

---

48. Buckley, "Christian Community," 204.

49. Barth, *CD* 4/4:40.

50. Ibid., 206–10.

51. For a helpful description of Barth's baptismal dichotomy in dialogue with an alternative vision see Mangina, *Karl Barth*, 161–72.

strong view of the primacy of God's grace. Just as many early Anabaptists understood the Christian life to be rightly characterized by obedience, Barth shows us that believers' baptism need not be promethean. The fact that it is responsive and contingent as much as it is a voluntary act of discipleship helps us see the congruency of this initiatory rite with the tradition of Anabaptist pacifism. Baptism is not about making history turn out correctly; it is about responding appropriately to God revealed in Jesus.

A Non-Exclusive Account of Human and Divine Agency

Stressing Divine action as does Barth could lead some to worry that it might overrun the human element of the ordinance altogether and leave Anabaptists looking rather obtuse for not baptizing infants after all. It is certainly possible to overextend the determinative nature of God's initiatory action in baptism and lose sight of the place God marks out for human response as revealed in the biblical witness. Indeed, some might make this charge of the Barthian account just given. This has been done of Barth's work in general. Since this is a common response it is worth considering how John Webster, a particularly attentive reader of Barth, understands him on this point. In listening to Webster we will gain not just insight into Barth's theology, but more constructively, perceive an outline of how to construe the relationship of Divine and human agency. It is the fog that surrounds this relationship that produces the theological ambiguity I am attempting to dissolve. In gaining a view of the ethical space created for humanity within the will of God, we can see the essential parameters of the concurrence of divine and human action in the life of the church.

In *Barth's Moral Theology*, Webster vigorously argues against the common notion that in Barth's thought God's saving work overwhelms human action.[52] Webster proposes that for Barth human freedom and human action are both relative categories, neither absolute nor independent. Both are better understood as being contingent upon God and must be thought of as corollaries to God's freedom. Thus, the center of human selfhood and moral discernment is not the vague entity of the self; it is God's revelation and judgment, which grants it a proper specificity.[53] In Webster's analysis, Barth departs from the modern cultural turn toward inwardness and embeds human agency in God's action. Attempts to consider human agency

52. Webster, *Barth's Moral Theology*.
53. Ibid., 99, 114, 175.

merely in the context of human moral consciousness are, for Barth, wrongheaded. They amount to avoidance of God's prevenient acts of redemption. For Barth being a moral agent is to be shaped by an externality—God—rather than interiority, and therefore theological ethics must always bend itself toward God's judgment.[54] Webster writes that in Barth's thinking, "*All* worlds of discourse and *all* human perception are relativized by God's communicating self-presence, a presence which both forbids co-ordination or correlation of theology and other disciplines and also undermines theological arrogance."[55] This means that since humans are God's created creatures our lives are shaped by God's call and not by being our own projects. In this light we see that human self-determination or "freedom" for Barth is not merely synthesized with divine determination, but is brought under the definitional power of Christian theological language derived from the narrative of God's covenant with humanity.[56] The definitional power of this narrative gains clearer inflection through Christology. Through this lens the moral field is framed by the hypostatic union itself and divine subjectivity takes precedence over human.[57]

What form does this abstract language actually take in the Christian life? For Barth the paradigmatic human activity is not faith, not witness, not pacifism, not activism in its myriad of forms—it is *prayer*. In this activity humans are enabled by the Holy Spirit to call on God. Prayer is not only a request for God to work in creation, but it is itself a human work willed and made possible by God.[58] Webster summarizes Barth's understanding of human freedom by outlining his three key theological moves, which can be summarized as follows: (1) God's freedom is his own, and therefore it is God that takes the initial move of commitment to humanity; (2) human freedom is a gift from God, and in it we appropriate God's election; and therefore, (3) theological ethics is a reflection on human action in the context of God's calling.[59]

Webster's description of Barth here is clear and begins to provide the categories for understanding how baptism might be the product of God's work *and* of human freedom. The importance of this Barthian structure

54. Ibid., 42–45.
55. Ibdi., 47.
56. Ibid., 101–2.
57. Ibid., 169.
58. Ibid., 171–73.
59. Ibid., 101.

is that God is not introduced into a theology of the Christian life as an entity to fill gaps in a largely anthropocentric and voluntarist matrix, as, for instance, seems to be the case in Hubmaier's defense of the freedom of the will.[60] Instead, Barth's work describes the deep character of human action in relationship to God's. This provides a conceptual clarity lacking in the Anabaptist denominational statements. What we can take from Barth at this point, despite his disavowal of a strong form of ecclesial mediation implicit in his rejection of the sacraments, is that approaching baptism with the assumption that its effectiveness must lie either with God or with humanity is wrongheaded. In couching human freedom within Divine freedom, Barth enables us to constantly affirm both. This does not, however, necessitate either a sacramental or a testimonial view of baptism since both of these views affirm that God and humans act, though it does exclude extreme versions of both. If human freedom is to come under the definitional power of the story of God's action in the world then baptism itself must adhere to this same axiom. This means that the determinative language for the emerging doctrine of ecclesial mediation should be primarily structured not by a highly developed theology of the sacraments or semiotic theory but by the narrative of God's relationship with humanity.

What Barth does not show very clearly is how the church participates in this economy. It is not immediately clear what the church does in conversion or baptism. This weakness has been diagnosed by Joseph Mangina who argues that while Barth maintains that the church is "securely anchored within the economy of grace," it becomes dehistoricized. Although the church's essential identity remains correlated to that of Christ, this is not transferred to the church's empirical or social life.[61] Mangina contends, "To be more precise, while Barth emphasizes the church's task as a witness to Christ, it is not clear that the church *as a configuration of human practices* makes much difference to this task."[62] It is interesting that this last statement in particular parallels my analysis in the previous chapter of contemporary Anabaptist denominational statements. It is therefore necessary to say, in much more direct ways than Barth, that God's enabling of human freedom occurs primarily, though not exclusively, through the church. Humans are enabled by the Spirit to pray, to use a favored example of Barth's, most directly in the context of the ministry of the church. It is through the

60. Hubmaier, *Theologian of Anabaptism*, 426–91.
61. Mangina, "Bearing the Marks of Jesus," 271–78.
62. Ibid., 278.

life of the community of those who acknowledge the lordship of Christ that individuals hear most plainly the call of the Spirit and learn to respond appropriately. Webster's account of Barth's moral theology does not present a consistent or clear doctrine of ecclesial mediation, even though it makes conceptual space for it. This is not Webster's intention. Upon first read Barth's *CD* 4/4 makes it difficult to believe that he consistently endorses such a doctrine. Yet, some Barth scholars, John Yocum most notably, have argued that a subtle form of this doctrine is woven throughout the *Church Dogmatics*.[63] Either way, my contention is that an Anabaptist theology of baptism is strengthened by Barth's doctrine of God and thereby less likely to melt into an anthropocentric ethical system incapable of formation or discernment that is particularly Christian. Webster makes it clear that Barth's doctrine of God leaves ample room for the integrity of human agency.

John Howard Yoder and the Sacraments

Barth's work helps to mark out a certain territory within Divine intention for the creaturely and ecclesial, situating human freedom within God's. We might say that this is to approach the question of ecclesial mediation from above, but the question can also be approached from below, from the social realm. This is necessary to begin the task of describing how the actual physical life of the church bears witness to Christ. A short book written by John Howard Yoder, one of Barth's students, facilitates an initial foray in this direction. This book, *Body Politics,* is more like an extended essay than it is a full monograph. While it is certainly not everything Yoder wrote about the sacraments, considering it in some detail will serve to outline what ecclesial mediation might be like from this second perspective. Yoder studied under Barth at the University of Basel. Though much of Yoder's work betrays Barth's influence, like any good scholar Yoder retained his own judgment. During his doctoral studies in Switzerland Yoder wrote a critique of Barth's position on war and presented it to him in the summer of 1957, shortly before Barth was to participate on a panel for Yoder's final oral exam.[64] Thus while Yoder's theological project is amenable to Barth's, we must not consider it a clone.

Yoder's work shares some of Barth's nervousness about using the language of mystery and sacrament to refer to the practices of the church.

---

63. Yocum, *Ecclesial Mediation*.
64. Yoder's critique has been published in *Karl Barth and the Problem of War*.

In Favor of Ecclesial Mediation

However, Yoder's aversion is neither as strong nor as fundamental. Yoder writes, "I have sometimes proposed to try to retrieve the term [sacrament] . . . distinguishing between 'sacramental' and 'sacramentalistic', but we are not always able to commend to others a corrected use of traditional terms."[65] Yoder's work is relevant to this project both because of its status within Anabaptist theology and because it takes as axiomatic God's creation of the church while maintaining the propriety of its voluntary character. Yoder's theology circles around the twin emphases of ecclesiology and Christology. This is not to the exclusion of other traditional doctrines such as creation, revelation, eschatology, and so on; but rather, a result of Yoder's conviction that God has revealed himself most clearly in Jesus and that it is in the church that the implications of this are continually discerned and lived. This is why Yoder is most well known for defending Christian pacifism in a broadly relevant way and why his work is not methodologically straight-jacketed or foundationalist. Uncharacteristically describing his own methodology in a memo to Mark Thiessen Nation, Yoder writes, "My position is stronger if/as/because it is not my own, not stated on the grounds of a basis I first lay out. A foundationalist beginning is by definition sectarian."[66] Like Barth's, Yoder's theology is dialogical—something of an ongoing conversation.

It is in the tone of this minimalist methodology that Yoder describes the practices of the church in his short book *Body Politics*. This work is not meant to be a full sacramental theology, and neither is Yoder attempting to describe all the sources necessary for performing the Christian faith. However, Yoder's work in this book is intriguing in the context of our present discussion because he describes five key church practices with an eye toward the political importance of each. His understanding of the basic character of the relationship between the Christian community's core practices and politics is revealed when he says: "The Christian community, like any community held together by commitment to important values, *is* a political reality. That is, the church has the character of a *polis*."[67] In saying that the church is a *polis* Yoder is indicating that it is a structured social body with defined roles, methods of making decisions and common goals. In this framework the five ecclesial practices—which he discusses using the non-traditional terminology of "binding and loosing," "breaking bread," "baptism," "the fullness of Christ," and "the rule of Paul"—are ways in which

---

65. Yoder, *Body Politics*, 44.
66. As quoted in Zimmerman, *Practicing the Politics of Jesus*, 180.
67. Yoder, *Body Politics*, viii.

the church is called to be a *polis*. These practices demonstrate the ultimate calling of the world.[68] Yoder envisions them to both serve as a set of goals or ideals and to be the very process for achieving these goals. For instance, what Yoder refers to as binding and loosing, a phrase meant to encapsulate both moral discernment and reconciliation as described in Matthew 18, is a practice that names both an ideal, a reconciled community, and a process, communal discernment. In the practice of breaking bread Yoder observes both the celebration of a common meal among the followers of Jesus and a sharing of goods. In baptism he sees the introduction of a new humanity, a new identity that surpasses old social boundaries. In the practice of the fullness of Christ Yoder sees that every member of this new community has a specific role to play, each has something to offer. The rule of Paul is a mode of interaction for community meetings. Each individual, regardless of role, has the right to speak in turn.

After explaining the first three practices in *Body Politics* Yoder synthesizes his preceding account by naming commonalities. Here is a portion of his description: "Of all three practices it is the case that the practices are ordinary human behavior. To reconcile through dialogue, to share bread with one another, or to fuse two cultural histories into one new shared community are not mysterious. No esoteric insight is needed for them to make sense. A social scientist could watch them happening. There are no necessary correct holy words to make the rites 'right'; no special chapter titled 'theology of sacraments' is needed to describe what is going on."[69] Yoder goes on to suggest that the discipline which could most aptly perceive what is happening in these church practices is neither semantics, aesthetics, nor dogmatics, but rather *sociology*. With this statement Yoder is not suggesting that the five practices he studies do not have roots in the work of Jesus. He is proposing that their ongoing effectiveness could be best understood sociologically. The advantage of this is that these practices are open to adoption by any community that observes their fruitfulness. Thus the social reach of the gospel can extend far beyond the Christian community itself. The anchoring of the community's social vision in practices instead of abstract ideals implies their inherent pedagogical character. Through these practices communities deepen their commitment to a way of life and create a strong tradition of embodied knowledge.

---

68. Yoder, *Body Politics*, ix.
69. Yoder, *Body Politics*, 44.

In Favor of Ecclesial Mediation

The attention Yoder pays to practices is generally aligned with a broad range of contemporary scholarship that emphasizes the importance of embodied practices and virtue formation.[70] The attention given to the work of Aristotle by philosophers such as Martha Nussbaum and Alasdair MacIntyre are examples of this. The weight that the moral theologian Stanley Hauerwas has placed on virtue and character is another.[71] Sarah Wenger Shenk, president of a Mennonite seminary, argues for the value of recognizing embodied forms of knowledge and learning, saying:

> We have often underestimated the importance and persistence of the bodily aspects of social memory, but we do it to our own peril. Those who understand the Christian tradition as primarily the social embodiment of the narrative and ethic of Jesus rather than the exposition of an abstract doctrine will pay particular attention to the assertion that we preserve the past most memorably in our bodies. The values we are most anxious to conserve we will entrust to bodily automatisms because the past can be best kept alive by a habitual memory sedimented in the body.[72]

Other scholars have explored similar themes with particular attention to the way in which religious ritual expresses and shapes knowledge.[73] In *Body Politics*, however, Yoder is not working on a general theory of knowledge or a full scale development of moral theory; he is endeavoring to show how sacramental and ethical questions are knit together.

Yoder aims to read the biblical accounts of these practices through his preferred hermeneutic of biblical realism, which means in part that he tries to attend to the historical and cultural background available without allowing the methodology of historical-critical study to dictate metaphysical parameters. Yoder's goal is to read Scripture by thinking along with the text, letting it provide the categories in which it is to be understood. Because of this methodology, questions like whether or not to use sacramental language are not crucial. With respect to the practices of binding and loosing, breaking bread, and baptism Yoder writes, "[I]t is formally said in the NT that when humans do it, God is doing it. This would justify our using the

---

70. For a description of the development of "practice" as a focus of ritual studies see Bell, *Ritual*, 76–83. A particularly prominent example from the field of anthropology is Bourdieu, *The Logic of Practice*.

71. For example, see Nussbaum, *Aristotle's De Motu Animalium*; MacIntyre, *After Virtue*; Hauerwas, *A Community of Character*.

72. Shenk, *Ways of Knowing*, 143.

73. Shilbrack, ed., *Thinking through Rituals*.

word *sacrament* if the term had not been burdened by mechanical or magical misreadings through the centuries."[74] Terminology aside, it is clear that for Yoder these practices effect what they signify.

For Yoder the meaning of baptism is clarified by the Pauline language of new creation, chiefly drawn from 2 Corinthians and Galatians. In Christ a disparate people are welcomed through baptism into a new humanity that joins the Jewish and Gentile narratives.[75] Yoder strains to find a term that describes what is going on in this rite. He rejects what he calls a "Zwinglian" or "Baptist" view that reduces baptism to a symbol. He argues that a symbol "does not make the world new."[76] As noted earlier, he also rejects what he terms a "sacramentalistic" view of baptism that relies on the play of mediated salvation against original sin. He is looking for a form of sacramental language that communicates baptism "is the formation of a new people whose newness and togetherness explicitly relativize prior stratification and classification."[77] There is resonance here with Webster's depiction of Barth's moral theology: the priority of Divine freedom in creating a new people takes precedence over human inclination toward fragmentation. Yet Yoder more forcefully shows that the world continues to encounter the apocalypse of Christ through the church's witness.

My search for language that clearly communicates what happens in baptism parallels Yoder's. It is the core of Yoder's proposal in *Body Politics*, however, that clarifies the type of ecclesial mediation that can help Anabaptists make sense of baptism. Yoder's affirmation about ecclesial practices, "when humans do it, God is doing it," is glib, but the center of his rationale—that the good news of the gospel is lived in the church—is crucial. The objective qualities of Christian initiation that believers' baptism so easily forgets can be recovered coherently through an ecclesiological affirmation that God chooses to act in, with, and under the work of the church. That is to say, the church's life participates in the gospel of Jesus Christ and is the primary media through which God is present in the world.

Yoder describes how this is not limited to baptism but is characteristic of biblical ecclesiology and politics generally. In the context of Yoder's

---

74. Yoder, *Body Politics*, 44. Yoder's regret at the history of the language of sacrament in some ways mirrors Barth's in *CD* 4/4; Yocum, *Ecclesial Mediation*, 146.

75. Yoder, *Body Politics*, 28–33.

76. Ibid., 33. Here Yoder's view is similar to Barth's in his 1943 baptism lecture, Yocum, *Ecclesial Mediation*, 144.

77. Yoder, *Body Politics*, 33.

description of the church as a *polis* the discussion of baptism quickly broadens beyond the usual study of liturgics or theology of the sacraments. This means that our present inquiry into the theology of baptism is a point of entry into the whole ecology of Anabaptist thought and practice. A serious problem with the contemporary practice of believers' baptism such as the inclusion of young children is indicative of a larger vulnerability. The first part of this chapter dealt with two possible alternatives to an Anabaptist affirmation of ecclesial mediation: a sort of rationalist humanism and an individualistic pietism. Yoder's socio-political vision is more concrete than either of these, and that is to its credit. However, it also contains a serious risk, one that may well be the rightful target of Dintaman's essay.

The Necessity of Theological Description

The troubling implications of Yoder's approach make themselves known in his assertion that the effectiveness of church practices is best understood *sociologically*. Why does he think sociology is the superior explanatory discipline? His dismissal of *dogmatics*, described earlier, is particularly revealing. In a version of this same essay published a year before in the journal *Theology Today*, Yoder speaks of the disciplines which are *not* needed to perceive these practices as semantics and philosophy. In the earlier venue he forgoes the dismissal of dogmatics, which is later included in *Body Politics*.[78] It is doubtful that the increased precision of Yoder's writing is accidental. His privileging of the discipline of sociology and the explanatory power of the social scientist represent a deliberate description of how these ordinances are effective. Additionally, in Yoder's scheme there is nothing about these practices that uniquely places them within the life of the church. They can be practiced by non-church entities with equal effectiveness. This is what Yoder intends to emphasize by saying that no particular language is required for their proper function. The sacraments are universally available social practices and are *themselves* the good news. What are often thought of as unique ordinances or rituals of the church constitute social practices such as sharing, peaceful conflict resolution, and so on. In Yoder's view these are not results of the gospel—they are the gospel.[79] Thus, Yoder universalizes a ver-

---

78. Yoder, "Sacrament as Social Process," 40. For a provocative description of the development of Yoder's thinking on the sacraments, see Martens, "The Problematic Development."

79. This is implicit throughout the book, but most clearly stated in, Yoder, *Body Politics*, 75.

sion of the Christian faith that is practically rich but, on the surface at least, is virtually devoid of theological content, which is to say it is unclear how God remains involved. Yoder's ostensive sacramental rhetoric is undercut by deflating the notion of sacrament into a universal social program. The charge of sociological reductionism applies in a particular way to this particular text of Yoder's.[80] The problems with the position he takes here have already been hinted at through the work of William Connolly in terms of the poverty of secularism. As I will suggest, other portions of Yoder's own body of work question the privilege he grants sociology in *Body Politics*.

Oliver O'Donovan, in his book *The Desire of the Nations*, also raises a concern relevant to this discussion about Yoder's ecclesiology.[81] He worries about the centrality of "voluntariety" to Yoder's "characterization of the church."[82] This worry is seconded by the well-known advocate of Yoder's work, Stanley Hauerwas, who along with coauthor James Fodor say rather breezily in a footnote that O'Donovan is "on to something."[83] I assume these comments are directed at statements like this in *The Priestly Kingdom*: "The model toward which the Protestant Reformation initially began to move, and which so-called 'free churches' sought to incarnate more thoroughly than official Protestantism, is the voluntary community which has about it neither the coercive givenness of establishment nor the atomistic isolation of individualism."[84] Others have engaged this specific issue in Yoder's work and so that need not take up space here.[85] Nevertheless, the general theme applies in this context, that is, the downplaying of the immanent work of God and the inflated assumptions about the potential of the human being.[86] Yoder's *Body Politics* compellingly illustrates that ethics and church practices

---

80. For a provocative discussion of the sacraments in Yoder's thought, see Martens, "The Problematic Development."

81. O'Donovan, *Desire of the Nations*, 223-24.

82. Ibid., 223.

83. Hauerwas and Fodor, "Remaining in Babylon," 224n15.

84. Yoder, *Priestly Kingdom*, 25.

85. Epp Weaver, "After Politics," 637-73; and Kroeker "O'Donovan's Christendom and Yoder's Voluntariety," 41-64.

86. It is worth noting that the charge of voluntarism laid against Yoder bears striking resemblance to an inversion of the charge against Barth. Epp Weaver, in his defense of Yoder against O'Donovan, suggests that it is not Yoder's optimism about the individual's potential that makes the voluntary church a real possibility, but it is his confidence in the redemptive character of God's grace that allows the kingdom of God to be manifest in the church ("After Politics," 659).

are one and the same topic. My analysis of contemporary Anabaptist confessional statements supports this point, indicating that the challenge of human voluntariety, a virtual semi-Pelagianism, occurs in both.

The voluntariety implicit in the sociological reductionism of Yoder's *Body Politics* can be scrutinized from two angles. The first is the Barthian framework described earlier. Yoder's description of the practices of the church as universal political goals and methods leads him to seek a universalizing set of linguistic categories with which to describe them. His solution, found in the discipline of sociology, holds only if sociology is itself such a universally accessible discourse—if it is a precise and open-minded enough science to interpret these practices appropriately. From a Barthian perspective Yoder's sociological language can only rightly describe human action if it acknowledges that human action is dependent upon God's initiative—human freedom resting on the surer foundation of Divine freedom. Thus, only through the recognition of Divine priority can an interpretive lens approach the universal character Yoder seeks. In his book *Theology and Social Theory* John Milbank presents a congruent, if more biting, perspective. He argues that sociology of the twentieth century can be seen as an attempt by the secular to police the sublime. Through his tracing of the genesis of sociology, Milbank argues against the reduction of religion to the social. Yoder's account of baptism treads dangerously close to doing this very thing. Milbank also denies in a technical sense that there is something called the "social" to which religion could be reduced. He asserts that the idea of the social or society is itself problematic in that it never allows itself to be doubted. On the other hand, "religions" are necessarily objects of suspicion. Indeed, Milbank locates the emergence of the idea of the social within the construction of the "secular" and the state. The propagation of this concept is itself the secular's attempt to legitimate itself—to create space for itself.[87] If we read Milbank and Barth alongside each other it becomes apparent that human religious activity inevitably is interpreted within a more comprehensive matrix, and we are presented with a choice between the secularity of sociology and the theological axiom of providence. Yoder's avoidance of a thick theological description from

---

87. Milbank, *Theology and Social Theory*, chaps. 3–5. Through this Milbankian lens Yoder's account of baptism as a sociological phenomenon can be seen to be an opportunity for the incursion of the force-dependent modern secular into the church's own account of its being. If Milbank's analysis of sociology is correct then Yoder's description of church practices opens the door for the community based on the peace of Christ to be redefined as a polity based on force and violence.

above in *Body Politics* makes this construal of church practices vulnerable to the charge of being sociologically reductionist. It fails to appropriately contextualize human action with reference to divine initiative, the triune economy. It fails to recognize that description is inseparable from doctrine.

By considering the issue from another angle, we can see that Yoder's own work questions the notion that sociological description might be universal enough to carry the interpretive load he lays on its shoulders. In his book *The Priestly Kingdom* Yoder dedicates an essay to describing how Christians ought to respond to the perennial challenge of relativism.[88] Yoder begins the search by referring to Lessing's ditch and enumerating six possible strategies of responding to the unnerving realization that extrapolating from particulars to universals is, to speak optimistically, tenuous. Yoder observes that most options share the assumption that the priority of truth always lies in what is wider or more universal. Here he is critical of this and writes, "One adolescent's breath of fresh air is another's ghetto. Any given wider world is still just one more place, even if what its slightly wider or slightly more prestigious circle of interpreters talk about is a better access to 'universality.'"[89] Yoder rejects these sorts of options on the grounds that the NT demonstrates an alternative model. In this model, Yoder observes that the response of early translocated Christians was to become at home in their new linguistic world, learn its conceptual structure and perennial points of uncertainty. Christian witness in this new plausibility structure avoided flatly placing claims about Jesus into the obvious, but inevitably distorting, cosmological slots. Instead, the witness of these early Christians placed Jesus, the suffering servant, in a position of lordship over that cosmology. In this spirit Yoder affirms the importance of Abrahamic particularity and the necessary inculturatedness of the Christian faith—of course one should speak Greek in Greece. By putting it this way, Yoder wants readers to see that the question is not whether or not Christians should proclaim that Jesus is Messiah and Lord, but rather *how* this should be done in any given context. "What we are looking for . . . is not a way to keep dry above the waves of relativity, but a way to stay within our bark, barely afloat and sometimes awash amidst those waves, yet neither dissolving into them nor being carried only where they want to push it."[90]

---

88. Yoder, *Priestly Kingdom*, 46–62.
89. Ibid., 49.
90. Ibid., 58.

In Favor of Ecclesial Mediation

The question that Yoder's argument about relativity brings to his description of baptism and other key practices in *Body Politics* is to what extent he leaves open the possibility that the cosmology implied in the discipline of sociology might limit a possible articulation of the lordship of Christ in the practices of the church. In dismissing the usefulness of theological language for describing the sacraments and describing these church practices as the good news, Yoder violates his observation of the character of NT witness. He places the practices of good news, and thereby Jesus himself, into an available cosmological slot within a secular discipline. This fails to maintain the properly Christian location of Jesus as Lord of that cosmology. Yoder's dismissal of dogmatics in explaining the working of ecclesial practices limits the potential success of his description.

In sum, the particularity of the incarnation calls into question any description of baptism that allows that such a practice can be reduced to a universally applicable social phenomenon. This is the case because such reductionism concedes epistemological priority to what *appears* to be the wider world. In his appeal to wider relevance, which is represented by the discourse of sociology, as that which most clearly interprets baptism, Yoder fails to follow this with an explanation of how the Lordship of Christ undoes the metaphysical assumptions and universalist pretensions of that discipline. In theological terms Yoder's description of baptism is in danger of losing its recognition of God as the grounding of all that is and all that humans do. This leaves no room for a description of how God acts in baptism, and we are left to create the new humanity alone.

Everything turns on the word "description" in this case, for both the social scientist and the theologian are attempting to depict what goes on in church practices and how this takes place. As Nicholas Adams and Charles Elliott have put it with reference to Hauerwas's project in *Sanctify Them in the Truth*, "[A] problem arises precisely because it is possible to think that theologians and anthropologists have different jobs. At the risk of oversimplifying, we think that it is one thing to distinguish dogmatics from ethnography, and another to separate them."[91] In the view of Adams and Elliott both disciplines are primarily dedicated to providing true descriptions of the world. Therefore, they "insist that ethnography is dogmatics because *description already includes a metaphysic*."[92] The shortcoming of

---

91. Hauerwas, *Sanctify Them in the Truth*; Adams and Elliott, "Ethnography is Dogmatics," 362.

92. Adams and Elliott, "Ethnography is Dogmatics," 363.

Body Politics is not that it forgets that the importance of baptism is invisible; I believe that Yoder is right to suggest that it is not. Rather, the issue is that the descriptive license granted to sociology is set apart from dogmatics as though its task was something altogether different.

The danger of Yoder's sociological reductionism is a warning flag related to the use of the concept of ecclesial mediation. It casts doubt on the ability of generic sociological categories to capture the dynamics of the creaturely mediating the divine. In contrast, the language necessary to describe this must be able to rightly name the social elements through which God chooses to work and to be present in the world. Descriptions of baptism and other church practices must not glaze over the sociological or avoid empirically quantifiable modes of study, but to provide descriptions that are useful or true they must be rendered in terms that take into account the apocalyptic and eschatological elements of the Christian view of the world.[93] In short, a description of baptism as an act of ecclesial mediation must remain ardently *theological*.

Through this exploration of aspects of the work of Barth and Yoder we now have in place at a conceptual level the parameters within which a constructive Anabaptist elucidation of the church's mediatorial role can proceed and a key qualification that the descriptive language must meet. The necessity of contextualizing human freedom within God's, and therefore human action as responsive participation in God's initiative, represents the doctrinal parameters within which the subsequent work will move forward. The action of God in baptism must be understood to have clear social effect, for this is the very character of the gospel. Descriptions of church practices that fail to retain these features fail to depict robustly that the gospel matters. This is particularly true in the context of a metaphysically minimalist cultural milieu where the pragmatism of a necessarily pluralist politics threatens to cascade into all corners of life. Yet the language we use to describe this character of the gospel needs to remain theological in order to employ the necessary analytic and descriptive categories.

To say with respect to Yoder that there is a danger of reducing baptism to its social function begs the question of what shape a thicker theologically framed and socially attentive description might take. Within this husk lie the

---

93. Also see Scharen, "Ethnography as Ecclesiology," 141. Scharen writes, "Ethnography, although dominated by the domain of anthropology and sociology today, in fact has been and should be a skill available to the theologian as a theologian. What after all, was Tertullian up to in his classic critique of the Roman games in *Spectacles*? It was ethnography as ecclesiology, in the sense that he intended it for use in baptismal catechesis."

seeds of the next step of my argument, for despite the helpful outline from Barth we have yet to describe with any specificity how God is involved in baptism. Simply affirming that God does something to initiate or underwrite baptism and that human freedom finds its source within God's is not sufficient to avoid a complete spiritualization of Divine work. It is not enough to flatly affirm, as some popular accounts do, that God invisibly covers over human limitation by adding an extra magical ingredient. This would risk a vague spiritualism out of step with the God of Scripture whose instinct is manifestly toward loving, fleshly incarnation. In the following chapters I seek to give a vital and more nuanced theological account of how Anabaptists might affirm God's participation in the rite of Christian initiation.

3

On the Ecclesial Character of Divine Presence

So then you are no longer strangers and aliens, but you are citizens with the saints and also members of the household of God, built upon the foundation of the apostles and prophets, with Christ Jesus himself as the cornerstone. In him the whole structure is joined together and grows into a holy temple in the Lord; in whom you also are built together spiritually into a dwelling place for God

(Eph 4:19–22)

During the winter of 1940–41, amidst the height of the power of the Nazi regime, the Lutheran theologian Dietrich Bonhoeffer cloistered himself in the Ettal Monastery in the Bavarian Alps. He had recently taken on the sham identity of a member of a German military intelligence agency, the *Abwehr*. During the previous years he had made the difficult decision not to remain in the safety of an appointment in the United States, but to return to Germany to continue his subversive church work. At the monastery he worked on *Ethics*, a book he may well have intended as his magnum opus. Bonhoeffer had been prohibited from public speaking and would shortly be denied the freedom to publish. The *Ethics* manuscript would not be published in his lifetime.

Clifford Green, the editor of the English translation of the critical edition of *Ethics*, introduces the text and outlines its driving goals and concepts. Two of the central themes are relevant here. They are the complimentary concepts of "vicarious representative action" and "freedom."[1]

---

1. Green, "Editor's Introduction to the English Edition," in Bonhoeffer, *Ethics*, 10.

Vicarious representative action, alternately translated "deputyship," speaks to the ethical analogy between God's action on behalf of humanity in Jesus, and human action on behalf of others that takes the form of Christ.[2] The concept of freedom links God's freedom in the incarnation to its analogical embodiment by Christians whose actions are free from predetermined ethical systems.[3] Both of these themes implicate the church. It might be that, as Bonhoeffer worked through these ideas, he had in mind the original vision of the Barmen Declaration, which was written in large part by his mentor Karl Barth. It set out the Confessing Church, as opposed to the German Christian Church, as *the* Protestant church in Germany. Part of the Barmen Declaration reads as follows: "The Christian Church is the congregation of the brethren in which Jesus Christ acts presently as the Lord in Word and sacrament through the Holy Spirit."[4] The Barmen Declaration may not have come from Bonhoeffer's pen, yet his ongoing work to support congregational ministers affirmed the sense of this extract. In a paper written in 1935 called, "The Confessing Church and the Ecumenical Movement," Bonhoeffer argues that The Barmen Declaration and the Dahlem Confession had authority and thus demanded a clear Yes or No of support from the broader ecumenical community. The church beyond Germany's borders could not recognize both the Confessing Church and those the two documents accused of heresy. In the same paper, written while Bonhoeffer presided over the underground seminary in Finkenwalde, he cites *baptism* as the ground for the relationship between the two ecclesial bodies mentioned in the document's title. On account of their participation in one baptism, these diverse churches were able, even obligated, to concern themselves with the integrity of the other. The life of the church mattered to Bonhoeffer, and the faithful exercise of its sacraments was a crucial resource for sustaining its opposition to the Reich. In the drafts of the *Ethics*, written roughly six years after the landmark Barmen Declaration, Bonhoeffer says that to be "drawn into the form of Jesus Christ" is what it means to enact the good.[5] Bonhoeffer goes on to state that this is not simply another task to be achieved through the power of the will: "This does not happen as we strive 'to become like Jesus,' as we customarily say, but as the form of

---

2. Bonhoeffer, *Ethics*, 12.
3. Ibid., 14.
4. As quoted in Metaxas, *Bonhoeffer*, 225.
5. Bonhoeffer, *Ethics*, 93.

Jesus Christ himself so works on us that it molds us, conforming our form to Christ's own."[6]

The responsible life for Bonhoeffer is the one that wholly and selflessly answers to the reality of Christ.[7] Bonhoeffer's view of the responsible life bears elements of similarity to the way I described Barth's theology of baptism in the previous chapter inasmuch as Barth considered baptism at its most basic level a response to God's redemptive work. For Barth, even its voluntary quality is enabled by the grace and initiation of God. Therefore, baptism fits with the larger ecology of the Christian faith. Divine and human action need not be held in a zero-sum tension, in which one excludes the other. In the previous chapter, I used this Barthian concept to show that the objective and subjective qualities of baptism need not be viewed as competitors; rather, these qualities indicate baptizands both act and are acted upon. Through this rite of initiation Christians are formed into Christ's mold. For Bonhoeffer this meant resisting dominant ideologies, speaking truthfully about the powerful, naming the church's shortcomings, and engaging in concrete forms of resistance—from training ministers illegally, to aiding Jews attempting to flee Germany. Ultimately, such resistance would even mean association with those directly attempting to overthrow the Nazi regime. Bonhoeffer's life and that of the companions he worked with display the topic of this chapter well: the sacramental character of the church as the community through which Christ now acts.

The line of inquiry of this chapter is an attempt to consider how this might be possible while at the same time providing further theological content to the formal structure developed through my engagement with Barth and Yoder. This structure will be carried forward as two axioms: first, that human freedom, or agency, is a relative category subordinate and not inherently opposed to that of God; and second, that the practical thrust of the gospel is enacted in the church's practices, which not only signify good news but participate in it. This last supposition means that in considering baptism the appropriate question is not, "What does baptism mean?" but rather, "What does baptism do?"[8] I have used the shorthand "ecclesial mediation" to describe an affirmation missing from current Anabaptist con-

---

6. Ibid.

7. Ibid., 254–55.

8. By asking what baptism does I am not attempting to align myself with either functionalist or neo-functionalist schools of ritual interpretation, both of which flow from the work of sociologist Émile Durkheim. For an overview of these developments, see Bell, *Ritual*, 24–46.

struals of baptism. These two axioms gleaned from Barth and Yoder give structure to this concept, tying it to the gospel and contextualizing it within the redemptive work of God. However, this structure still has little content. This chapter will supply a portion of this in hopes of further relating how it is that God acts through the church, or how we might say that in baptism God cleanses and welcomes candidates.

I am proposing that contemporary Anabaptist theology should affirm that God acts through the church and that people encounter God through the lives of congregations as these communities continue to respond to Jesus Christ in worship and the training of those apprenticed in his way of life. Such a claim focuses our attention on this relationship of God to the church and requires closer examination of several biblical images, or models, that depict the dynamics of God's use of the church as the primary locus of his presence and work in the world. However, this chapter can only indirectly treat traditional theological definitions organized around themes such as *ecclesia* and *koinonia*. The center of my argument is that as the church is in Christ it constitutes the ongoing presence of God in the world in an objective though always subordinate sense.

The following two parts of this chapter consider the work of Dietrich Bonhoeffer and that of the sixteenth-century Anabaptist theologian and church leader, Pilgram Marpeck. My explication and analysis of key elements of Bonhoeffer's early work *Sanctorum Communio* will describe how the concrete social character of the Christian community is an extension of the narrative identity of Christ. Exploring the work of Marpeck will demonstrate that there is precedent within the Anabaptist tradition for understanding the practices of the church as acts of God. Marpeck's work describes how these practices can be consonant with and can even participate in the incarnation. Both theologians emphasize the christoform character of the church. Their work and my analysis of it will not only depict the church as a way in which God remains present to the world, but will also help render the sacramental question in christological and ecclesiological terms. Such a theological lexicon is the antidote for the deforming temptation of sociological reductionism. It will prove useful for an investigation of the practices of the church that can advance my argument for the necessity of understanding baptism as an ecclesial event mediating God's redemptive work. It will also counter a temptation to use an independent sacramental vocabulary, the hearing of which in Believers Church circles often aborts consideration of the way God works in, with, and under the life of the church.

DIETRICH BONHOEFFER

On February 4, 1906, Dietrich Bonhoeffer was born into a highly educated and well-connected German family. On April 9, 1945, he was executed by the Nazi government for treason. Between these brackets lies an impressive body of intellectual and pastoral work that many, including Anabaptists, find very compelling. Bonhoeffer's response to the idolatrous ideologies of his day was prophetic and practical. It displays the ideals of the pastor-theologian. To Anabaptist eyes often sceptical of the discipline of dogmatics, the attraction of such a life gives reason for his formal theology to be taken seriously. Bonhoeffer's work has long been appreciated by Anabaptists. Harold Bender even suggested that Bonhoeffer would actually make a pretty good Anabaptist himself. Incidentally, Bender had studied alongside the teenage Bonhoeffer at Tübingen in 1923.[9]

The opening of this chapter described Bonhoeffer's belief that the question of ethics really is a christological question, an issue of formation. Bonhoeffer's treatment of Christian ethics is intended to proclaim this and to assist the church's formation.[10] He believed that if congregations are not places where Christ actually takes form among the people of the world then they are just religious associations. The only freedom or authority that the Christian community has is granted through the one who dictates its form.[11] This line of thinking from *Ethics* echoes a theme clearly present in Bonhoeffer's much earlier, and more overtly academic work, *Sanctorium Communio*. Both texts are driven in various idioms by the theme of the church's christoformity.

In *Discipleship*, the book for which Bonhoeffer is most famous, he includes a short chapter on baptism. Bonhoeffer rarely addresses he topic deeply, and here he devotes less than ten pages to his claim that baptism functions for Paul the way discipleship functions in the Synoptics. Being baptized marks one's break with the old self and the old world. Bonhoeffer struggles to hold the passivity and grace implied in infant baptism together with his guiding instinct that the command of Jesus demands a "visible act of obedience."[12] His thinking on the subject may not be highly developed,

---

9. Keim, *Harold S. Bender*, 152, 320.

10. Bonhoeffer, *Ethics*, 102.

11. Ibid., 96–97. I take this to also be one of the central tenets of the Barmen Declaration.

12. Bonhoeffer, *Discipleship*, 207.

but its actual role is to emphasize the importance of the church and frame his subsequent discussion of the body of Christ. Another instance where Bonhoeffer treats the topic of baptism is in a letter he wrote from prison in May of 1944. This was less than a year before Bonhoeffer would be hung in the last days of one of the most devastating wars in human history. The letter marked the occasion of the baptism of the son of Eberhard and Renate Bethge, Bonhoeffer's close friend and niece respectively. The child's name was Dietrich. In this letter Bonhoeffer reflects on the difference between his generation and little Dietrich's. The war had brought significant changes, and even its welcome end promised only uncertainty and instability for Germans. Speaking directly to the child, Bonhoeffer wrote:

> You are being baptized today as a Christian. All those great and ancient words of the Christian proclamation will be pronounced over you, and the command of Jesus Christ to baptize will be carried out, without your understanding any of it. But we too are being thrown back all the way to the beginnings of our understanding. What reconciliation and redemption mean, rebirth and Holy Spirit, love of one's enemies, cross and resurrection, what it means to live in Christ and follow Christ, all that is so difficult and remote that we hardly dare speak of it anymore.[13]

Bonhoeffer goes on to wonder what the church eventually might be like when this child is grown. In this dark moment of confinement Bonhoeffer is unsure of the specifics of the church's future, but is confident that whatever God calls the future church to be or do, its proclamation will be as liberating and redeeming as Jesus' original ministry. Bonhoeffer's extraordinary confidence can be seen as a refinement or a deepening of convictions evident years before in *Sanctorum Communio*. The themes Bonhoeffer refers to in 1944—reconciliation, redemption, regeneration, the Holy Spirit, love of enemies, cross, resurrection, life in Christ, Christian discipleship—are themes that resonate deeply with Anabaptists. Though they gain energy in Bonhoeffer's mature work, they are formally present, and more than merely embryonic, in *Sanctorum Communio*.

Bonhoeffer's *Sanctorum Communio* is an exploration of the sociological character of the ecclesial presence of Jesus. It is a refashioned version of his 1927 dissertation, written when he was not much more than twenty years of age.[14] He revised it, shortening it radically, during his pastoral in-

---

13. Bonhoeffer, *Letters and Papers from Prison*, 389.
14. The dissertation was titled *Sanctorum Communio: Eine dogmatische Untersuchung*.

ternship in Barcelona and finally published it in 1930. Few took notice. It is true that later in his life Bonhoeffer expressed reservation about some of his early academic work, yet *Sanctorum Communio* remains an important text. Karl Barth would later comment glowingly on the book:

> If there can be any possible vindication of Reinhold Seeberg it is to be sought in the fact that his school could give rise to this man and this dissertation, which not only awakens respect for the breadth and depth of its insight as we look back to the existing situation, but makes far more instructive and stimulating and illuminating and genuinely edifying reading today than many of the more famous works which have since been written on the problem of the church... I openly confess that I have misgivings whether I can even maintain the high level reached by Bonhoeffer, saying no less in my own words and context, and saying it no less forcefully, than did this young man so many years ago.[15]

The laudatory review from Barth and foundational nature of *Sanctorum Communio* for Bonhoeffer's later work are not the only reasons for considering it closely. The strengths of this text will help describe the mediatorial role of the church and its weaknesses will highlight important elements of Marpeck's theology that are relevant to my proposal.

On a programmatic level *Sanctorum Communio* is intended to be a theological treatment of the church that makes deliberate use of the disciplines of philosophy and sociology.[16] Although Bonhoeffer recognizes that the use of these two supporting disciplines is what lends his ecclesiology distinction as well as currency, he makes it clear that theological concerns drive the project.[17] In the last chapter I criticized Yoder's lack of clarity in preferring sociology as an analytical tool for understanding the life of the church. In the case of Bonhoeffer it is important to recognize that he does not think that the methodological appropriateness of using sociological and philosophical tools is based on general warrant stemming from a doctrine of creation, nor from reductive assumptions about the church. Bonhoeffer believes that the use of these analytical tools is warranted only through revelation—by which creation more generally is itself rightly known.[18] In the face of these limits the fact that the church can and should be described

---

15. Barth, *CD* 4/2:641. In Barth's view Seeberg was an arch-Protestant liberal.
16. Bonhoeffer, *Sanctorum Communio*, 21.
17. Ibid., 22, 32.
18. Ibid., 65.

sociologically remains one of Bonhoeffer's central claims in *Sanctorum Communio*, and it is this point of tension that drives the argument of his book. This may also be one of the keys to Bonhoeffer's thought that prompted him to see the risks of National Socialism and the Reich Church in advance of many of his colleagues, even committed Christians such as Martin Neimöller. The crucial difference between Bonhoeffer's affirmation that the life of the church is concrete and material and Yoder's obfuscation in *Body Politics* is that Bonhoeffer believes the sociology of the church only comes into focus theologically. In this way Bonhoeffer's sociological analysis meets the criteria derived from Barth in which creaturely elements are understood through their ordained service to God. We will also see that it meets the criteria derived from Yoder in that the life of the church is not made external to the gospel.

Critical Development of Idealist Themes

It is not surprising that a book developed from a dissertation would clearly evidence its intellectual context. In *Sanctorum Communio* this is the legacy of German idealism. In particular one notices the heavy influence of the work of G. W. F. Hegel. Charles Marsh reminds us of the challenge implicit in taking issue with Hegel's philosophy. He cites Barth's dictum that we "must always think three times before contradicting Hegel's system, 'because we might find that everything we are tempted to say in contradiction to it has already been said within it.'"[19] One example of Bonhoeffer's critical appropriation of idealism is his leveraging of the concept of spirit to develop his construal of the relationship of the individual to the community and ultimately his description of the church.[20] Bonhoeffer was particularly dissatisfied with the ecclesial implications of German idealism, and attempted to position his vision of the church in opposition to it. This can be seen by his initial decision to differentiate what he understands as a Christian view of the person from the idealist version.[21] Bonhoeffer believes that idealist philosophy fails to grasp a Christian concept of the person because it

---

19. As quoted in Marsh, "Human Community and Divine Presence," 427.
20. Bonhoeffer, *Sanctorum Communio*, 65–80.
21. Ibid., 45. It is not always clear what Bonhoeffer means by "idealism," though he generally seems to have virtually the entire German idealist tradition in view. He frequently cites Kant, Fichte, Schelling, Hegel, Schleiermacher, Scheler, and occasionally Leibniz.

has no room for either sin or a responsive, active God. This shows itself in the inability of idealism to appreciate movement or struggle; it tends to be static, ruling out both the distressed conscience and anxious turmoil in the face of decisions.[22] By contrast, Bonhoeffer's understanding of Christian anthropology asserts that the human becomes a conscious being "in the moment of being moved—in the situation of responsibility, passionate ethical struggle . . ."[23] In Bonhoeffer's judgment, idealism wrongly removes the human from the concrete situation and from the dynamics of existence in relation to divine transcendence.[24]

Within the conceptual space created by his dissatisfaction with the German idealist tradition, Bonhoeffer places his own constructive theological anthropology, which is fundamentally relational and assumes that personhood arises only in relation to the otherness of God. Bonhoeffer says the fact that the human creature is constituted by and directed toward God implies sociality as a basic feature of human existence.[25] The individual stands before God simultaneously alone and a part of corporate humanity. This lays the foundation for being able to uphold in the doctrine of the church, which is sanctified community, both the individual and the corporate human. This marks the beginning of Bonhoeffer's epic narrative of the christoform church. By beginning in this way, Bonhoeffer asserts his concept of true community in parallel with the Genesis narrative not only as an eschatological hope, but also as the primal state of humanity. This establishes the theological baseline from which Bonhoeffer will use his socio-philosophical tools to fashion the narrative arc of old and new adam, the story that links Christ to the church. In the context of his constructive theological anthropology Bonhoeffer observes that the collective human and the individual human bear structural similarity. Just as people are at the same time individual and social, so is the collective person. This means that corporate humanity is inter-relational.[26] Bonhoeffer ties this concept to Scripture to develop a substantive theological claim: "God does not want a community that absorbs the individual into itself, but a community of

---

22. Ibid., 49. Portions of Bonhoeffer's response to idealism here anticipate his engagement with the work of Martin Heidegger in his second major work, *Act and Being*. For more see Marsh, "Bonhoeffer on Heidegger and Togetherness," 263–83.

23. Bonhoeffer, *Sanctorum Communio*, 49.

24. Ibid.

25. Ibid., 63.

26. Ibid., 77–78.

human beings. In God's eyes, community and individual exist in the same moment and rest in one another."[27] This assumption in turn will support Bonhoeffer's development of the concepts of religious community, a *negative* concept, and the church community, a *positive* one. The simultaneous nature of humanity as individual and corporate makes room for an act such as baptism that can at once be the voluntary decision of an individual candidate and an act of the community as a whole. Baptism can be both an individual's response to God and, through ecclesial participation in the life of Christ, God's reclamation of humanity.

The Theological Necessity of the Life of the Church

Bonhoeffer's inclusion of an account of sin in his ecclesiology marks another of his criticisms of idealism. Sin creates the problem to which the church community is a part of God's solution. Bonhoeffer believes sin comes to be through the fall as humanity allows love to be replaced with selfishness. This creates a rupture not only within the relationship of humans to God but also between members of the human community itself. Subsequently, the human creature no longer lives in giving relationships; but instead, lives in voluntary isolation and tries to be individually complete, relating to others only through demands. The result is that humanity no longer lives one life in God.[28] Therefore Bonhoeffer says, "Sin must be conceived as both a supra-individual deed and, of course, as an individual deed; it must be simultaneously the deed of the human race and of the individual."[29] The existence of sinful human beings is one of solitude. They share only sinfulness.

God chooses to address the sin of all humanity within history through Jesus. The sinful adam represents the collective broken human that can only be superseded by a new adam—"the new humanity in Christ"—or "Christ existing as church-community."[30] In Christ, God does not approach humanity in a demanding posture, which would mirror the results of the fall, but with open arms, ready and able to resolve the isolating and self-protective rift. The result of this restoration is the community of the church, or as recent translators render Bonhoeffer's use of the German

---

27. Ibid., 80.
28. Ibid., 107–8.
29. Ibid., 108.
30. Ibid., 121.

term *Gemeinde*, "church-community."[31] In Bonhoeffer's thought the "ontic basic-relatedness" of humanity is paired with the "pre-volitional sociality of the human spirit" to the effect of locating the church as a sanctified form and re-manifestation of this basic feature of humanness.[32] The power of Bonhoeffer's work here is his demonstration of how God's will to restore relationship implies both the work of Jesus *and* a concrete church that takes up social space. Bonhoeffer believes that God's redemptive will is a will for community, such that as a community the church does not exist to fulfill objectives ulterior to its own being. As strange as it sounds, Bonhoeffer believes that restored community exists for its own sake. It is made possible by the will of God actualized in divine self-surrender and only contingently by the divinely enabled self-surrender of human beings.[33] Despite its peccability the church represents the possibility of true postlapsarian community because, and *only* because, of its unique involvement in the life and redemptive work of God.[34]

All this echoes Yoder's description of the church's practices as gospel. Yet, in the context of that discussion it is important to realize that the reality of the church for Bonhoeffer is not a logical deduction that necessarily follows from socio-philosophical analysis. He writes, "The concept of the church is conceivable only in the sphere of reality established by God; this means it cannot be deduced. The reality of the church is a reality of revelation, a reality that essentially must be either believed or denied."[35] This means that judgments of the claims that the church makes about itself and its relationship to God cannot be made independently from the outside,

---

31. Ibid., 145. In the Dietrich Bonhoeffer Works edition of *Sanctorum Communio* the German term *Gemeinde* is translated as "church-community" where other versions have used either "church" or "community." Clifford Green explains: "It is used as a theological term that emphasizes the communal character of the sanctorum communio and high lights the link to its sociological counterpart, *Gemeinschaft*. Simultaneously, it links by translation the words *Kirche* and *Gemeinde*, so that Bonhoeffer's intention to define and constitute the former by the latter is honoured. The hyphen will repeatedly remind the reader of the theological point Bonhoeffer is making" ("Editor's Introduction to the English Edition," 16). Though I have maintained this awkward English construction in direct quotations from this translation of *Sanctorum Communio*, I think that Bonhoeffer's point is well made and therefore use the terms "church" and "community" independently in my own description.

32. Bonhoeffer, *Sanctorum Communio*, 124–25.

33. Ibid., 173, 176.

34. Ibid., 214.

35. Ibid., 127.

since its actuality does not follow logically from some generally observable order of creation. Bonhoeffer is similarly adamant that the church community cannot be deduced from a general concept of religion, religious community, or some transcendent notion of the holy.[36] The church is visible, yes, but not generically or totally so.

This assertion about the limitation of the church's availability to analysis is not to say that in Bonhoeffer's mind the church remains outside history. Rather, "The history of the church is the hidden center of world history . . . For the church is Christ existing as church-community."[37] God intends that the church be an empirical reality—the presence of Christ in history. Yet, we might wonder how the history of the church can be the center of world history if the observability of the church's true nature is not generically visible, if, as Bonhoeffer says, its preeminent status is hidden. We must think about the possible alternatives. One would be to the response of spiritualism, saying that the true church is at most invisible, or if viewed in an even lesser light, completely unnecessary. Another would be the reasonable, materialist response, saying that the church is simply another sociological entity. It has been primed with a unique set of practices, yes, but the doing of these is completely within human potential. These possible responses of course map onto the two general alternatives to the concept of ecclesial mediation. In these two approaches the Christian life is either rationalized, and eventually severed from the need for God, or spiritualized, and its physicality and concrete character are viewed as accidental.

In Christ, Bonhoeffer says with Paul, the church community is elect from eternity.[38] Christ is the foundation, cornerstone, and builder of the church. Bonhoeffer understands Pauline theology to say that Christ and the church community can be identified together—to be in Christ is to be a member of this community.[39] "The church," Bonhoeffer writes, "is the presence of Christ in the same way that Christ is the presence of God."[40] The term "presence" is critical. Bonhoeffer is not suggesting that the church is divine. His language is more controlled than Augustine's, who, in his homily on John 21:8, says, "Let us rejoice, then, and give thanks that we are made

---

36. Ibid., 127–28, 133. A corollary here is that the generally observable spirit of the church, a social phenomenon, cannot be equated with the Holy Spirit (ibid., 214).

37. Ibid., 211.

38. Here Bonhoeffer has in mind Eph 1:4ff and 2 Thess 2:13 (ibid., 135–37).

39. Here Bonhoeffer is thinking of 1 Cor, 2 Cor, Col, and Eph; also see ibid., 139.

40. Ibid., 140–141.

not only Christians, but Christ. Do ye understand, brethren, and apprehend the grace of God upon us? Marvel, be glad, we are made Christ. For he is the head, we are the members: the whole man is he and we."[41] Nevertheless, the central concept is similar: the *totus Christus* includes the church, Christ together with the church makes up the whole Christ. Though Bonhoeffer advances his ecclesiological assertions with the language of idealism, his thought is profoundly Augustinian.

The church is the presence of Christ not because God depends on humanity, as though God did not exist before creatures, but because God has willed it to be so. Bonhoeffer understands election to be actualized within the church as it is established by Christ and gathered through the Spirit.[42] Pentecost is the time when the church was established in time and geography; at that moment the Spirit became the spirit of the community of Jesus.[43] But the relationship here only goes one way, it is not correct to say that the Spirit is *merely* the spirit of a "religious community." Bonhoeffer is adamant that Jesus is not the founder of a religious community in the sense of a generic sociological category. That is, God did not establish a religious community at Pentecost, but rather an utterly unique body.[44] Bonhoeffer writes,

> In and through Christ the church is established in reality. It is not as if Christ could be abstracted from the church; rather, it is none other than Christ who 'is' the church. Christ does not represent it; only what is not present can be represented. In God's eyes, however, the church is present in Christ. Christ did not merely make the church possible, but rather realized it for eternity. If this is so, then the significance of Christ must be made the focal point in the temporal actualization of the church. This is accomplished by the Spirit-impelled word of the crucified and risen Lord of the church.[45]

If we are to appropriate Bonhoeffer's insight we must remember that the actions of church members, if they are to be true acts, must correspond to the church's establishment in Christ, which they can only be as they are enabled by the Spirit. Christ not only established the church and is its Lord, but just as the material, human body of Jesus Christ became the resurrected body, so the body of adam became the body of Christ through the

---

41. Augustine, *Homilies on the Gospel of John* 21.8 (140).
42. Bonhoeffer, *Sanctorum Communio*, 143.
43. Ibid., 153.
44. Ibid.
45. Ibid., 157.

Spirit.[46] The second part of this statement has a dual meaning constituting two movements: first, Christ takes on humanity through the Spirit, and thereby adam became the body of Christ; second, human creatures become a new creation through the Spirit, they are made new in Christ and become part of the church, and thereby *adam* becomes the body of Christ. This twofold work of the Spirit catches the importance of the embodied or physical character of the church. It shows that what this community does is not unimportant. It is the work of humans, yes, but it is not merely that. As it allows God's Spirit to work through it, the church community is the leading edge in the creation of a new humanity. Therefore, Bonhoeffer acknowledges "the concrete, empirical church in which the word is preached and the sacraments are celebrated" is "God's own church-community" and "Christ's presence in the world" in which God's Spirit is working.[47] The action of the Spirit is not limited to the church's origin, but is ongoing in the community's embodiment of Christ. Established in Christ and enabled by the Spirit, the practices of the church have a life beyond their generic social character, though they are certainly not less than social acts. The being of the church in the context of its life in the triune God is a life of action, and therefore anchoring the church's being in the life of God is not a temptation for passivity. Chief among the actions of the church are its core practices which both identify it and constitute its social and supra-social existence.

As we begin to appropriate Bonhoeffer's theology toward the goal of this book we recognize that this Spirit-indwelt character of the church's identification as the body of Christ is what gives the church's ordinances their paradigmatic status. Within the life of the church people learn the virtues necessary to relate to others in more loving ways than they might otherwise.[48] This effectiveness is not found in the social uniqueness of the church's practices, as though they were just 'good ideas' creatively developed by Jesus and his disciples. Their effectiveness comes through the fact that God is doing something in, with, and under what would otherwise be ordinary acts of bathing or sharing a meal.

---

46. Ibid., 147.
47. Ibid., 280.
48. Ibid., 167–68, 182, 184.

Toward an Anabaptist Appropriation of Bonhoeffer's Early Ecclesiology

There are two prominent shortcomings of the ecclesiology developed in *Sanctorum Communio*. The first is that it remains abstract and theoretical. Despite his emphasis on the church's sociality and his negative appraisal of many idealist themes, Bonhoeffer mostly fails to describe a church that concretely or empirically participates in the world. Given the fact that Bonhoeffer's participation in church life before writing *Sanctorum Communio* was probably rather limited, this is not surprising. His later work, particularly *Life Together* and *Ethics,* are very different in this respect. *Life Together* was written to share with the wider church what he had learned from his experience running the experimental seminary at Finkenwalde. In this text Bonhoeffer describes Christian community in very practical, even methodical ways. Though it displays some ecclesiological features that *Sanctorum Communio* does not, *Life Together* is a development rather than a repudiation of the earlier text.[49] It represents a rounding out of the core convictions described above. In many ways *Ethics* is similar. The second shortcoming of *Sanctorum Communio* is that it risks giving the impression that the church can be the presence or body of Christ in a static, institutional sense. In *Ethics* Bonhoeffer more clearly states that the church community participates in the *totus Christus* in its representative action on behalf of others.

The theme of christoformity is important for understanding the contribution of *Sanctorum Communio*. Jacob Holm has observed that one of the key features of Bonhoeffer's critical appropriation of Hegel is that Bonhoeffer's concept of the church is christocentric, while Hegel's is theocentric. The reclamation of community in the church is important for Bonhoeffer, yet he denies that theology should sublate God into either society or the church. This denial accounts for the church's sin and maintains divine alterity.[50] We have already observed that this critical response to Hegel is developed by Bonhoeffer into a sort of cloverleaf ecclesiology in which each outward line of thought loops back to a christological center. Bonhoeffer asks that we understand the significance of the church in its broadest

---

49. In his introduction to *Life Together* Geffrey B. Kelly writes, "[T]he interpretive key to so much of Bonhoeffer's ecclesiology and, therefore, of his understanding of the nature of community was set in his doctoral dissertation on the church, *Sanctorum Communio*, and in his second dissertation, *Act and Being*, which grounded his interpretation of the church as a primary form of God's self-revelation" ("Editor's Introduction," 6).

50. Holm, "G.W.F. Hegel's Impact," 189n184.

sense as a recovery of humanity's essential social character as participating in the new adam. Its mission is congruent with the mission of Jesus, and its life is an ongoing act of reconciliation. Baptism participates in this work. It is an ongoing act of recreation: each baptism makes the subject, another member of adam, new.

There are significant ramifications of this segment of Bonhoeffer's thought for baptism: baptism into Christ's body changes the social landscape, which is to say that it participates in God's restoration of community. Without obliterating the freedom of personhood, therefore precisely as *believers'* baptism, this ordinance renews the possibility of the collective subjectivity of humanity as the new adam in relationship to God. This is starkly opposed to revivalist visions of baptism that view it as secondary to the individual's inner commitment, which is prompted by the invisible and ineffable working of the Spirit the rite is said to publicize. Therefore, revivalist baptism as extra-ecclesial baptism is unable to fully participate in the new humanity because it perpetuates the disunity of the old adam. It does this by denying that the very physicality of the church's rite of initiation is constitutive of the gospel.

To this extent Bonhoeffer is successful. In view of this project it follows that through the ongoing gift of God's presence in the church persons who undergo baptism encounter God's grace in this practice of washing with water and its related experiences of catechesis, the communion meal, and so on. In these practices people encounter God objectively and divine grace takes visible, tangible shape. As we have observed in the last two chapters, contemporary Anabaptists, in contrast, generally construe baptism according to the parameters of a testimonial rubric. Though Anabaptists may share much of Bonhoeffer's christoform ethic, they are less likely to share the ecclesiological assumptions that support it. While many Anabaptist denominational statements speak to the purpose of baptism for the individual candidate, the role of ecclesial and divine action is nebulous. My attempt in preceding chapters to reclaim on a conceptual level at least the mediatorial role of the church has doubtlessly made it clear that I favor a more sacramentally informed description, something more akin to, though not identical with, Bonhoffer's.

When I suggest that baptizands experience God's grace through baptism I am consciously diverging from the later work of Barth where he reserves the title of "sacrament" for the unique event of the incarnation. At its core the Barthian assumption, that grace flows through the apocalypse of Jesus, should be roundly affirmed. Nevertheless, though Barth's rejection of the sacraments is not without merit, it runs the risk of depicting God as perpetually distant, even though this is something Barth doubtlessly wanted to avoid. I am suggesting that the way forward in the quest to develop an appropriate contemporary construal of believers' baptism is to more clearly name the church as the location of the ongoing presence of God in a way similar to Bonhoeffer. In Bonhoeffer's theology God addresses the brokenness of humanity through Jesus and now wills to do so through the church. On a conceptual level this follows a denial of the ubiquity of Christ, emphasizing instead a reading of Matt 18:20 that privileges the localized, though still transcendent, presence of Christ where two or three gather in his name. More immediately relevant is the preliminary conclusion that believers' baptism should be viewed and practiced in a more objective way, as a rite that is determinative instead of merely expressive. A more pronounced affirmation of sacramental objectivity, a rediscovery of the sense in which people are *acted on* in the church's practices, holds potential to support the distinct moral life of Christian communities at risk of stumbling in the late modern mist of vague moralism and ambiguous religiosity.

This proposed sacramental construal of baptism does not, however, demand that Anabaptist churches need to develop a list of rituals called sacraments and determine criteria for the validity of each. Instead, we would do better to begin by considering how the life of the church as a whole is sacramental, how God's presence is manifest through it, and how it renders God's grace visible. The Catholic theologian Karl Rahner does something similar when he calls the church the "primal sacrament."[51] Bonhoeffer does this in sweeping fashion. He gives us a way of understanding the sacramental character of the church that maintains the centrality of Jesus. We might also be reminded of Calvin who writes that "Christ is the matter or the substance of all the sacraments; for in him they have all their firmness, and they do not promise anything apart from him."[52] The point is that it is the life, death, and resurrection of Jesus of Nazareth that is determinative, not an independent ecclesiology or concept of a sacrament. For Bonhoeffer the church's social ethic is founded in the work of Christ

---

51. Rahner, *Church and the Sacraments*, 18–24, 39–41, 76–82. Similarly, the opening paragraph of *Lumen Gentium* includes the phrase, "the church is in Christ like a sacrament." Second Vatican Council, *Lumen Gentium: Dogmatic Constitution of the Church* (1964), 1.1, http://www.vatican.va/archive/hist_councils/ii_vatican_council/documents/vat-ii_const_19641121_lumen-gentium_en.html.

52. Calvin, *Institutes*, 2:1291.

On the Ecclesial Character of Divine Presence

and teleologically oriented toward his form. Through God's grace it is the manifestation of renewed sociality. Thus the church's life is sacramental in nature, as by extension are its central practices. Contemporary Anabaptists are comfortable speaking of *discipleship* as a formative feature of their ethic, yet to the extent that this term loses the corporate dimension of the body of Christ it fails to capture the its sacramental character. The sacramental function of the church's participation in the *totus Christus* runs counter to the individualized and spiritualized versions of discipleship adopted from either pietist or rationalist derivations of modernism. It does not, however, deny the voluntary character of Anabaptist communities. It does not follow from an affirmation that God acts through the church that anyone should be made to participate or be baptized into this body without their truly free decision to do so.

The NT refers to many aspects of ordinary life as pictures, or perhaps even icons, of God's relationship to humanity: marriage depicts the relationship of Christ to the church; water, the vitality of new life in Christ; viticulture, the care of God for his people; warfare, the struggle against the fallen powers of the world. Yet two activities—communion and baptism—are uniquely ordained by Jesus himself for the community of his followers. The special status of these practices is universally recognized by the church. In Scripture there are at least two others that are similarly mandated: proclamation and binding and loosing, the last of which includes both moral discernment and reconciliation.[53] My argument in favor of a general sacramental understanding of the life of the church does not mitigate the special status of these ordinances, but neither does it require a precise list of them. It provides, instead, a conceptual key to understand their function and theological location.

Bonhoeffer's christoform ecclesiology also helps us answer an important question arising from the NT. A crucial turning point in the biblical account of God's presence to humanity is the story of the ascension as recorded in the first chapter of Acts. This event coupled with Pentecost, recorded in the following chapter, serves as the hinge between the accounts of the gospels and the letters of the early church that make up the rest of the NT. A cursory evaluation might conclude that the former are accounts of Christ's presence and the latter accounts of his absence. This prompts readers to wonder where Jesus is now. However, the NT motif in which the

---

53. Regarding the mandate to preach and teach consider Matt 10:27; 28:19–20; regarding that of moral discernment see Matt 16:19; 18:15–20; John 20:21–23.

church is described as the body of Christ stands against the presumption that the apparent absence of Jesus is determinative.[54] Bonhoeffer's attention to this motif against the backdrop of sin's effect of alienation and separation reminds us of the importance of bodies for reconciliation. Like Bonhoeffer, fellow Lutheran Robert Jenson believes that this NT motif is particularly important for understanding the life of the church. He endeavors to take the ontological implications of the motif seriously when he writes, "the body Pilate hanged, and the embodiment of gospel-speaking among us, the ensemble of the gospel's sacramental reality, *are one thing*." Just as vigorously he says, "the whole object-reality of our community is the body of Christ."[55] Understanding the church to be the body of Christ in a world of disunity and alienation helps make sense of a practice such as baptism. As an act of Christ's body it is an act of God's redemption that continues the objective presence of God and mitigates claims of absence.[56]

This claim about Divine presence must be qualified, however, and several key criteria will be introduced in the final section of this chapter. Nevertheless, at a formal level these qualifications do not lead to a dialectical opposition of the presence of Christ in the church and his absence following the ascension. That the sacramental life of the church continues Christ's presence is an affirmation that exists precisely because the ascension is an event of absention, though the result is not the absence of Christ. The practices of the church have meaning as God's presence to the world because this presence is particular and localized. This form of presence is thus veiled, and the corrective that this thesis offers to contemporary Anabaptist ecclesiology is not one that baldly exchanges the absence of Christ for a total objective mediation of the Divine through the church community. Neither the totalized category of ubiquitous presence nor that of absence is ultimate.[57] Instead, what is axiomatic is God's redemptive work in which the localized presence of Christ in the church is significant because of the particular form of divine absention. In other words, baptism and the other ordinances of the church's life are given roles as instruments of God's presence in the time spanning the events of ascension and parousia.

---

54. This central Pauline motif can be found most prominently in Rom 7; 1 Cor. 6, 12; Eph 4–5; Col 1.

55. Jenson, *Visible Words*, 44, 46.

56. Cf. the way Karl Barth aligns God's subjective revelation with the Spirit, and objective revelation with Christ in *CD* 1/1:448–49.

57. Cf. Farrow, *Ascension and Ecclesia*; and Schillebeeckx, *Christ the Sacrament*, 40–45.

On the Ecclesial Character of Divine Presence

Before exploring the necessary qualifications that the veiled nature of this presence requires, I would like to consider the work of a theologian from a very different tradition and era—the early Anabaptist leader, Pilgram Marpeck. This will prove beneficial on two counts: First, Marpeck was an influential, though non-professional theologian who possessed a remarkably nuanced familiarity with the broader Christian tradition. As such he can serve as a model for contemporary Anabaptist theologizing. Second, Marpeck shows that a more sacramental understanding of the church's practices, particularly baptism, is not without precedent in early Anabaptist thought. It is interesting that Anabaptists find the lives of both Marpeck and Bonhoeffer compelling since they share some important social and theological similarities. The reason for their theological complementarity, though, is due to their common Protestant roots. Bonhoeffer was deeply influenced by the Protestant dogmatics of Barth and Luther. Marpeck, like most early Anabaptists, shared similar debts to Luther and Zwingli. Marpeck aligns more closely with Bonhoeffer than some other Anabaptists because of his strong rejection of spiritualism. Both of these figures would likely affirm Luther when he writes, "For our whole life should be baptism, and the fulfilling of the sign or sacrament of baptism, since we have been set free from all else and given over to baptism alone, that is, to death and resurrection."[58] Like Bonhoeffer, Marpeck's baptismal life lends credibility to his thought.

PILGRAM MARPECK

It is disappointing that many of the details of Pilgram Marpeck's life are lost to us.[59] We do know that he was likely born in the Austrian Tirol late in the fifteenth century. He was an engineer by vocation who worked as a civil servant and supervised significant projects in mining, lumber procurement, and hydrology. He was educated and wealthy enough to be mobile and to own his own home. This was an uncommonly urbane background for an early Anabaptist. Though it was unknown to many of his civil contacts at the time, he possessed an extensive circle of influence within the Anabaptist movement, one that is only now being fully appreciated.[60] Marpeck engaged in public debates about religious freedom, the sacraments, and civil

---

58. Luther, *Babylonian Captivity*, 70.

59. For a thorough account of Marpeck's life, see Klaassen and Klassen, *Marpeck*.

60. Rothkegel believes that Marpeck participated in something like a denominational network ("Pilgram Marpeck," 7–36).

authority. In recent years both historians and theologians have begun to pay increased attention to his legacy.[61]

Marpeck and Bonhoeffer were both public leaders whose influence overflowed those roles and seeped through clandestine channels. Both assumed pastoral responsibilities in one form or another and both engaged in significant written theological discourse. Both Marpeck and Bonhoeffer lived much of their lives at odds with prevailing civil authorities. Most readers are likely familiar with Bonhoeffer's correspondence through the famous collection, *Letters and Papers from Prison*. Less know that Marpeck also maintained correspondence with a wide variety of interlocutors. He engaged not only recognized church authorities such as Martin Bucer, a leading reformer and ecumenically-minded cleric in Strasbourg, but also a number of lesser known Anabaptists, his most lively exchanges being with those under the sway of spiritualism. The multi-facetted nature of Marpeck's correspondence and public engagement makes reading his work somewhat ponderous. It is made more difficult because it is not always clear if works bearing the stamp of Marpeck's influence came solely from his hand or were products of a circle of co-conspirators. If we are patient enough to hear him, however, Marpeck offers us an example of early Anabaptist thinking that takes the need for sustained and patient—though always spirited—reflection seriously. In Marpeck and his community we see a welcome model for Anabaptist theologizing that is appropriately self-critical and yet willing and able to engage the complexities of local social realities and the many-sided Christian tradition.

In the analysis of the Marpeck scholar Neal Blough, the significance of Marpeck lies in the fact that he went beyond the simple biblicism of other early Anabaptists like the Swiss Brethren and situated his convictions within the context of the broader Christian tradition. He took seriously medieval theological concepts such as the incarnation and the Trinity and used them, Blough tells us, as "theological guideposts along the way for reading and interpreting Scripture."[62] Our attention is demanded in a particular way by the dexterity with which Marpeck navigates the relationship of christology and ecclesiology, for, as we've seen in the work of Bonhoeffer, it is this convergence that ultimately defines the rites of the church.

---

61. For an overview of the development in Marpeck studies, see Klassen, "Legacy of the Marpeck," 7–28.

62. Blough, *Christ in Our Midst*, 19.

Marpeck understood his task to be one of reclamation, like that recorded in the book of Ezra. The early chapters of Ezra describe how a significant number of those exiled from Jerusalem were allowed to return during the reign of the Persian king Cyrus. These returnees quickly set about restoring the worship life of that city. They restored the facilities, ceremonies, and ordinances that had been interrupted by the long and spiritually disconcerting captivity. Marpeck suggests that just as these ancient children of Abraham restored neglected ceremonies, so too were Christians in his day returning from an exile in which the right exercise of their rituals had been forgotten. Against those who would reject these rites as unsalvageable after their captivity to the Roman church Marpeck writes, "The ceremonies, duly instituted, are valid in themselves and cannot, as a result of the Antichrist's impurity and abuse, become impure for the pure."[63]

The fact that Marpeck's defense of these ceremonies would in the end prove highly sacramental stands in contrast to other Anabaptists past and present. The contemporary preference for the testimonial view is not out of step with the greater part of the Anabaptist tradition. Therefore, it is only fair to present some of that argument here before exploring Marpeck's thought more closely. The most prominent reason for the denial of the sacramental view is biblical, or more pejoratively, biblicist. This argument holds that Scripture does not support a sacramental theology.[64] In this perspective the question of the sacraments amounts to a decision between two competing sources of theological authority. We must choose between tradition and the Bible. Harold Bender's description of the conversion of Menno Simons, who was a contemporary of Marpeck though separated geographically, illustrates this stance well: "In the very first year of Menno's priestly service, in 1525 . . . a grave doubt arose to disturb his carefree, frivolous life with its formal religion. As he was celebrating the mass, suddenly the thought arose that possibly the bread and wine were not actually changed into the flesh and blood of the Lord as he had been taught, and as he was teaching the people."[65] Bender goes on to describe how Menno, after spending two years in anxious deliberation, finally decided to search the Bible for an answer to his question. In Bender's words:

63. Marpeck, *Writings*, 45.

64. A little known example of especially vigorous polemics from the Anabaptist perspective can be seen in the following stream of literature: Bergestresser and Bashor, *Waynesboro Discussion*; Funk, *Reviewer Reviewed*; Moore, *Trine Immersion*; Quinter, *Vindication of Trine*; Quinter and M'Conmell, *Debate on Trine Immersion*.

65. Bender, "Brief Biography," 5.

> Now the decision of Menno Simons to search the Scripture for help in solving his doubts about the mass was not a decision to give up the authority of the church, for he probably hoped to find in Scripture a confirmation of the teaching of the church. The real problem came when Menno, having dared to open the lids of the Bible, discovered that it contained nothing of the traditional teaching of the church on the mass. By that discovery his inner conflict was brought to a climax, for he now was compelled to decide which of two authorities was to be supreme in his life, the church or the Holy Scriptures.[66]

Bender's description of the conversion of Menno Simons is notable as a marker for an important epoch in Anabaptist self-awareness. In Bender's description we see an early Anabaptist leader colored as an arch-Protestant. This becomes even clearer as Bender continues, "Menno's progress in the Gospel was slow. One pillar of his Catholic faith had broken down, namely, the mass, but he continued nevertheless, out of fear of men, to celebrate the mass as before. He might never have left the Catholic Church had it not been that a second pillar of his Catholic faith also broke down, the pillar of baptism."[67] In Bender's telling, the struggle of Menno turned on a question of authority. His conversion to true Christianity and his view of sacramental theology were inversely correlated. Though this view represents a prominent stream within Anabaptism, it contradicts the thought of Pilgram Marpeck.

In his book *The Lord's Supper in Anabaptism* John Rempel suggests that the chief goal of Marpeck's theology is to demonstrate that the practices of the church, even though they are outward events and often disparaged in the circles of the Radical Reformation, are of one essence with the inward reality to which they corresponded.[68] Marpeck seems to have been concerned that the reforming spirit might go too far. He was worried that the essence of the incarnation might be disavowed and that matter would be dismissed as a possible mediator for things eternal and spiritual.[69] Marpeck believed that in his time God was renewing the ceremonies of baptism and the supper, ensuring their ongoing vitality just as the vitality of Scripture was also assured.[70] The historical typology mentioned earlier,

66. Bender, "Brief Biography," 5.
67. Ibid., 6.
68. Rempel, *Lord's Supper,* 97.
69. Ibid., 125.
70. Marpeck, *The Writings,* 46.

in which Marpeck paralleled the post-exilic re-establishment of worship to the renewal of the rites of the church during the Reformation, shows his understanding of the task facing his community. It also shows his willingness to engage the OT as a resource for understanding how God is present to his people. It hints at the way Marpeck's theology is more fully anchored in salvation history than some streams of contemporary Anabaptist thought that longingly flirt with the quasi-gnostic and anti-Jewish theology of Marcion. Marpeck's arguments for the enduring importance of the church's practices, which I will organize around three main themes, are less philosophically sophisticated than Bonhoeffer's, but we will see that his conclusion is no less challenging for Anabaptist theology.

Practices as Co-Witnesses

Based on Marpeck's connection of the Christian community's ritual life to the OT one might think that he had much in common with Reformed streams of early Protestantism. And in a way he did, due in no small part to the fact that he was a theological borrower. His Anabaptist orientation did not preclude his sharing assumptions with any number of other church leaders. Calvin, in his *Institutes of the Christian Religion*, describes a sacrament as a word and a sign appended to a promise. In a general sense Marpeck's thought is amenable to this link between God's work and human acts.[71] However, a key distinction from the Reformed theology under development at the time is evident in Marpeck's *Confession*, a document published several years before Calvin's magnum opus and likely a response to Bucer and the city officials of Strasbourg. Those leaders looked to the reform movement in Zurich under Zwingli for direction. Zwingli's theology of baptism emphasizes the continuity of the old and new covenants. Zwingli understood baptism to be analogically related to circumcision, and he bluntly declares, "baptism is the circumcision of the Christians."[72] Zwinglian theology holds that Christian baptism is chiefly derived not from Jesus' command in Matthew 28 but from the baptism of John the Baptist.[73] This stands in continuity with Calvin's belief that the Jews of the OT felt the same power in their sacraments that Christians do in theirs.[74] Calvin

71. Calvin, *Institutes*, 2:1278.
72. As quoted in George, *Theology of the Reformers*, 141.
73. George, *Theology of the Reformers*, 140–143.
74. Calvin, *Institutes*, 2:1299.

tightens the link when he says, "The promise is the same in both [baptism and circumcision], namely, that of God's fatherly favour, of forgiveness of sins, and of eternal life. Then the thing represented is the same, namely regeneration."[75] For Calvin the two differ only in outward form. In his *Confession* Marpeck differentiates his view from the Reformed position by calling this parallel into question. Marpeck understands circumcision as a sign to which God is the witness. He does not, however, think that baptism is this type of a sign. It is not a sign like circumcision because, Marpeck believes, grace itself does not need a sign.[76] Marpeck claims that in the NT baptism is not a sign but a *witness*. It is a creaturely witness that is *of one essence* with what takes place internally.[77] The old practice of circumcision signalled an inclusion in God's future-oriented promise, but baptism is a witness along with the Spirit to what occurs in the believer's heart and is manifest in her life. The words sign and witness play in related semantic fields. Yet Marpeck's assertion that the creaturely witness is of one essence with the internal witness of the Spirit suggests a stronger connection than does Zwingli, for whom a sacrament is likened to a monk's cowl, or Calvin, for whom it is a seal or a guarantee.

In Rempel's view this notion of co-witness, or *mitzeugnus*, is "Marpeck's primary innovation in defining the sacrament."[78] In Marpeck's thinking baptism and the Spirit witness together. Again, there is similarity to Calvin, who writes, "If the Spirit be lacking, the sacraments can accomplish nothing more in our minds than the splendor of the sun shining upon blind eyes, or a voice sounding in deaf ears."[79] Marpeck was wary of the Spirit being construed to be dependent on baptism. To say that the Spirit waited for the mechanics of baptism to do its work would, in his view, make the Spirit "dead" or powerless. In opposition to magisterial Reformers such as Bucer, Marpeck sought to show that the Spirit's initiation is prior to the church's act of baptism, and by implication he affirms the dissimilarity of the old and new covenants. The OT implied a necessary fulfillment within time and history accomplished in Christ. Indeed, Marpeck insists that the ancients themselves were waiting for Christ. Although always existing as the second person of the Trinity, Christ fulfills the promises of the covenant in time

75. Ibid., 2:1327.
76. Marpeck, *Later Writings*, 75.
77. Ibid., 85–86.
78. Rempel, *Lord's Supper*, 120.
79. Calvin, *Institutes*, 2:1284.

and space through his incarnation, death, and resurrection. The faith of those ancient people of God was founded on God's promise and brought to fruition in the humanity of Christ. Therefore Marpeck believes that the epochs before and after the life, death, and resurrection of Jesus are distinct and unequal. Baptism and circumcision are not simply two mirrored sides of one event; rather, they look from opposing directions and disproportionate positions to the event of the incarnation. It makes a difference on which side of the life of Jesus, before or after, the ritual is located. The incursion of God into time in Jesus is not merely an event in history—it *defines* history.

We see that Marpeck's theology of baptism is carefully positioned. The incarnation is used both against the spiritualist rejection of ceremonies and against Bucer's flattening out of the covenants.[80] This positioning is important. Marpeck's co-witness concept maintains that baptism responds to God's work; it proceeds alongside the Spirit testifying to divine initiative. Baptism is not an act of an individual's self-assertion. In Rom 8:16 Paul says that God's Spirit testifies along with our spirit regarding our adoption as children of God. In chapter fifteen of the same book Paul describes how the Spirit provided amazing signs and miraculous events to make the mission to the Gentiles possible. Furthermore, in the second chapter of Hebrews the author describes how God testified to the gospel through signs and gifts of the Spirit. In Marpeck's Anabaptist theology baptism falls in line with this pneumatic NT precedent, *not* with the OT sign of circumcision. A crucial difference between "sign" and "witness" for Marpeck is that as a co-witness baptism is a practice empowered in ways that exceed the simple referential ability of a sign like circumcision. Circumcision signalled inclusion in the promise of God—a fulfillment that had not yet occurred—while baptism is an active witness with the Spirit to inclusion in the present manifestation of the family of God. Therefore, Marpeck breaks with the various iterations of the Reformed position through his understanding of salvation history manifest in the dissimilarity of the old and new covenants and in his preference for the concept of witness over that of sign. Of course he also breaks with Anabaptists of spiritualist persuasion who disparage such rituals.

---

80. Regarding Marpeck's connection to the spiritualist leader Caspar Schwenckfeld on this issue, see Blough, *Christ in Our Midst*, 51.

Uniting Inner and Outer through the Doctrine of the Trinity

Against a backdrop of covenantal distinction that anchors baptism within salvation history, Marpeck's thought on baptism can also be understood through a second theme: a phenomenological unfolding of the relationship of the inner and outer aspects of personhood. This inner/outer distinction is roughly equivalent to a distinction between the spiritual and physical.

Marpeck's deployment of these categories can be illuminated by observing how Menno Simons deals with the same. Menno's most recognized work, *Foundation of Christian Doctrine*, illustrates another type of Anabaptist objection to the sacraments. Menno wrote this piece both to educate his flock and to break down the harsh negative stereotypes propagated against Dutch Anabaptists. He wanted to show the biblical foundation of their convictions. In a section of the document that outlines the biblical case for believers' baptism, Menno writes:

> Paul also calls baptism the washing of regeneration. O dear Lord, how lamentably thy holy word is abused! Is it not most lamentable that men attempt with these plain passages to support their idolatrous and invented baptism of infants, asserting that infants are regenerated in baptism, as if regeneration were simply a matter of immersing in water. Oh, no! Regeneration is not such an hypocrisy but it is an *inward* change which converts a man by the power of God through faith from evil to good, from carnality to spirituality, from unrighteousness to righteousness, out of Adam in Christ.[81]

In this excerpt from *Foundation of Christian Doctrine* the debate about baptism centers on the mode of regeneration. For Menno, regeneration is fundamentally an act of God's invisible grace. Therefore, it is to be positively identified with the spiritual realm and opposed to the carnal. The carnal is visible while the spiritual is invisible. Menno, like a number of other early Anabaptists, ties sacramentalism to infant baptism and disposes of both.

Marpeck's metaphysical sympathies are different. He tries to maintain the unity of the Christian experience and in most of his work rejects the notion that the external and physical are unnecessary or mask true reality. He says, "Whoever has been inwardly baptized, with belief and the Spirit of Christ in his heart, *will not* despise the external baptism and the Lord's Supper which are performed according to Christian, apostolic order; nor will

---

81. Simons, *Complete Writings*, 123 (emphasis added).

he dissuade anyone from participating in them."[82] In the broader context of this remark Marpeck has in view, not only baptism, but also other "external witnesses" such as proclamation, martyrdom, and the Lord's Supper. None of these are to be rejected, nor is participation in them to be discouraged.

For Marpeck the relationship between inner and outer elements of our humanness is severed only at the price of dividing the Trinity.[83] This argument is made in a complex document now called *The Admonition of 1549*. Historians believe that this text was created through the Marpeck group's reworking of a Münsterite confession—the longest early Anabaptist treatment of the sacraments.[84] What is particularly interesting about this piece is in a section of the text *added by the Marpeck group* where it is proposed that just as the Spirit acts *internally* in a person, so water baptism acts *externally*. This assertion is grounded in the trinitarian observation that "the external essence of the Son is one in essence, and works in the Father and the Spirit."[85] Blough summarizes the understanding of baptism in this text this way: "The Father acts internally through the Holy Spirit in the heart of humans and the Son acts externally, through water, 'at the same time.'"[86] The person of Christ is linked to outer, physical rites like baptism. By tying the inner and outer baptisms to different members of the Trinity, Marpeck and his peers believe a denial of the importance of external rites is a denial of the triune character of God. This is one of the reasons why the stakes for Marpeck with respect to the sacraments are so high.

---

82. Marpeck, *Writings*, 65 (emphasis added).

83. Marpeck's thought on the Trinity is not without problems. He appears at times to confuse the Spirit with the divine nature of Christ. Blough describes this peculiarity rather gently: "Marpeck's simultaneous identification of the divine element with the Holy Spirit and the Word in the inner/outer union is at times rather confusing" (*Christ in Our Midst*, 147). Furthermore, Rempel suggests that Marpeck's description of God often verges on being binitarian when he identifies the agency of the Spirit directly with the first or second persons. While this binitarian tendency may be related to Marpeck's reliance on John's Gospel, the conflation is still extraordinary in light of his general sensitivity to trinitarian doctrine (Rempel, *Lord's Supper*, 105–8, 148–49). Even if it is handled with the softest of gloves, as Blough does, Marpeck's strange transposition is a substantial divergence from traditional Christian trinitarian thinking. It may be that this confusion is a manifestation of Marpeck's lack of formal training or the dialogical nature of his theological exposition (Blough, *Christ in Our Midst*, 180).

84. Blough, *Christ in Our Midst*, 108.

85. Marpeck, *Writings*, 195–96.

86. Blough, *Christ in Our Midst*, 108.

Participating Witness

In a letter to a woman named Helena von Streicher, Marpeck reaches further in his exposition of the necessity of physical rites by exploring what humans need in order to understand. He suggests that because of humanity's need to comprehend things through physical and material elements, wherever the Spirit works there is new life in the physical realm. When Marpeck reasons this way one hears similarities to Calvin, who writes: "The sacraments, therefore, are exercises which make us more certain of the trustworthiness of God's Word and because we are of flesh, they are shown us under things of flesh, to instruct us according to our dull capacity, and to lead us by the hand as tutors lead children."[87] In Marpeck's reasoning this anthropological observation is joined to his commitment to the centrality of Christ. What emerges from the union of these ideas is a claim that the physical voice of Christ cannot be separated from the Spirit, or even stronger—the claim that Christ's witness implies the participation of the Spirit. Marpeck is triangulating to the mandate that human reasoning ought not to divide what God does not divide.[88] Therefore, Marpeck's use of the co-witness concept moves beyond descriptions of baptism as a testimony, at the same time as his deployment of trinitarian logic advances his approach to the rite of baptism beyond the semiotic and ties it to the very life of God. This means that what happens outwardly in baptism is ontologically linked through the being of God to the Spirit's inner work. It is not merely a sign of it.

Church and Incarnation

We have focused thus far on Marpeck's description of the church's practices as co-witnesses, as well as his way of anchoring both the inner and outer aspects of personhood in the triune nature of God. Another important and very relevant theme in Marpeck's thinking relates to his understanding of Jesus. Earlier I suggested that in most of his work Marpeck is committed methodologically to maintaining the propriety of human physicality and the needs such an existence produces. It is his christology that unfolds his understanding of the triune nature of God and shows further how his construal of baptism is grounded in something more theologically sturdy than anthropology. In the context of his dispute with the spiritualists, Marpeck lays out his logic this way: "Where Christ has come in the flesh by faith (Eph 3; Gal 2), that same man, with his flesh and all external members,

87. Calvin, *Institutes*, 2:1281.
88. Marpeck, *Writings*, 379, 388–389.

indeed, the whole man obedient in external ceremonies, will confess the instruction and the life of Christ. But today these spirits desire to make the kingdom of Christ far too spiritual, and make too great a leap, just as, on the other hand, the Antichrist has made it too physical."[89] Marpeck is trying to extend the spiritualist reasoning to show how such commitments undermine the logic of the incarnation. He identifies this inversely with the problems of the Roman Catholic Church, which his audience took for granted. Marpeck believes an outward access point is needed to attain spiritual knowledge.[90] He is trying to hold a mediating position between medieval Catholicism and the spiritualism of his contemporaries.

In some of his later work Marpeck uses the concept of the "unglorified Christ," Christ before the ascension, in a complementary way. Although now glorified, Christ continues to also act through his unglorified body, which Marpeck identifies as the church.[91] This is an attempt at working out the logic of Christ being present through his body to the world in the community of believers while simultaneously being seated at the right hand of the Father. In the terminology used earlier, the church is Christ's presence after his ascension. Marpeck believes that the life of the church continues the humanity and presence of Christ upon his absention.[92] This is a point about revelation, but just as importantly it is a point about the ongoing action of Christ's body. Blough summarizes part of Marpeck's argument from a tract called "A Clear Instruction," by saying that he aligns "the visible church with the humanity of Christ," and thereby considers "the presence of the Christian community on earth as a prolongation of the Incarnation."[93] In various ways Marpeck uses these theological strands to support the claim that baptism should not be considered merely a sign of some more important invisible, spiritual event. Since the rite participates in "divine reality" it is much more.[94]

Marpeck believes the incarnation shows God's willingness to work transformatively with material reality in history. The church continues this.

---

89. Ibid., 52.
90. Blough, "Church as Sign or Sacrament," 33.
91. Ibid., 37.
92. Rempel, *Lord's Supper*, 107, 109, 161.
93. Blough, "The Church as Sign or Sacrament," 149.
94. Ibid., 34. To emphasize the fact that baptism is not just a symbol, Marpeck says, "In Christ there is only essence and truth, not sign or figure . . ." (Marpeck, *Later Writings*, 107).

It follows then that the individual's life of discipleship in the context of the church is participation in God's triune life. The church's life is God's love for the world made available to human perception and enacted "materially within history."[95] Therefore, the ceremonies of the church are important in that they "prolong God's presence in time and space, thus serving humanity in the same way as did Jesus of Nazareth."[96] To contemporary Anabaptists still under the influence of revivalism, Marpeck's thought represents an estranged part of their spiritual lineage. Yet for Blough the implication of the thinking of this sixteenth-century Anabaptist is clear: "The humanity of Christ refers first to the Incarnation, the person, words, teaching and work of Christ; second to the teachings and deeds of Jesus and the apostles, and finally to the words and acts of those who make up the church throughout history."[97] The conceptual structure of Marpeck's employment of the christological category of incarnation is congruent with the more formal affirmations in this project of the mediatorial character of the life of the church.

Toward an Appropriation of Marpeck's Sacramental Ecclesiology

What emerges from this overview of Marpeck's thought is, at the very least, clear evidence that there is precedent within the Anabaptist tradition for taking the practices of the church seriously as a means of Christ's ongoing presence among us. Through his use of salvation history to highlight the co-witnessing quality of baptism, his affirmation of the Trinitarian binding together of both inner and outer, and the link he sees between the incarnation and the church, Marpeck argues that the church's sacramental life plays a role in the ongoing physical presence of Christ in the world. The boldness of Marpeck's position is highlighted by comparison to other early Anabaptists. According to Thomas Finger, though most of them insisted that the inner and outer elements of baptism were interconnected, like the inner and outer elements of participation in Christ, they tended to commend water baptism out of sheer obedience to Jesus' command.[98] Marpeck's rationale, as we have seen, possesses much greater explanatory density.

If part of the answer to the question of baptism's possible participation in the sacramental character of the church is found in the way Jesus is

95. Blough, "Church as Sign or Sacrament," 36–37.
96. Blough, *Christ in Our Midst*, 37.
97. Ibid., 38.
98. Finger, *Contemporary Anabaptist Theology*, 165.

now present to the world, then it is evident that for Marpeck, Jesus is present through the Christian community.[99] More clearly than for Bonhoeffer, Marpeck realizes that this ongoing presence requires the dynamic work of the Spirit. In Bonhoeffer's *Sanctorum Communio* it is unclear at times how he distinguishes the life of the Holy Spirit from that of the church. Marpeck's ecclesiology does a better job maintaining the alterity of the Spirit and thus the potential for the church to be affected from without. It is precisely because the Spirit cannot be reduced to the invisible qualities of the church that congregations can bear witness to Jesus. However, Marpeck's ecclesiology focuses so directly on the individual's response to the Spirit, as do contemporary Anabaptist construals of the church, that the church as a community threatens to drop from view. It is held in place by the simple fact that its constitutive practices cannot be carried out alone and by his view that the church in some way amounts to the continuation of the humanity of Jesus. Here Bonhoeffer, with his emphasis on church-community, is a helpful conversation partner. Bonhoeffer upholds the necessarily corporate nature of the church in a way that Marpeck does more by accident than by intent. Describing the church as the continuation of the incarnation, while correct in its affirmation of the importance of the church in this time between the ascension and parousia, risks an ecclesial positivism so idealized that it loses contact with the actual church, or even worse, an idolatrous worship of the community itself. However, if we are to affirm that the church's life takes on a sacramental character we must also state how the community's mediatory role remains submitted to Christ—how the primary narrative in which baptism occurs is that of Jesus and only secondarily the story of the church and the baptizand.

An additional weakness of Marpeck's theology is his assumption that the Spirit's work is limited to the dimension of human interiority. Despite his efforts to restore the sacramental life of Anabaptist communities, he still concedes too much. He affirms the visible, social life of the community, but seems reluctant to think that the Spirit works through it. This is evident in his thoroughgoing assumption that water baptism and the inner change that the Spirit prompts are separate events. Though Marpeck goes to great length to bind these two together through the doctrine of the Trinity, his dualist presuppositions betray him. One result of this can be seen in his

99. Though my reading of Marpeck is mostly guided by Blough and Rempel, it is largely congruent with the more recent analysis of Dalton, whose essay on the subject was published after I wrote this chapter. See her essay "A Sacramental Believers Church," 223–36.

conservative approach to civil authority. Though, as he argues in *Exposé of the Babylonian Whore*, Marpeck wishes civil authorities to give up coercion in matters of faith, he sees little problem with them exercising it in all other areas of life. Like many subsequent modern theorists, Marpeck's default position is to cleanly hive the world into matters of faith and matters secular. Only in matters of faith are Christians permitted to counter the wishes of the civil authorities, and the only mode of response available to Christians living under unjust rulers is simple and sparing admonishment.[100] Unlike Bonhoeffer, Marpeck fails to see the socio-political critique of fallen social structures inherent within the life of the Christian community. This wall of separation does not cohere with more central themes of Marpeck's thought. If Christ's humanity is prolonged in the believing community through the work of the Spirit and if discipleship is the "primary sacrament of God's presence in the world,"[101] it is difficult to see how this does not clash with the extensive claims of civil authorities.[102] Latent within his understanding of the practices of the church is the recognition that matters of faith are not only those commonly thought of as spiritual. The humanity of Jesus, which cannot be divorced from his divinity, along with his ongoing presence through the church, mean that the dichotomy between spiritual and physical is ultimately as misplaced as is the assumption that the Spirit only works through invisible, spiritual means.

Notwithstanding the shortcomings of Marpeck's thought, his work is an example of early Anabaptist sacramental ecclesiology that demonstrates my suggested revisions are not as novel as they might first appear. Marpeck shows how such a theology can be developed by emphasizing baptism's character as a witness alongside traditional trinitarian and incarnational themes. Of these three themes it is Marpeck's construal of baptism as a co-witness that is most beneficial to carry forward and the one that I will develop further.

A SUBORDINATE OBJECTIVITY

Bonhoeffer and Marpeck agree that the life of the church is central to the ongoing work of God in the world. They show that ecclesial mediation is

---

100. Marpeck, *Later Writings*, 29, 38.

101. Blough, *Christ in Our Midst*, 226.

102. William Cavanaugh's critique of the theology that enabled the Pinochet regime in Chile is relevant here. See his *Torture and Eucharist*.

compatible with the central Anabaptist pillars of believers' baptism and a Christ-centered ethic of discipleship. Bonhoeffer sees more clearly than Marpeck the importance of the community as such. At the same time Marpeck realizes that this work relies upon the dynamic and vital activity of the Spirit. Marpeck articulates the way in which this involves the practices of the church within the paradigm of the incarnation. Bonhoeffer locates the church in the cosmic narrative of creation, sin, and new creation in Christ. In light of this we can now say much more about the role of the church's practices in the Christian life. Baptism allows us to see and feel that the work and presence of God continues. It is a practice in which the ongoing presence of the incarnate Son of God among believers continues to take shape. In this case the Spirit's renewing takes the form of cleansing through water and welcoming into the community. Believers' baptism then is a rite much more significant than testimony or self-identification. It is not a mere public confession on the part of the candidate or just an outward symbol of an inward reality. Through both Marpeck and Bonhoeffer we see that believers' baptism is initiation into the community that embodies Jesus' presence to the world. With the Spirit it witnesses to the transformative power of Christ, and as a co-witness it participates in this transformation that is both inward and outward. Through baptism candidates are acted upon by God and incorporated into the Divine life, and through it they become members of Christ's body. Believers' baptism is an act of God through the community of those who have been and are still being made right.

If the preceding exploration demonstrates the theological soul of ecclesial mediation oriented toward an understanding of the church as the objective presence of God, it remains necessary to further articulate some of the limitations of this proposal. Namely, it is necessary to explain the ways in which this objectivity remains a subordinate objectivity. I will argue that christological doctrine furnishes useful tools for doing this. Christology determines the church's mediatory role not only positively but also negatively; it limits or properly subordinates it. This is no radical change of course, as much of the argument thus far has revolved around the christoform character of the church. More specifically, though perhaps still indirectly at times, it has relied on the NT motif of the church as the body of Christ. We begin to see the christological limitation of this, however, when we remember that the NT uses a variety of models to describe the church. Each of these enumerates something of the multifaceted characterization of the relationship of God to the church. Each supports the thesis of this chapter and aids our present task of refinement. A cursory review of some of the most notable models will also help to ground the conceptual work of this chapter biblically.[103]

In 1 Peter 2 believers are described as "living stones" in a "spiritual house." Citing Isa 28:16, Jesus is named as the "cornerstone" of this house. Though the fact that both believers and Jesus are cast as stones implies a level of similarity, there remains here an unmistakable inequality between the living stones and the cornerstone. It is through the singular Christ that the many living stones offer "spiritual sacrifices" acceptable to God. Jesus is the bridge between the one and the many. Nevertheless, an implication is that through the work of Christ believers participate in him, both as structural elements and as the passage also states, "priests." Further in this passage the description of the church as priesthood is paralleled by the church depicted as the "people of God." This is a reference to the role of Israel, a people called to bless the world as a peculiar nation living in covenant relationship with God. God dwelt in their midst, and their community life was intended to facilitate the welcoming of the nations into the covenant blessing. Israel's social ethic was not an addendum to God's presence in the world: it was to be its manifestation. In Christ's covenant faithfulness vicariously imparted to all of Israel and in the extension of this work through time by the Spirit's work in the people of God, the gap between the particularity of Israel's life and the universal character of God's healing mission is narrowed.

The architectural imagery of 1 Peter is part of a common NT model of the church in which it is described as the temple of God. Paul invokes this model in 1 Corinthians 3, 2 Corinthians 6, and Ephesians 2, as does John to some extent in Rev 3:12. This description of the church denotes not only the process that the church undergoes—it is being built—but just as important, the dwelling place of the Spirit of God. To describe the church as the temple of God is to say that it is the place where God's presence is scandalously localized. It is the place amidst the complexity of fallen creation in which God identifies himself. Like the body motif, the picture of the temple points toward the church as a particular media in which God is present in the world.

The NT also describes the church as Christ's bride or spouse.[104] Second Corinthians 11, Ephesians 5 and Revelation 21 in slightly different

---

103. The field of comparative ecclesiology is clarified by several key texts: Kärkkäinen, *Introduction to Ecclesiology*; Dulles, *Models of the Church*; Minear, *Images of the Church*.

104. See Jenson, "Bride of Christ," 1–5.

ways identify the church this way. This type of description is not unique to the NT. Hosea 1 and Ezekiel 16 exemplify this descriptor with respect to God's relationship to Israel. This motif describes not only the care and commitment God maintains toward the church and Israel, but also God's anticipated union with this community. This marital imagery highlights a problem that arises if Jesus' life is *reduced* to the church. Christ becomes both bride *and* groom, differentiation collapses into identity, and alterity into unity. In the dissimilarity held by the marital model we are reminded of corollary limitations of the body motif.

In describing the church as the bride of Christ, NT writers push back against ecclesial descriptions that would assume total identification of the church with Christ. We are also reminded of the risks of describing the church as an extension of the incarnation. Like the motif of body, the more theologically abstract language of incarnation threatens to move in the idolatrous direction of total identification. To carry forward the caution implicit in the description of the church as bride in a phrase would be to affirm the *differentiated unity* of the church with Jesus, or we might point out that the classic Augustinian language of the *totus Christus* is useful precisely because it implies the unity of still differentiated entities. To speak of the "whole Christ" is not equivalent to speaking of "all of Christ," or what is sometimes technically referred to as the *totum Christi*. To define the church exclusively and exhaustively as the *body* of Christ surpasses biblical warrant, and to fully transmute Christ's being into that of the church dissolves the tension produced by the range of biblical metaphors related to the question of unity and alterity. It sharply reduces the witness of Scripture. Thus a sacramental leveraging of the biblical concept of the church as body of Christ, even as we observed in both Marpeck and Bonhoeffer, is bound to remain below this register. The language of mediation does this because a thing does not mediate that which it is; rather, it mediates what it is not. It makes present a form or an aspect of something absent.

An additional qualification that will prevent the overextension of this dominant motif comes from Ephesians. The description of the church found in Ephesians 4–5 is one of the most extensive in all of Scripture. In Eph 4:11–16 Paul develops the body motif by describing Christ as the *head* of that body. This shows both a similarity and a dis-similarity between Christ and the church, as Christ bears a uniquely privileged position with respect to the body's identity. The life, death, and resurrection of Jesus are the visage that provides its identity. In addition, through his authoritative position Christ provides orientation and direction. The disproportionality of this relationship is ignored if Christ and the church are conflated unequivocally. In other words, if we say Christ's present life is fully identical with that of the church—rather than saying that the life of the church is included in the life of Christ—the eschatological thrust of the NT is ignored. Likewise, if we describe the relationship of Christ and the church as one of full identity we deny the possibility of critiquing the church. Such critique requires the uniqueness of Christ as an independent plumb line. Therefore, we cannot say that the church is the body of Christ and that the actions of the community are God's actions *without at the same time* holding the community accountable to what we know of the character and will of Jesus. The logic of Paul works this way in Ephesians, and it is particularly evident from 4:17 to the end of the letter. This upholds the central elements of Anabaptism's discipleship ethic, which is to follow Christ's lead. This priority of the body's head can also keep in proper perspective Marpeck's view of the church as the incarnation's extension. The church extends the incarnation non-identically. It adds an appendix to the story of redemption, but does not further develop the plot with a subsequent chapter.

Even with these limitations, we need not say the church is *less* than the body of Christ. The life of the church is not inconsequential to the working of the gospel. Though the author of Ephesians vigorously reminds us of the church's dependence on Christ, this community is still affirmed as the dwelling place of God and the body of Christ. There remains no clear reason to doubt that God chooses to act through the church as it takes the form of Christ. To assert that Christ is the head of the body is to affirm that the church is *his* body. Worries about ignoring the fallibility of the church and the complete identification of Christ with the Christian community notwithstanding, the NT language of the church as the body of Christ is a key motif for understanding the present relationship between Jesus and the church. It is the common ground for Marpeck and Bonhoeffer and represents a biblical mandate for the concept of ecclesial mediation substantially absent from contemporary Anabaptist denominational statements. Marpeck's work shows that taking this image seriously for construing the practices of the church adheres to trinitarian logic and has Anabaptist precedent. The work of Dietrich Bonhoeffer shows its ecumenical promise, narrative import consistent with the theme of Christ as the new *adam*, as well as its accessibility to a theologically shaped sociological description.

The various NT models attune us to the fact that an argument in favour of ecclesial mediation has the potential to become overly inflated and lead to the collapse of christology into ecclesiology and the reduction of the activity of God to that of the church. Such over-inflation would be theologically aligned against the axiom that God—not the church—is the one who freely redeems in grace. It would contradict the first commandment, in which God's identity is asserted as unmatchable. It would also contradict the essential salvation narrative in which God reaches out in Jesus to a fractured world in need of redemption. These guiding dogmatic principles affirm the traditional tenets that God exists independent of humanity, is unique, and redeems the fallen world through grace. Nevertheless, the collapse of christology into ecclesiology and the reduction of the activity of God to that of the church remain reasons for being careful in embracing the mediatorial or sacramental quality of the church's life.

Bonhoeffer's way of reining in these problematic possibilities is to remind readers of the impurity of the church. Though the church plays a crucial role in the economy of salvation, Bonhoeffer is profoundly sceptical of any human attempts to purify it. In *Sanctorum Communio* he argues that because of its historical nature the church will always be impure and therefore ought not to judge—even its own members. Instead it should, in good Augustinian fashion, allow weeds to grow in its midst and await the final judgment of God.[105] Here Bonhoeffer is opposed to traditional Anabaptism, or at least the more strict separatism of Schleitheim and Dordrecht. Bonhoeffer's appropriation of Augustine's logic, though, is undeveloped and out of step with the abstract purity of his system. We can posit that his critique of his own idealist intellectual milieu was not radical enough at the time he wrote *Sanctorum Communio*.[106] Though Bonhoeffer's denial of the puritanical implications of his approach to ecclesiology are well intended, there is a more helpful way to consider the question besides simply asserting the Augustinian reading of Matthew 13, a reading that most Anabaptists reject. Bonhoeffer's later work directing the seminary at Finkenwalde yields a more helpful perspective on the nature of the church's holiness and impurity. In *Life Together* we see his embrace of various formational practices, from solitary meditation on Scripture, to confession, corporate worship,

---

105. Bonhoeffer, *Sanctorum Communio*, 222, 281.

106. There is some important development along these lines in *Act and Being*, where Bonheoffer more fully, though not uncritically, appropriates Barth.

and participation in the Eucharist.¹⁰⁷ Even if only considered at a glance, the semi-monastic regimen implemented at Finkenwalde demonstrates more clearly that the church's response to impurity and the reality of its sinfulness ought to be careful discipleship and not hedging theorization.¹⁰⁸

The underlying issue here, the church's impurity, connects us to the way early Anabaptists like Balthasar Hubmaier and Peter Riedemann understood baptism to be related to the office of the keys. For them baptism functioned as a signal of the individual's voluntary submission to and participation in the church's disciplinary practice.¹⁰⁹ The presence of sin in the church is not a glitch in the system. It is an opportunity for the Spirit working in, with, and under the life of the community to form it into the likeness of Christ. Both sin and the Spirit's presence are manifest throughout the life of the church, and thus the traditional question of how a sacrament can be valid when the church is impure applies to the community's entire life together. This parallels the idea that the term "sacrament" applies most fundamentally to the church's life as a whole.¹¹⁰ We wonder how the body can effect what it signifies when it falls short of the form of Christ. That the objectivity of Divine presence in the church remains subordinate is a reminder that its sacramental character is dependent and derivative. This is signalled practically by the ongoing disciplined and penitential nature of the community. As an event of death to sin and cleansing, baptism takes part in this repentance.¹¹¹

Martin Luther's classic description of the Christian from his lectures on Romans—at once sinful and righteous, or *simul justus et peccator*—can be read as a static and somewhat speculative picture of the Christian life: the fact of sin is theoretically covered by the imputation of Christ's righteousness.¹¹² In this case the concept is not congenial to Anabaptist thought because it depends on understanding salvation as the abstract imputation of righteousness. This model of soteriology is contrary to much of historic Anabaptist theology. Luther's description appears to be a final, stagnant statement about

---

107. Bonhoeffer, *Life Together*.

108. The theological groundwork for *Life Together* is evident in Bonhoeffer's *Discipleship*.

109. Finger, *Contemporary Anabaptist Theology*, 160–165.

110. Cf. Rahner, *Church and Sacraments*.

111. Bergen argues that the church's holiness is seen precisely in its repentance. It is worth noting that ecclesial repentance, as a function of the doctrine of the community of saints, follows from baptism. See Bergen, *Ecclesial Repentance*, 153–241.

112. Luther, *Lectures on Romans*, 260.

On the Ecclesial Character of Divine Presence

the life of the human creature. It undercuts the self-involving dynamic of discipleship and risks ontologizing grace, turning it into an invisible quantity trafficked by the sacraments and functionally detached from following in the way of Christ. Marpeck, though, inclines us to consider that grace need not be understood as an invisible quantity in need of a sign, and on the other hand, Luther's reflections related to Rom 4:7 can be understood differently. If we focus on the Reformer's analogy of God as a physician, his description of the Christian life is more amenable. Luther says, "For we believe Him who promises to free us, and in the meantime we strive that sin may not rule over us but that we may withstand it until He takes it from us. It is similar to the case of a sick man who believes the doctor who promises him a sure recovery and in the meantime obeys the doctor's order in the hope of the promised recovery . . . But now if this sick man should like his sickness and refuse every cure for his disease, will he not die?"[113] Here we see room for the community's life. Discipleship can be understood as the obedient corporate response to the physician's prescription for the restoration of health. Of course sin remains and the restorative work of God in the lives of individuals continues, but seen in this light the gathered community is not inert and Luther's famous description is less fatalistic.

The effects of sin on humanity are thoroughgoing, and subsequently the healing attention of the physician is as well. The limitation made evident by the church's sin is one of chronology—the extent to which a patient God has bound himself to time, withholding ultimate restoration and allowing the brokenness of creation to persist until the final judgment. This can be seen by analogy in the comparison of Jesus' pre- and post- resurrection body. After the resurrection, though Jesus' body was identifiable and retained the marks of his suffering, it possessed a new and astonishing quality that differentiated it from its precursor. The Gospels describe the physicality of the post-resurrection Jesus as one that dramatically appeared to and even startled the disciples. Despite the apostolic, catholic, and Spirit-indwelt character of the church community, it is analogically congruous with Jesus' pre-resurrection body—still under the care of the physician.[114] The *res signata* of the sacramental character of the church, the thing it signifies, is Christ's conquering of humanity's disease *and* future, ultimate resto-

113. Ibid.

114. That my use of this reference to the body of Christ is analogical in a way that the previous uses in this chapter are not can be explained by the fact that Paul's more univocal reference to the church as Christ's body in Ephesians 4 focuses on growth and not on any distinction between death and resurrection.

ration. Anticipating the latter, the church's proleptic life under the doctor's care is good news to the extent that it is hospitable. In Marpeck's terms, the community's life is a witness to the gospel of Christ, even as it participates in the gospel as Christ's body.

The thesis of this chapter has been that the objective presence of God that occurs in Jesus Christ continues in subordinate fashion through the life of the church. The objectivity of God's presence in the church is not equal to the objectivity of the life of Christ before his ascension. The preceding paragraphs can be summed up by stating that the objectivity of the church can only be the presence of Christ as it remains subordinate to the incarnation. This qualification of subordination requires of the baptismal community a continued openness to the Spirit and a submission to the witness that the apostles bear to the gospel of Jesus. The qualification of openness to the Spirit and submission to the witness of the apostles mean the church's mediation of the presence of God is never a forgone conclusion. It means, furthermore, that it cannot be mechanistically deployed. Continuing in rote the historic practices of the church is no guarantee of their involvement in God's self-presentation to the world. These qualifications protect the church's self-understanding from idolatry and remind congregations that they must constantly seek to embody the form of Christ and not presume to possess it.[115] Finally, the objectivity of God's presence in the church is qualified by the fact that it is the *life* of the church community that exhibits objectively the presence of God. It is not, to the extent that these can be considered separately, a genealogy or a structure as such. While institutional continuity may be a presenting identifier of the location of God's ongoing self-presentation, there is no necessary link between the two. Rather, the link is found only in the extent to which congregations take the form of Christ and rightly steward the memory of his ministry.

Within the logical structure of understanding the church as Jesus' ongoing presence in the world it is coherent to posit that God continues to welcome disciples into the community of his people. Membership in this new community is premised on an active acknowledgement of Jesus' Lordship and a willingness to participate in his reconciling body. As the church is the presence of Christ in the world, so the acts of the church—baptism central among them—are acts of God. Yet only through God's gracious taking on of human flesh are they possibly true acts, or acts that fit with God's

---

115. Paul's words in Gal 4:19 express the attentiveness this requires: "I am again in the pains of childbirth until Christ is formed in you . . ."

world and God's ongoing restoration of it. This has significant implications for baptism. It means that, though a rationalist, testimonial description of this practice may well fend off some of the unfortunate "magical" or "cultic" distortions of popular sacramentalistic views, this move comes at significant ecclesial cost, and therefore relying on the testimonial understanding of baptism alone is problematic. By contrast the discussion of this chapter has shown the richness of a more sacramental account of the church's life.

To carry forward the theology to which this chapter points, I suggest that baptism be understood as a *participating witness*. This is an outworking of the thesis of this chapter relevant to baptism, and it does at least two things. First, it carries forward Marpeck's language of co-witness. Baptism is a tangible witness to the successful work of Christ in each new participant in the community of the church. The agent of this witness is Christ's Spirit working through the church. Second, this description indicates the way in which the act of baptizing participates in the drama of grace. Unlike passive observation, baptism is an ecclesial activity through which God's restoration effectively proceeds. As a participating witness baptism partakes in the mediatorial role of the church. When baptism leads to right participation in the continued presence of Jesus, it displays the ongoing healing work of God in the world. Humbly practiced under the headship of Jesus it is an epic practice that strikes at the core of how we imagine and enact our humanity. Baptism is involved in the continual mad scramble to make sense of Jesus anew in our individual and corporate lives. To be baptized, to baptize, or to affirm baptism is to participate in the ongoing apocalyptic life of Jesus of Nazareth. It is to be brought into the concrete presence of Christ in the world and to be transformed into a member of that presence—to be as Scripture says in an impossible metaphor, "living stones."

4

The Spirit and the Problem of Fratricide

There are three that testify: the Spirit and the water and the blood, and these three agree.

(1 JOHN 5:7)

ACCORDING TO THE MARTYRS *Mirror*, George Wagner was killed on the eighth of February, 1527 in Munich. He died in the center of the city after being tied to a ladder with a bag of gunpowder around his neck and pushed alive into a bonfire. His crime was failing to recant his controversial beliefs, including his disavowal of the ability of priests to forgive sins, his denial of Christ's bodily presence in the Eucharist, and his rejection of the idea that baptism had salvific power. While Wagner was in prison, authorities tried to convince him to renounce his heretical views. His wife and children were brought to visit in an attempt to remind him of what he was in danger of abandoning if he chose to continue rejecting official doctrine. Wagner gave up his life instead of his convictions, and, as it was remembered, just before his death he said, "Be it done in the name of the Father, the Son, and the Holy Ghost."[1] Wagner's words echo the traditional baptismal formula, yet this was not a baptism in water but in his own blood.

Many of the stories of the sixteenth-century Anabaptist martyrs are stunningly and fantastically violent. The bodies of these Christians were tortured—stretched and torn on the rack, their tongues squished in screw devices, strung up by their wrists; and they were killed—drowned,

---

1. van Braght, *Martyrs Mirror*, 416.

beheaded, and burned alive. In the case of Michael Sattler, the well-known ex-Benedictine and framer of the Schleitheim Confession, the prosecuting court's decision read: "In the case of the Governor of his Imperial Majesty *versus* Michael Sattler, judgment is passed, that [he] shall be delivered to the executioner, who shall lead him to the place of execution, and cut out his tongue; then throw him upon a wagon, and there tear his body twice with red hot tongs; and after he has been brought without the gate, he shall be pinched five times in the same manner."[2] This was carried out and his body—his "heretical" body—was burned to ashes. A number of his friends were killed as well. Several days later, Margaretha, his wife, was drowned. Stories like Wagner's and Sattler's, which may well number in the thousands, are all the more haunting because the cruelty was inflicted on Christians *by* Christians.

Throughout history and across the breadth of geography, Christians have victimized and killed each other. The North African rigorist movements inspired by Novatian and Donatus in opposition to Catholicism were the occasion for some of the earliest. The so-called "Wars of Religion" in Europe, as well as civil wars in England, France, and the United States, even both World Wars, are additional examples. The twentieth-century Rwandan genocide is a terrible and recent witness to the fact that this feature of Christian existence continues. As Lee Camp reminds us, before falling into monstrous chaos, Rwanda was thought of as a shining example of the success of Christian mission.[3] Yet, without forgetting this litany, the violence of the sixteenth century uniquely challenges the thesis of this book. This is because it is from that tearing apart of Christianity in Europe that the Anabaptist movement emerged. The frame of Anabaptist life and thought was bent by the experience of those generations, and contemporary Anabaptist theology must take this into account.

However, the mode of intra-Christian relationship has not remained static since the sixteenth century. In the almost 500 years between that century and the present, Protestants, Catholics, and Anabaptists have generally come to recognize each other as Christians, or at least as "separated brethren." In light of this mutual acknowledgement, we must admit the century in which the Protestant Reformation began was, in all its upheaval, a century not only of the fracturing of the church and of martyrdom but also one of fratricide. Seen from the twenty-first century, the painful irony, then, is

---

2. Ibid., 418.
3. Camp, *Mere Discipleship*, 19–21.

that baptism, the sacrament of cleansing and welcome, was contested in such a diabolical way that the boundary between martyrdom and fratricide evaporated. In the drowning, decapitation, and burning of "heretics" at the hands of Christians, the waters of baptism joined many to the death of Christ. As self-professing followers of Jesus tore at each other's bodies, they ripped apart the body of Christ—the same community about which the last chapter spoke so idealistically. Given this history *and* our contemporary view of it, a troubling question presents itself: How can we say God is at work in the baptisms of this conflicted body? In prior eras, when it was not accepted that the other's claims to the Christian faith had any serious validity, this question might not have arisen. Now it cannot be avoided.

In this chapter I will consider Anabaptist responses to the questions raised by the martyrdom of Wagner, Michael and Margaretha Sattler, and others. My suggestion is that the legacy of Anabaptism's sixteenth-century origins in the context of ecclesial persecution have allowed for a view of the church that is pneumatologically underdeveloped. Evidence of this can be found in the denominational ecclesiologies surveyed in chapter 2. There I tried to demonstrate that the theology of contemporary Anabaptist communities fails to clearly locate the church with respect to either the work of God or the performance of the Christian life. The result is a low view of the church and the assumption that baptism can only be the work of the human creature. The argument of this chapter, then, is that the classic Anabaptist response to the question of the historical character of the Spirit's presence in the church is in need of revision.

In the first part of this chapter, I will describe and critique the *Martyrs Mirror* as the classic Anabaptist *theological* response to the sixteenth-century persecution. In the second, I will engage two prominent twentieth-century efforts to refashion this classic position. In the third, I will outline a corrective that I believe is more capable of coherently affirming the Spirit's presence to the church through time without minimizing the deplorable—indeed, heretical and anti-Christ—nature of sixteenth-century fratricide. I will do this by sketching the orienting principles of a more pneumatologically attentive ecclesial memory. The goal is to not fall victim to an idealized vision of how it is that believers' baptism can be an event in which God acts by the Spirit through the church.

PNEUMATOLOGY AND ANABAPTIST MEMORY

It is believed that the largest book published in the American colonies before the Revolutionary War was a German translation of *The Bloody Theatre*, a book better known today as the *Martyrs Mirror*. In 1745 German-speaking Mennonites in eastern Pennsylvania wrote to members of the Mennonite community in Amsterdam asking for assistance in producing a German translation of the text originally published in Dutch by Thieleman Jansz van Braght in 1660.[4] The Mennonites in Pennsylvania were concerned about the rising threat of war. They were worried that many of their members would not remain true to their traditional ethic of non-resistance, and it was their hope that the *Martyrs Mirror*, with its stories of the faithful witness of numerous Christian martyrs—many but not all of them Anabaptists—would serve as an inspiration. To the Dutch Anabaptists they wrote:

> As the flames of war appear to mount higher, no man can tell whether the cross and persecution of the defenseless Christians will not soon come, and it is therefore of importance to prepare ourselves for such circumstances with patience and resignation, and to use all available means that can encourage steadfastness and strengthen faith. Our whole community has manifested a unanimous desire for a German translation of the [*Martyrs Mirror*] of Tieleman Jansz van Braght, especially since in this community there is a very great number of newcomers, for which we consider it to be of greatest importance that they should become acquainted with the trustworthy witnesses who have walked in the way of truth, and sacrificed their lives for it.[5]

In 1748–1749 the massive book, all 1512 pages, was printed in Ephrata, Pennsylvania, then the frontier of European settlement, on presses operated by a peculiar Protestant community of monastic vegetarians. This was not the only time the *Martyrs Mirror* was re-published. Even before

---

4. The book was identified in the 1660 edition with the title, *Het Bloedig Tooneel Der Doops-gesinde, En Weereloose Christenen (The Bloody Theatre of the Baptism-Minded and Defenseless Christians)*. The layout of the title page was reworked in the 1685 edition to feature the Martyrs Mirror phrase more prominently. It is this edition that was widely translated and this title by which the book is now widely known. Also, though I refer to Thieleman Jansz van Braght as the author, and though he did write some of the material, a significant amount was borrowed from a variety of sources, including martyr accounts, both by Anabaptists and more famous church historians such as Eusebius, court documents, and even prison letters. See Covington, "Paratextual Strategies," 1–29.

5. *GAMEO*, s.v. "Martyrs' Mirror."

the twentieth century, it went through several editions in Dutch, German, and English. This is a text of singular importance for understanding the development of Anabaptist identity. It represents a classic Anabaptist understanding of the history of the church, a view that held for centuries.[6] It is far from clear that it has even now been superseded. Though contemporary Anabaptists in North America recognize the diverse, global, and historical nature of the church, their doctrinal statements include little if any theological explanation for the dissimilarity of various traditions. These documents are even strangely reluctant to provide reason for the unique existence of Anabaptism. They present a faith eerily suspended in the world of ideas, free of history or context. Thus the account of history and relationship to other Christian bodies that the *Martyrs Mirror* provides retains significant influence. Its value endures not least because it offers a plausible narrative within which a community's identity might be located.

Framing the Question

In the last chapter, I argued that baptism is the practice in which Christ's body welcomes new members and participates in the incarnational presence of Jesus and thereby the creation of a new humanity. In the context of this project's skepticism about spiritualist interpretations of baptism it is important to remember that baptism as just outlined is all that it is *within* history. Therefore, grievous moments in the church's life cannot be ignored if our considerations of Anabaptist baptism are to take account at all for the actual, social existence of this community. There is then a question as to how this destroying and destroyed body could be that of Christ, and there is also a question as to how the Spirit of God could have allowed this deep evil to reside in that same body. If God's Spirit resides in the Christian community throughout history, how is it that this body could be disassociated to the point of self-mutilation? If God's Spirit does not reside in this body then baptism as it has been described has ceased to exist. This is the question this project now puts to the *Martyrs Mirror*.

The question assumes two things. First, that the three relevant sides of the sixteenth-century violence, Protestant, Catholic, and Anabaptist, assumed themselves to be Christians, and furthermore, that their spiritual

---

6. For an account of the relationship of historiography and identity in North American Mennonite circles, see Sawatsky, "History and Ideology."

descendants continue to hold this assumption.[7] Second, this question assumes that the Spirit does indeed accompany the church through time. The first assumption probably does not need to be argued, and the second is only slightly less widely held. A quick defence of the second assumption is simply to expand it by saying that the pneumatology undergirding this chapter will proceed in the direction pointed by the following five biblical markers: (1) as indicated in Eph 1:13, the Spirit is both active in the present outworking of God's redemption and has a role in the eschatological unfolding of salvation in history; (2) as described in Titus 3:3–8, redemption itself is inseparable from the Spirit, who has been poured out through the work of Christ; (3) the power of the gospel, as 1 Thess 1:5 tells us, is the power of the Spirit; (4) in line with John 14:15–27, the teaching work of the Spirit is implied in the life of the Christian community across time; and (5) as we read in 1 Cor 12:13, this same Spirit brings about the unity of the church as the body of Christ.

Prior to this chapter most of this project's constructive work in favor of the sacramental mediation of God's presence and work through the life of the church has been conceptual, oriented through the biblical witness, and yet almost entirely independent of temporal context. Now we must address the question stretched through time, asking not just how *a* community of Jesus' followers might constitute God's ongoing presence, but how *this* community—the Christian community as Anabaptists have known it—can be said to do the same. The challenge is to address the question not with a generic notion of time but in a specific history, the history of the church. We cannot expect to develop more than an outline of such a response in a single chapter. Nevertheless, if this project is to be convincing, its Anabaptist account of believers' baptism must be compatible with a way of narrating the Spirit's presence, and summarily the church's viability, across time and in history. If there is no theological way to narrate this troubled history the only coherent alternative is to embrace an idealistic, abstract, and spiritualized ecclesiology. The affirmation of baptism as a participating witness requires an account of how this body has remained the body of Christ despite episodes of obvious discontinuity. We would do well to remember, however, that the need for such a narrative is not new to either the Jewish or Christian traditions. It is similar to the task of finding

---

7. Cavanaugh, *Myth of Religious Violence*, has convincingly undermined the standard myth that the modern nation state arose as the solution to theological competition between these groups. His work suggests that the incipient nation state itself engendered much of the violence.

a coherent story within the continuity and discontinuity of the biblical chronicles of divine presence, which stretch from figural fires encountered by the ancients through the tabernacle and temples of the Israelites to the body of Christ and the church that gave birth to the NT.[8]

The Classic Anabaptist Account

The classic Anabaptist response to these questions is found in the *Martyrs Mirror*. This book expounds a history counter to the dominant churches in which the faithfulness of minority groups is contrasted to the wayward propensity of the mainstream. It tells us much about how Anabaptists have understood their historical relationship to the universal church. This sort of narrative is by no means unique to Anabaptism. All lasting communities have their own way of understanding history that serves a mythological function in supporting their identity, explaining their uniqueness and giving rationale for the effort it takes to maintain their existence.[9] This understanding of history supports and forms the community's worldview as it is transmitted either through formal educational methods or storytelling and traditional practices. A key feature of an Anabaptist reading of history is how this community's at times tortured relationship with the larger Christian faith is understood. The essential problematic arises from having been persecuted by Christians and yet not wanting to be other than Christian.[10] The classic answer, which the *Martyrs Mirror* exemplifies, traces the general arc of a declension narrative in which the mainstream church falls while Anabaptist-like groups persist as true followers of Jesus. This reminds us that for Christian communities such as Anabaptists, their ecclesial memory not only explains their existence but also affects and is affected by the possibility of reconciliation.

It is with these concerns in mind that we will consider the *Martyrs Mirror* more closely as one of the most important sources for understanding Anabaptist memory. This text recently celebrated its 350th anniversary.

---

8. The Catholic theologian Yves Congar has taken up this challenge in one form in *Mystery of the Temple*.

9. Plato recognizes this in book III of his *Republic*.

10. It is not uncommon to find Anabaptists so allergic to being identified with American evangelicals that they prefer to discard the Christian identifier altogether. This is discussed briefly in Matthew Krabill, "Mennonite, not Christian?" *Mennonite Weekly Review*, Sept. 28, 2009.

From its inception the *Martyrs Mirror* was intended to be historically sound, yet its primary reason for existence has always been formational, or we might even say, devotional. In the preface van Braght addresses readers directly and frames the book's purpose: "This book, the humble work of our hands, but which is nevertheless a precious jewel, in view of the persons and matters contained therein, we have dedicated to you . . . Read it again and again, and with the same attention and emotion with which we have written and re-written it. We are fully confident that, if you do this, it will not be unfruitful to you. But, before all things, fix your eyes upon the martyrs themselves, note the steadfastness of their faith, and follow their example."[11] Van Braght invokes the martyr stories, which were cobbled together from a variety of sources and contained in his compendium, for the spiritual profit of his readers. The power of this martyrology, though, is inseparable from the overarching narrative of the decline of the church. Van Braght writes, "As there are two different peoples, two different congregations and churches, the one of God from heaven, the other of Satan and from the earth; so there is also a different succession and progress belonging to each of them."[12] This dichotomy serves as the context for each and every martyr story. Faithful Anabaptist Christianity is juxtaposed to the diabolic fall of the mainstream church.

Van Braght chronicles the history of believers' baptism and of the persecution that was intended to uproot it. He gives an account of the growing influence of infant baptism and the suppression of the original credobaptist practice from the first century through the sixteenth. Van Braght suggests the origin of the suppression of believers' baptism lies in the fifth century in the decrees of Theodosius and Honorius. He highlights an ecclesiastical canon that anathematized anyone who spoke against infant baptism.[13] These fifth-century developments were prompted by the Donatist controversy and the fallout from Augustine's debate with Pelagius. Therefore, in van Braght's view, the liturgical mistake was perpetuated by the development of a sweeping account of original sin that gave theological urgency to the baptism of infants. After the fifth century the picture van Braght paints becomes increasingly dark as the true church—baptizing adults only—was

---

11. van Braght, *Martyrs Mirror*, 8.

12. Ibid., 21.

13. Ibid., 197, 201. Though the specifics are unclear in the *Martyrs Mirror* it seems as though van Braght has in mind imperial decrees given in support of the ecclesiastical canon 110/112 of the synod held in 418 in the North African city of Carthage under the authority of Bishop Aurelius.

hidden from view. Here the *Martyrs Mirror*, which up to this point had related the stories of well-known Christian martyrs, begins to specifically track those killed as "Anabaptists."[14] In English, van Braght's use of the term "anabaptist" seems anachronistic when applied to pre-sixteenth-century figures. This highlights the counter-historiography of the volume, which argues that Anabaptism can be traced institutionally to the early church. Van Braght defends his anachronism by saying that "there have been persons in every century . . . who have believed and taught the article of holy baptism . . . in the very same manner as the Anabaptists . . ."[15]

The *Martyrs Mirror* seeks to remind readers that persons practicing the true apostolic faith existed throughout the church's history. It informs them that many of these, such the Waldensians, where labeled "heretics" by the Roman Church, as the *Martyrs Mirror* labels the Catholic tradition, and killed. The force of the narrative of the *Martyrs Mirror* is to not only encourage the reader to live rightly in light of the gospel of the apostles, but also to deny dominant churches' claims to apostolicity. Van Braght believes true apostolicity is doctrinal, and in this vein cites the Apostles Creed as a distillation of true doctrine.[16] In the introduction to the second part of the text, which is entirely devoted to martyrs of the sixteenth century, van Braght suggests that the most prominent mark of deviation from this center, the mark of *true heresy*, is the willingness to kill the so-called heretic. This is the real register of the mainstream church's depravity and its most abominable teaching.[17] The story he tells of this heresy, which is also the counter-story of martyrdom, reaches its nadir in the sixteenth century. This period is introduced dramatically: "A great door is opened unto us to the arena of the martyrs and blessed followers of Jesus. None of the previous persecutions endured by the orthodox martyrs are to be compared to the present one. We have come through the time of fifteen centuries, each consisting of one hundred consecutive years; but we must confess that we did not meet with what we have seen, or, at least, that which we shall see here. The length of the time, the severity of the persecution, and the number of

---

14. The texts links the English term "Anabaptist" with the Dutch *Doopsgesinde* and the German *Taufgesinnte* and suggests that it might be better rendered in English as "baptism-minded" (ibid., 16n*).

15. Ibid., 18.

16. Ibid., 27.

17. Ibid., 357–58.

the martyred persons shall testify to this."[18] Here the suffering of sixteenth-century Christians at the hands of other Christians is purposefully placed in line with the sufferings of early believers. The latter would have been acknowledged as martyrs and true witnesses to the gospel by all the factions of the Reformation. The bare act of binding the two groups of martyrs within the covers of the same book is an effort to link them. Van Braght argues this point more overtly by establishing a direct line of succession from the early universally acknowledged martyrs to the Reformation-era Anabaptists. Written in the seventeenth century, the *Martyrs Mirror* is a monument to the sixteenth-century martyrs and a defense of their sacrifice in the face of those who understood them not as martyrs but as heretics endangering the faith. The sixteen-hundred-year narrative counters the mainstream interpretation of the Anabaptist movement as a heretical sect and is an apology for the value of their struggle and the appropriateness of their witness. Van Braght writes that the whole Bible itself seems to be a book of martyrs, "replete with numerous, according to the flesh, sorrowful, but according to the spirit, happy, examples of the holy and steadfast martyrs..."[19] He lists a number of characters from the OT and 2 Maccabees, and writes, "The honor... due to the holy martyrs, is infinitely greater and better than that of earthly heroes..."[20]

The account of the first fifteen hundred years is something like a prolegomena to the sixteenth century, which makes up the bulk of the volume. A representative entry from this later period appears as follows:

> CHRISTINA HARING, A. D. 1533
>
> In the year 1533, a sister, named Christina Haring, was apprehended, taken to Kitzbuehl, and there fastened to a chain; she, however, remained steadfast in the faith. But as she was with child, and was soon to be confined, they let her go home until she should be delivered of her child; and though she knew that she would be apprehended again, and might have escaped ten times, or even more, she did not flee, but boldly remained. When she saw the officer coming, she went out to meet him, and asked him what he desired. He said, "I have come to take you away again;" and thus they again took her to the town of Kitzbuehl, where shortly afterwards she was executed with the sword for the faith to which she steadfastly adhered. Her body was afterword burnt (Matt 24:13).

18. Ibid., 410 (punctuation altered).
19. Ibid., 12.
20. Ibid., 14.

> This courageous, heroic woman or sister in Christ, who forsook her husband, infant, house and home, and all temporal things, strengthened her womanly heart with such valiant manliness, and by the grace of God so armed herself in the faith, that she paid her vow unto the Lord, and joyfully went to meet Christ her bridegroom, with her lamp burning, and her light shining so that many were filled with astonishment (Matt 25:1).[21]

The stories in the *Martyrs Mirror* are bluntly recounted hagiographies depicting not only the purity of the Anabaptist witness but also the depravity of the savage attempts to crush it. The starkness of these stories and the way they are interwoven with Scripture is part of the book's formational power. Readers learn to expect resistance to their faithful practice. Anabaptist readers are given a picture of the hero as well as a possible explanation for their own trials. Part of the lasting success of this text is surely due to its ability to engage the reader as a believing and moral subject.

The *Martyrs Mirror* is about religious persecution and baptism. It is about the apostolic church and its impostors. The *Martyrs Mirror* is overtly anti-Catholic, and thus it is not surprising that the story it tells about the "true" church places the papacy in the role of chief antagonist. The papal office is given responsibility for the ongoing deviation of the "Roman Church," and is challenged both theologically and historically over some dozen pages.[22] At the conclusion of the topic van Braght writes, "It is enough for us to know, that their succession, of which the papists boast so much, is confused and vain, or, at least, without tenable grounds."[23] The *Martyrs Mirror* presents the decline of the mainstream church as gradual but perceivable, and van Braght names clear signs of how the mainstream church went wrong: pedobaptism, the violent suppression of heresy, and so on. In this liturgical and moral account of the church's fall a breach is opened in the biography of Christ's body. Within it Anabaptist identity is established in opposition to the larger church, making it dependent on the very story of that unfaithfulness. It is the muddied corruption of the mainstream that shows the purity in the counter-currents. Yet most importantly in the context of this chapter this decline is described without direct

---

21. Ibid., 441.
22. Ibid., 49–60.
23. Ibid., 59.

The Spirit and the Problem of Fratricide

reference to the Holy Spirit. The fall is described as willful failure and the deceptive work of the devil.[24]

The *Martyrs Mirror* succeeds in four prominent ways: (1) it profoundly engages readers at a devotional level, (2) it establishes a prominent record of the stories of those who died, (3) since it is a narrative it presents the church as a concrete community in history, and (4) it locates Anabaptism with reference to other Christian traditions. It may have been possible at one time to argue, as the *Martyrs Mirror* does, that Anabaptist baptisms exclusively were true baptisms because that community represented the body of Christ when no others did. In such a reality the pneumatological question is not raised because competing ecclesial claims are "settled" through the de-churching of the other. In this paradigm the baptisms of the church can continue to be carried on in assurance that God acts in them because the presence of God is not identified with the contravening claims of other church bodies.

This triumphalist option is no longer available to Anabaptist communities. The problem arises in the instance of the *Martyrs Mirror* because the story it tells is theologically rash. This leads to an unsatisfactory relationship with other Christian traditions, which alone would be reason enough to address the problem. What is more, this shortcoming is of a piece with the lack of clarity manifest in the breakdown of the practice of believers' baptism named earlier. In sidestepping pneumatological questions, the *Martyrs Mirror* describes the church anthropocentrically. Even for those who accept the negative diagnoses of the features of the mainstream church that van Braght presents as evidence for its fall, a crucial theological gap remains. The *Martyrs Mirror* does not give a clear theological description for how such a deep apostasy came about or why some could remain faithful while others did not. The breach opened in ecclesial history is presented without frame or limitation. Without substantive theological explanation it threatens to undo the whole doctrine of ecclesiology. At the very least its theology fails to remain viable in an ecumenical age. Most obviously it is unclear how the Spirit maintained or failed to maintain a presence among those who gathered in the name of Christ.

One wonders what van Braght thought had happened to the guiding function of the Spirit. How are we to understand the absence of the Spirit's reconciling power and guiding role in the unfolding of the history of God's people? The martyrological genre of the text lets readers down, leaving

24. Ibid., 21.

them with an over-and-against reading of history in which the mainstream church is fallen and corrupt, no longer bearing the presence of God in its midst. Contemporary readers cannot help but wonder where God is in all of this bloody and dualistic rendering of past events. What are the workings of the Spirit? Were those baptized as infants in the mainstream church welcomed into the body of Christ or not? More pointedly, did baptism occur outside the stream of the "faithful" Anabaptists and the various proto-Anabaptist groups? If we say that those baptisms were but shams and imitations, do we not fit Augustine's caricature of the rigorist whom he describes when he writes, "the clouds roll with thunder—that the house of the Lord shall be built throughout the earth—and these frogs sit in their marsh and croak, 'We are the only Christians.'"[25] In practice the dominance of this response among contemporary Anabaptists has waned, yet the theology of the church and of baptism has yet to take this into account.

TWENTIETH-CENTURY REVISIONS TO THE CLASSIC ACCOUNT

Sociological changes in Anabaptist existence in the twentieth century prompted a new type of theological reflection. The adoption of the dominant English language along with an increased interaction with other Christian traditions precipitated a revisiting of the declension narrative assumed by the *Martyrs Mirror*. Within the Mennonite community particularly, the work of J.C. Wenger and John Howard Yoder stands out in this regard. At the respective times of their writing, the work of these two men represented some of the most informed and sophisticated theological reflection being done by Anabaptists in North America. I will survey portions of the work of these theologians to develop my case that an ecclesiological lacuna remains.

J. C. Wenger's System

In 1954 J. C. Wenger published what may have been the first Anabaptist systematic theology in the four hundred and some years since Peter Riedemann's.[26] Alongside this distinction, Wenger's work is also notable because

---

25. As quoted in Harrison, *Augustine*, 154 (punctuation altered).
26. Finger, *Contemporary Anabaptist Theology*, 58. This claim depends in part on how Daniel Kauffman's work is evaluated.

of its positioning as part of the first wave of series theological reflection on Anabaptism in twentieth-century North America. The work of Harold Bender is more well-known and from roughly the same period, but Wenger's systematic focus pushes him to consider normative questions in a more comprehensive fashion. The full title of Wenger's book is apt, if not a bit cumbersome: *Introduction to Theology: A Brief Introduction to the Doctrinal Content of Scripture Written in the Anabaptist-Mennonite Tradition*. Like the German translation of the *Martyrs Mirror*, Wenger's book was commissioned. The Mennonite Publication Board had requested the production of a "Mennonite theology." More specifically, Wenger was asked to write an introductory text that would initiate readers to Anabaptist theology through accessible language and systematic organization.[27] The volume's approach to theology, then, represents the commitments of more than just one intellectual. Wenger was educated at several Mennonite colleges as well as Westminster Theological Seminary and the universities of Zürich, Basel, and Michigan. In Europe he studied with such luminaries as Emil Brunner and Karl Barth. His education had alienated him from some Mennonite leaders, but in the minds of the Publication Board it had prepared him for the task of writing a theological treatise in the Anabaptist-Mennonite tradition.[28]

Wenger's volume, like the German translation of the *Martyrs Mirror*, is consciously part of a program of Anabaptist recovery. In this case it is from what Wenger calls "disorientation." The disorientation arose during the late nineteenth century as Mennonites switched from German to English in both their churches and homes. This change cut Mennonites off from key formational texts and traditions, which put the life and worldview of their community at risk. Wenger writes of this period, "Although the brotherhood was saved by the introduction of the Sunday school, and was greatly revived by the ensuing interest in Bible study and missions, there arose a generation of leaders who were but superficially acquainted with the fundamental doctrines and insights of their Anabaptist forefathers."[29] Wenger's use of the phrase "fundamental doctrines" should not be overlooked, for *Introduction to Theology* is theology done in the key of Protestant fundamentalism.

27. Wenger, *Introduction to Theology*, v.
28. Ibid., viii.
29. Ibid., vii.

The significance of Wenger's book can be understood in view of its contrast to the earlier translation and printing of the *Martyrs Mirror*. Where the martyr stories were considered appropriate responses to the destabilization of Anabaptist churches in the run-up to the American Revolution, the request for Wenger's text demonstrates an assumption that assuring the availability of these same stories in English was not adequate for the demands of the twentieth century. This was despite the fact that the basic challenge was similar: the maintenance of Anabaptist identity and practice against the tenacious forces of assimilation. A fundamental feature of both responses is also similar: the attempt to construe Anabaptism through its relationship to other streams of Christianity. The important difference is that Wenger's text goes about this by making use of systematic tools and more abstract, propositional formulations of doctrine. His book, unlike the *Martyrs Mirror* and Harold Bender's *The Anabaptist Vision*, avoids narrating church history almost altogether.[30] Perhaps in this sense we might, against his self-understanding, view Wenger's central move as a liberal one. It is an attempt to develop an identity without any substantial reference to tradition. In this way the publication of *Introduction to Theology* is a marker of the Americanization of Anabaptist memory. I do not mean, of course, that Wenger fails to engage key voices in early Anabaptism—he does. Yet his engagement with them is consistently mediated by the probes of a systematic approach to doctrine as foreign to the *Martyrs Mirror* as it would have been to most sixteenth-century Anabaptists.

If Wenger's theology can be said to be an Americanized version of Anabaptism, it is so inasmuch as it is a clear Protestantization of it.[31] In part, this represents Wenger's way of coming to terms with Augustine's caricature of the sectarian rigorist. Wenger's conservative Protestant moorings are evident in several ways: first, as already mentioned, in the highly modern and systematic approach to theology to which he avails himself. Quite early on in his book he writes, "[T]o date no *systematic* theology has been written by a Mennonite."[32] He intends to break new ground. While Wenger does not mean to say that no previous Anabaptists have written theology as such, his claim implies the unique value of systematic proce-

---

30. Bender's classic essay was published in various formats and translated into a number of languages. It can be found online at GAMEO, s.v. "Anabaptist Vision (Text, 1944)."

31. As opposed to the more recent characterizations of Anabaptism as neither Catholic nor Protestant. See Klaassen, *Anabaptism*; and Snyder, *Following in the Footsteps of Christ*, 24–28.

32. Wenger, *Introduction to Theology*, 11 (emphasis added).

dure and the novelty of his approach for Anabaptists. What Anabaptists require to recover from their disorientation in the Anglophone world, in Wenger's view, is an approach to their faith more abstract and rightly ordered. This assumes a structure in which ethics and pastoral work, what Wenger thinks of as practical theology, is understood as a discipline that rests on the developments of systematics. Systematic theology in turn occupies a third tier, making the conclusions of biblical theology coherent, with biblical theology finally being built upon actual exegesis.[33] Virtually absent are the controls of community and the formative requisites of piety. Instead, Scripture is understood to interpret Scripture. The unity of the Christian community is found in doctrine understood propositionally as derived by the individual from the biblical text.

Wenger is trying to approach the biblical text via a path that avoids the dangers of both rationalism and Catholicism. His worries about modernism are standard issue for the mid-twentieth century and not significant for our discussion. His approach to Catholicism, however, is more germane. On the topic of Scripture Wenger states, "The right of interpretation, according to Catholicism, does not reside with the individual but with the authoritative church, which means concretely the hierarchy. Protestants, on the other hand, hold that the final authority in faith and life is the Word of God as interpreted by the Holy Spirit to the individual conscience."[34] While Wenger's verdict on Catholicism is still negative, the landscape clearly changed since the writing of the *Martyrs Mirror*. He opposes the notion that the interpretation of the biblical text should be delimited by the church hierarchy, but absent are vitriolic comments against the papacy and the maligning of hundreds of years of Christian practice. In fact, Wenger sees Catholicism as something of an ally against the rationalist attack on the doctrine of inspiration.[35]

Wenger's use of the basic assumptions of conservative Protestantism can also be seen in the logic of the book's organization. *Introduction to Theology* begins with prolegomena and traditional theistic proofs for the existence of god. It then moves through the topics of "God as Creator," "God as Revealer," "God as Redeemer," "God as Sanctifier" and concludes under the heading "God as All in All." At several points Wenger deals directly with the topic of Protestant fundamentalism. While he concedes that this

---

33. Ibid., 5.
34. Ibid., 20.
35. Ibid., 18.

movement has shown itself to be too narrow in its social conservativism, he writes, "Nevertheless it must be admitted that the Fundamentalist theologians of the twentieth century, in spite of their limitations, stand closer to the great reformers such as Luther and Calvin, than do the modernists and semi-modernists with their undue preoccupation with philosophy and its categories."[36] This approach is liberating for Wenger. It allows him to write a theological text that primarily cites biblical references while taking up few philosophical or historical problems. His is a fundamentalism that, in opposition to rationalism, allows for the immediate appropriation of the product of biblical exegesis, assuming its authority. Scripture can be cited verse by verse, read simply and plainly.

The Anabaptist turn to systematization represented by Wenger's *Introduction to Theology* indicates a conviction that martyr stories and counter-historiography are no longer sufficient to maintain the spiritual health of the community. This essential project is continued by Mennonite theologians like C. Norman Kraus in his book *God Our Savior*. Though he is writing in 1991 and engaging a different set of perceived threats than Wenger, his response to Anabaptist history is conceptually congruent.[37] Therefore it is at the point of this methodological judgment that Wenger's development of the classic approach must be evaluated. The softer rejection of Catholicism in Wenger's book is not a mere rhetorical shift from the language of the *Martyrs Mirror*. It draws our attention to the fact that he is attempting to articulate an Anabaptist view of the Christian faith in a new landscape. The cartographic contours have changed and Wenger, probably without knowing it, anticipates the shifting relationship between conservative Protestants and Catholicism that would accelerate at the end of his century. It is true that the old Mennonite settlements that requested the translation of the *Martyrs Mirror* into German had, since their emigration, existed in the religiously plural and progressive environment of William Penn's colony.[38] However, language barriers, the lack of proximity to Catholics, and the isolation of the frontier probably delayed the need for reconsideration of their triumphalist and exclusive narrative. It is not surprising that the

---

36. Ibid., 14.

37. Kraus, *God our Savior*, seems to be worried about precisely the sort of conservative Protestantism Wenger lauds. In Kraus's favor is his more developed pneumatology; however, Kraus's work lacks the paradigmatic status, which Wenger's and Yoder's hold, to warrant fuller consideration here.

38. For a description of some of these challenges, see Sawatsky "History and Ideology," 22–38.

The Spirit and the Problem of Fratricide

conviction of the insufficiency of the classic approach arose concurrently with the rise of the use of English and a general openness to the populist methods of North American Christianity. As the protective power of these distinctions disappeared after the American Civil War, a new set of anchors was required to stave off assimilation.

Whatever the effect of *Introduction to Theology* in 1954, we must ask if Wenger's solution to the problem remains sufficient. The central change to the classic approach of the *Martyrs Mirror* is the view that the narration of the community's history does not give appropriate orientation to the larger church. In the preface to the fourth printing of *Introduction to Theology* Wenger acknowledges he has learned much from other historical Christian traditions and remarks on the continued "phenomenal" sales of the *Martyrs Mirror*. He writes, "Though I am deeply immersed in Anabaptist studies, my final appeal in this work has been to the living 'Oracles of God,' especially to the books of the NT."[39] He is conscious of the relationship of his work to questions of the church's history and van Braght's classic interpretation. Initially this rendering of the systematic approach may well have been useful in allowing twentieth-century Anabaptism to stand apart from the sensational categories of the *Martyrs Mirror's* narrative of ecclesial decline. One would assume that it was beneficial to Wenger and the communities he served to establish an identity on the map of American religious life apart from the failures of others and the increasingly less believable triumphalism of Anabaptism's classic historical narration.

If Wenger's approach was at one time sufficient, it is no longer so. As a system it avoids the concrete task of historical narration and thereby idealizes the church. Wenger's attempt to establish the validity of Anabaptism through its relationship to the wider world of Protestant systematics fails to account for the current situation in which Anabaptists are willing to acknowledge that Catholics too are Christians. The point is not to blame Wenger, perhaps he could not possibly have anticipated this, but the fact that his Anabaptist theology rests on the paradigmatic status of the great Protestant Reformers, especially Luther and Calvin, continues to tie it to the assumption of the decline of Catholicism through the middle ages and denies the possibility of Catholic reform. The difficulty this presents is that to the extent that Protestantism continues to repudiate Catholicism, it cannot escape the need for a declension narrative. This type of denominationalism implies, in the provocative phrase of Ephraim Radner, the

---

39. Wenger, *Introduction to Theology*, x.

ongoing "separative logic of division."[40] In addition, the fundamentalist variety of the Protestant tradition Wenger endorses locates another fall in the mainstream church with the acceptance of modern historical-critical biblical scholarship. All of this is masked in Wenger's volume by the use of a systematic order and mode of appeal to Scripture that leaps across the life of the church. It is an attempt to transcend the problems of history by ignoring them. In this light the attempt to establish Anabaptist identity in abstraction beyond the fall of the mainstream church is unsuccessful.

A second significant shortcoming of Wenger's book is that it is unclear how in adopting the worldview of Protestant fundamentalism his theology remains Anabaptist. I think Wenger anticipates this critique by making two distinctions between his theology and that of the Protestant Reformers and their fundamentalist heirs. These relate to baptism and the Christian's relation to government. The latter distinction is not developed. Instead, Wenger commends the work of scholars John Horsch, Guy F. Hershberger, and John H. Yoder among others. Yet he does little to integrate their treatment of politics into the larger trajectory of his book. Similarly, Wenger quotes the "Schleitheim Confession" at length, but provides few points of connection between that historical articulation of belief and his work. Regarding the former distinction, related to baptism, Wenger is more forthcoming. He tells readers that he understands the NT to describe water baptism as a symbol of cleansing from sin and of one's death to it. It also constitutes a "covenant of discipleship with God through Jesus Christ," and symbolizes the baptism of the Holy Spirit.[41] In addition, Wenger writes, "the description of baptism given in the Scriptures eliminates any thought of infants participating in this ceremony."[42] Both baptism and relation to the state are secondary doctrines for Wenger. It is not apparent how they are constitutive of the community for whom he writes. Evidently for Wenger, to be Anabaptist is to be Biblicist, and the experience of that community does little to color its hermeneutics.

Wenger's *Introduction to Theology* is an attempt at not only providing a useful introduction to the topic of Christian life and belief, but also, if unwittingly, an attempt at answering the questions of history and the Spirit raised at the beginning of this chapter. The answer to the question of how Christian baptism makes any sense in the context of the body of Christ

40. Radner, *End of the Church*, 86, and elsewhere.
41. Wenger, *Introduction to Theology*, 234–35.
42. Ibid., 235.

killing and torturing itself is for Wenger twofold. First, Wenger implies that the question can be downplayed in light of the contemporary challenges to right belief and practice. In seeing himself and Anabaptist communities at large as essentially conservative Protestants, Wenger allows the question to disappear. Second, Wenger's pneumatology in *Introduction to Theology* is spiritualized and individualistic. The chief work of the Spirit in Wenger's view is convicting individuals of sin. This conviction precedes salvation; it is what adds members to the church.[43] The Spirit's work is extended through conversion in conforming the believer to the character of Christ.[44] A second function of the Spirit is to affirm the effectual power of God's promises to the believer. The Spirit allows the believer to rest in the results of God's mercy.[45]

Sanctification, in Wenger's view, includes the traditional Anabaptist distinctives of non-resistance and non-conformity. However, a curious feature of *Introduction to Theology* is that even though pneumatological language plays a key role in the doctrine of redemption, it fades in Wenger's subsequent discussion of ethics.[46] This implies that although Wenger readily declares the importance of the Spirit in conversion—that is to say, the individual's reception of and initial allegiance to the gospel message—he declines to view the Spirit as a prominent actor in the development of the Christian community across time. This frees his theology to take on the timeless pretensions of conservative Protestantism and ignore the questions of the Spirit, ecclesiology, martyrdom, and baptism. Though this might be useful in the ways alluded to, it simply ignores a fundamental aspect of the Spirit's role and sidesteps crucially important ecclesial questions. In addition, it is painfully insufficient to make sense of Anabaptist identity. Without a way of narrating, and in at least some minimal sense upholding, Anabaptist history as a faithful witness to the gospel, there is no clear reason why the theology Wenger presents should be Anabaptist at all. This supplements my general critique that *Introduction to Theology* fails to provide a clear sense in which God's Spirit has been active in the corporate body of Christ throughout history. His use of the language of "covenant" notwithstanding, baptism for Wenger is reduced to a fungible marker of the individual's coming to faith.

43. Ibid., 262, 272.
44. Ibid., 272.
45. Ibid., 304.
46. Ibid., 313–15.

Participating Witness

John Howard Yoder's Declension Narrative

Wenger's systematic approach is not symptomatic of a thoroughgoing shift in Anabaptist thought away from more historical and narrative construals of the doctrine of the church. For example, in 2007 Tripp York published *The Purple Crown* through Herald Press, a Mennonite publishing house. In this book York explores the logic and implications of Christian martyrdom. He explicates martyrdom as a political act of witness in which the body becomes the field of contest in the cosmic battle between God and rebellious powers. Using the *Martyrs Mirror* as a primary source, York describes martyrdom in the sixteenth century. He notes the challenges highlighted at the beginning of this chapter by acknowledging that those whom the Anabaptists may have thought of as *persecutors* would have considered themselves *prosecutors*. In his assessment of Christian martyrdom York employs George Lindbeck's theory of doctrine and claims that visible performances of the faith narrate claims of relationship to the gospel more truly than do words. And seemingly with a tone of reluctance, York concludes that the martyr follows in the footsteps of Christ.[47] *The Purple Crown* represents, among other things, the enduring nature of the problem raised in this chapter and its continued relevance for Anabaptist theology. In addition, the book points us again to the seminal work of John Howard Yoder. York's book appears in the Polyglossia series, which is described as growing "out of John Howard Yoder's call to see radical reformation as a tone, style or stance, a way of thinking theologically that requires precarious attempts to speak the gospel in new idioms."[48] York's book relies heavily on Yoder's thought, as well as the work of scholars influenced by it. With York's book as a reminder of the widely acknowledged importance of Yoder's work in this arena, we turn now to what I suggest is Yoder's refashioning of the classic Anabaptist narrative of ecclesial decline. In comparison to J. C. Wenger, Yoder represents a more current Anabaptist attempt at coming to terms with the leading questions of this chapter: how to understand the pneumatic character of the church in light of the body's autophagic episodes.

The focus of Yoder's doctoral study was not pacifism or even Anabaptist ethics generally; it was Anabaptist history. He researched and wrote on the topic of sixteenth-century Anabaptism in Switzerland. Perhaps it is

---

47. York, *Purple Crown*, esp. chap. 3.

48. Dula, Huebner, and Sider, Series Introduction, *Purple Crown*, inside the front cover.

because of this training that his work in social ethics never strays far from history.⁴⁹ Indicative of this is the way his critique of Christian involvement in war often proceeds alongside his historical depiction of "Constantinianism." The importance of the link between this central issue of social ethics and history is particularly evident in *Christian Attitudes to War, Peace, and Revolution*, a text that has its origin in a course by the same name Yoder taught for almost thirty years. In this setting Yoder discusses the "meaning of the Constantinian shift" as the backdrop for the entire discussion of war, peace, and revolution.⁵⁰ The Constantinian shift is central to the narrative of the church that lies behind Yoder's theology and ethics.

Yoder's use of the term "Constantinianism" does not mean that he is laying the blame for the fall of the church on Constantine as such. Rather, in Yoder's words Constantine is a "symbol of an epochal shift."⁵¹ Elsewhere Yoder describes the shift this way: "Constantine neither initiated that shift nor concluded it, and our present interest is not in the extent to which he knew what he was doing. The shift is what matters. That it took place, was far-reaching, and changed much of the concrete social meaning of Christianity, all historians agree."⁵² This focus represents several key revisions to the classic Anabaptist account in the *Martyrs Mirror*. For Yoder the papacy is not nearly the problem it is for van Braght. In addition, Yoder does not stress the issue of baptism, but rather the larger "social meaning of Christianity." He describes the new epoch symbolized by the ascendency of Constantine: "This new era was to include far-reaching changes in Christian social ethics. For example, the pre-Constantinian Christians had been pacifists, rejecting the violence of army and empire not only because they had no share of power, but because they considered it morally wrong; the post-Constantinian Christians considered imperial violence to be not only morally tolerable but a positive good and a Christian duty."⁵³ In Yoder's telling, the Constantinian shift is far reaching, influencing ecclesiology and eschatology in prominent ways.

Before Constantine, intermittent persecution made adherence to the Christian faith costly. After the imperial changes Constantine inaugurated

---

49. Yoder's doctoral dissertation has been translated and published as *Anabaptism and Reformation in Switzerland*.

50. Yoder, *Christian Attitudes to War*, 57–74.

51. Yoder, *Priestly Kingdom*, 135.

52. Yoder, *Royal Priesthood*, 245.

53. Yoder, *Priestly Kingdom*, 135.

it took significant conviction to publicly disavow Christianity, the result of which was eventually Augustine's *ecclesia invisibilis*. In the pre-Constantinian world it took a measure of faith to believe in God's guidance of history, but in the post-Constantinian reality God's guidance was empirically observable. In other words, providence was a matter of faith and the true church was empirically visible before Constantine, but the shift to which his name is attached reversed this.[54] Yoder writes, "These profound shifts were also felt in the realm of liturgy and theology. The pagans who became Christians in great numbers after Constantine could not be expected to give up their crude or primitive (or elite) understanding of the services that religion ought to render to society, so such celebrations as Christmas and Halloween annex pagan rites."[55] Yoder goes on to name similar liturgical developments that relate Christianity to the cycles of nature. The role of the theologian also changed. Throughout the Middle Ages the loss of missionary encounter led theology to become "the business of people who had nothing else to do." Theologians became concerned with "encyclopedic" issues, putting every bit of knowledge in its proper place and "attempting to teach everything as part of a whole."[56] At the height of Christendom Yoder tells us the dominant assumption was that, "There was one Christian culture, and theology exposits it; theologians explain its unity."[57] Readers familiar with Yoder's work know it is not limited to this sort of narration. Yet in one form or another, this reading of ecclesial history underlies his understanding of what it means to be an heir of the Radical Reformation.

In some of his later work Yoder applies the same basic logic, which questions whether developments in the Christian tradition were in fact necessary, to a wider range of issues. He addresses the Jewish/Christian split and the project of Christian ecumenism most notably. He argues that the parting of ways between Judaism and the early Christian movement did not necessarily have to take place. Even more provocatively he suggests that Anabaptism can be understood as a reclamation of a pacifist and diasporic way of being the people of God that existed within Judaism prior to the life of Jesus.[58] With respect to Christian unity Yoder regularly tried to refocus the conversation on local congregations and on social divisions that were in

54. Ibid., 135–37.
55. Yoder, *Preface to Theology*, 232.
56. Ibid.
57. Ibid., 233.
58. Yoder, *Jewish-Christian Schism Revisited*.

The Spirit and the Problem of Fratricide

his view far deeper than could be addressed by an ecumenism preoccupied with denominational mergers. Yoder also pointed out the need for Scripture to function as a mutually recognized resource for a dynamic evaluation of difference. Without this canon ecumenical dialogue could not be much more than a static naming of differences.[59] The breadth of Yoder's work is linked by his concern for Christian moral unity across national boundaries and the practical gospel-shaped lives of church communities.

Like Wenger, Yoder's approach represents a development of the *Martyrs Mirror* story line in response to the realities of the twentieth century. However, where Wenger's theology sidesteps important questions of historical identity and where the traditional Anabaptist counter-historiography of the *Martyrs Mirror* ignores ecclesial complexity and nuance, Yoder's approach, emphasizing important developments around the time of Constantine, hints at a description that might be able to take into account later developments during the Reformation era. Yoder is conscious of the relationship of his work to that of the *Martyrs Mirror*. He describes this classic Anabaptist account of the church's story as relying on "public institutional succession."[60] In Yoder's view van Braght intends to beat Roman Catholicism more or less on its own terms by offering a counter-historiography of a true church. The *Martyrs Mirror* tries to show an alternative stream of faithful and genealogical pure Christianity. Though van Braght's tome claims to track doctrinal integrity, in Yoder's view it actually retains institutional succession as the chief accrediting feature of the church. By contrast, Yoder argues faithfulness is better understood as a "continuing series of new beginnings, similar in shape and spirit, as the objective historicity of Jesus and the apostles, mediated through the objectivity of Scripture . . ."[61] Yoder's Anabaptism is juxtaposed to Constantinianism, yet he does not propose a clandestine, genealogically integral institution that captures the Spirit when the corrupt mainstream church cannot. As a corrective to classic Anabaptist triumphalism, Yoder advocates an ongoing reformational impulse dependent on the Spirit and the Scriptures. In this the focus shifts from possessing the right lineage to critically responding to contemporary inadequacies, whether they be of our own making or handed to us by the tradition.

59. See the section of essays under the heading, "Ecumenical Responses," in Yoder, *Royal Priesthood*.
60. Yoder, *Priestly Kingdom*, 133.
61. Ibid.

Yoder's recasting of the martyr narrative reveals possibilities for the reconstrual of baptism attempted here because it means his Anabaptist reading of history is not limited to choosing to identify the Spirit's activity in one or the other—in *either* the mainstream church or a clandestine series of dissenting groups. Rather, it is the recurring presence of reforming movements that demonstrates the Spirit's faithfulness. Through ongoing reform, the Spirit works to make Jesus present to the world through real people in actual physical communities with concrete modes of welcoming new members. Thus, reformation in view of Scripture is itself evidence of the Spirit's work. From a Yoderian perspective only if reform does not happen would the conflict-filled history of the church jeopardize the more sacramental description of baptism advocated in this project. This reminds us that the recovery of the practice of believers' baptism itself indicates that Anabaptist groups take history and the Spirit's work within it seriously. Why else would they believe infant baptism was a heretical innovation and believe it was a problem worth the cost of correcting?[62]

Yoder's view of Scripture may well have appeared too "Catholic" to someone like Wenger since it located the hermeneutic task in the church community. However, Wenger would have been sympathetic with Yoder's intent to maintain the importance of this text for life of the church. Serious attention to Scripture provides grounds for genuine ecumenical engagement and even accountability across traditional denominational lines. In an ecumenical era the good news of Jesus as described in the Bible functions as the necessary standard against which subsequent ecclesial developments are evaluated. Centered on Scripture, as opposed to historical developments about which Christian communities hold strongly divergent views, Yoder's ecclesiology opens up these sorts of possibilities in ways that the much more caustic categories of the *Martyrs Mirror* do not. Yoder's method of foregrounding the role of the hermeneutic community also sets him apart from Wenger, whose view of hermeneutics is predictably more individualistic.[63] For Yoder, the phrase from Acts 15:28 "For it has seemed good to the Holy Spirit and to us . . ." encapsulates the vibrant character of the interpretive community under the guidance of the Spirit.[64] The payoff of this approach is that it provides the theoretical frame not just for making some sense of theological and practical diversity within the church, but

---

62. Ibid., 123–34.
63. See especially Yoder, "Hermeneutics of Peoplehood," in ibid., 15–45.
64. Ibid., 33, 35.

The Spirit and the Problem of Fratricide

for critically engaging it. Honest, critical engagement is crucial for rightly forming Christian memory.

Yoder's reading of history invokes the Spirit in important ways that Wenger and van Braght do not. This is particularly evident in the context of his view of the ongoing ethical life of the church. It is the Spirit, Yoder believes, that aids the church's discernment and creativity; the Spirit enables right interpretation of Scripture.[65] An additional example is evident in Yoder's critique of Reinhold Niebuhr. Yoder's response is most obviously focused on Niebuhr's underdeveloped ecclesiology and his rejection of Jesus' peace ethic. Therefore it is easy to overlook the way in which Yoder's assessment is pneumatologically driven. This aspect of Yoder's retort to the "realism" of Niebuhr is exemplified when he asserts, "In the New Testament the coming of the Spirit means the imparting of *power*, and that *power* is not a mythological symbol for the infinite perfectibility of human rationality but rather a working reality within history and especially within the church. This power opens a brand-new realm of historic possibilities; not 'simple possibilities', but *crucial* possibilities."[66] Though Yoder's theology rarely gives thick pneumatological description, his reaction to Niebuhr shows that it is precisely this doctrine that makes his ecclesiology possible. We see this developed similarly in a personal letter of Yoder's responding to J. Lawrence Burkholder's affirmation of Niebuhr's basic way of stating the ethical problem. Yoder writes, "What needs to be advocated against Niebuhr is not a new systematic ethical philosophy . . . but the reality of the Holy Spirit in the church, as the condemnation of all possible apologies for compromise . . ."[67]

The positive elements of Yoder's contribution are significant. His approach to the story of the church and by extension the instance of ecclesial sin that so festers in the memory of Anabaptist communities is historically attentive even if it glosses over details. He maintains this while abjuring historical positivism. In its opposition to Constantinianism it provides a reason for the continued existence of the Anabaptist witness. Yoder's historical sensitivity, dialogical method, and biblical focus provide criteria for ecumenical engagement that fosters the sort of critical openness necessary to deal honestly with the past. As a corrective Yoder's work is unlike Wenger's *Introduction to Theology* in that it is more thoroughly grounded

---

65. Ibid., 35, 38, 94; *Preface to Theology*, 339, 379.

66. Yoder, "Reinhold Niebuhr," 116.

67. As quoted in Zimmerman, *Practicing the Politics of Jesus*, 61, from a letter to J. Lawrence Burkholder and Paul Peachey on July 20, 1956.

Participating Witness

in the church's life and does not try to leap outside of history. Of course it may be that Yoder's development of the classic *Martyrs Mirror* storyline, his theological narration of ecclesial history, would not have been possible without the sort of systematization Wenger's work represents. This could be the case because the challenge of systematization raises questions that in-house, self-vindicating declension narratives do not. Though Yoder's work represents a shift away from systematization, other Anabaptist theologians such as Jim Reimer have continued to argue for its importance. Reimer writes, "[W]e need a systematic theology to help prevent us from becoming one-sided and truncated in our Christianity and our humanity; to guard us from reducing the whole of the gospel to one of its parts (ethics or the historical Jesus of Nazareth)."[68]

Neither Wenger nor Yoder offer contemporary Anabaptism a corrective that is substantial enough, in either dogmatic or narrative form, to account for the specifically pneumatological shortcomings of the *Martyrs Mirror* and the triumphalism it engenders. Yoder's approach to biblical ethics and his critique of Niebuhr identify the ecclesiological necessity of the Spirit's presence, yet Yoder fails to appropriately deepen this insight. In addition, Yoder's appreciation for ongoing reformation and new beginnings can obscure the question of the Spirit's presence in the church's history. The counter-history of the *Martyrs Mirror* and the Protestant systematic theology of Wenger both have pneumatological and ecclesial shortcomings. With respect to the question that opened this chapter about the presence of the Spirit in a body wracked by violence, the *Martyrs Mirror* posits an alternative church with an independent genealogy, while Wenger essentially denies the unique witness and history of Anabaptism, casting its lot totally with the futures of conservative Protestantism, of which far too many of its forbearers were complicit in killing other Christians. Yoder's way of telling the story is a positive development to the extent that it opens up ecclesiology and pneumatology as historically informed doctrines and reflexively allows these doctrines to shape the act of historical narration. However, to avoid the risks of rationalist anthropocentrism or spiritualist abstraction and to support the construal of baptism as a participating witness, we still require a story of the sixteenth century told in such a way that it is more thoroughly shaped by the life of the Sprit.

In the beginning of this chapter I put forward the claim that considerations of baptism and the Spirit are inseparable from questions of history

---

68. Reimer, *Classical Theology*, 179.

The Spirit and the Problem of Fratricide

and narrative. I suggested that if there is no way to narrate this troubled history then considerations of God's Spirit acting in baptism can be only intelligible in abstraction. The classic Anabaptist theology of van Braght and its twentieth-century revision at the hands of Wenger and Yoder show that Anabaptism and its central practice of baptism continue to require the context of a larger ecclesial narrative that assumes the concrete character of the work of the Spirit and can explain the relationship of Christian traditions that have made martyrs of each other.[69] Though the writers just mentioned do point us in a helpful direction, a gap remains. None provides a thoroughgoing account of the church that upholds the Spirit's accompaniment of it through time while remaining conscious of its fratricidal past. The key markers of such an ecclesiology have yet to be outlined. I am certainly not the first to make this observation. As noted earlier, Jim Reimer's work points in similar directions. Yet most of Reimer's engagements with the topic are framed as critiques of Yoder and the more extreme positions of Mennonite theologian J. Denny Weaver. Though Reimer has argued that the doctrine of the Trinity is underappreciated by Anabaptist academic theologians in in the late twentieth-century, he has not devoted significant effort to solve the problem nor explained how his views might differ significantly from the likes of J.C. Wenger. In some ways this entire volume is congruent with Reimer's view that Anabaptist ethics or practice is best grounded in a Trinitarian account of the Divine, even though I place less emphasis on the specifics of the classical formulations then he would.[70] Here I seek to show how an explication of the church's sacramental character and the objective nature of its practices are enhanced through overt attention to the third member of the Trinity.

REMEMBERING IN THE SPIRIT

How can Anabaptist Christians, as members of a community that made baptism the occasion for murder, continue the practice without severing

---

69. Wenger and Yoder have been particularly influential, especially in Mennonite communities with Swiss-German roots. However, other perspectives certainly exist. Regarding the disparity in the early part of the twentieth century between Mennonites of Swiss and Dutch origin see Juhnke, "Gemeindechristentum and Bible Doctrine," 206–21.

70. See parts two and three of Reimer's *Classical Theology*. My last conversation with Jim Reimer, who died in 2010, occurred over lunch in Toronto after he participated on the committee that approved the proposal for my doctoral dissertation, which would lead directly to this book.

themselves from this history? Given the painful and potentially divisive memories the *Martyrs Mirror* calls us to revisit, from where do we gather confidence that the Spirit will now fashion the form of Christ out of the baptismal community? The volume of these questions is amplified by our attribution of the act of baptism to God's Spirit. It is these sorts of questions that drive this chapter, and my task in this third part is to respond constructively, to gesture toward a way of addressing the pneumatological lacuna in contemporary Anabaptist thought.

To name the relevant marks of a concrete ecclesiology attentive to the Spirit we must be particularly conscious of those aspects of the church's life attributed to the third person of the Trinity. However, we certainly cannot describe directly or with complete confidence all that the Spirit may have been doing in the life of the church, particularly with respect to the thousands of murders in the sixteenth-century. It is not possible to provide a detailed history of the Spirit's work in the church. The hubris of such a narration of pneumatological immanence would lie in purporting to see through the skin of the church to the Spirit. It would amount to rendering the Spirit's life objectively revealed and would deny the Spirit's pointing to the determinative concreteness of Divine revelation in Christ. This would be opposed to the character of the Spirit's work, which is self-effacing, bearing the form of Christ.[71] Along this same line of thought, Barth suggests that whereas Jesus is the objective element of God's revelation, the Spirit comprises revelation's subjective element.[72] Whether or not Barth's specific terminology is ultimately helpful is unclear; however, the basic sense of his judgment furthers my point that the Spirit's role in the life of the church community, though it is not identical to Christ's, is never separable from it. We do not see the Spirit; we see Christ. All this must chasten any attempt at describing pneumatologically the church in history.

Nevertheless, what *can* be done here is to score the territorial boundaries of a theological space within which the strong ecclesiological claims made in the previous chapters can support an understanding of baptism as an ordinance through which God acts. It is within such a space that questions prompted by Anabaptist memory can be more appropriately expressed. My goal in articulating such an outline is to simultaneously

---

71. Though Scripture describes the Spirit as being both "of God" and "of Christ" (both appear in Rom 8:9), I take the character of God's self-revelation in Christ to be such that the Spirit does not point to God other than as revealed in Christ.

72. Barth, *CD* 1/1:448–49.

The Spirit and the Problem of Fratricide

name the key elements of a corrective to the classic Anabaptist telling of the church's story that neither forgets the body's pneumatic dependence nor avoids its conflicted history. Another way of conceiving the operative question is as an inquiry into how Anabaptist memory, compellingly formalized as it is in Yoder's work and the *Martyrs Mirror*, might be pneumatically amended. To transcribe these boundaries from the biblical witness I will highlight three important markers of the Spirit's engagement with the world, particularly as this economy impacts Christian communities. These markers are *conversion, unity,* and *promise*.[73] If there is any uniqueness to the perspective that I advance, it is simply in the overt employment of these commonly held assumptions toward a refinement of Anabaptist ecclesial self-understanding relevant to the practice of baptism. Attending to these elements delineates a pneumatic theological space for the life of the church that allows Anabaptist thought to more thoroughly take into account the Spirit's work. It is as we gain the ability to describe the violence of the sixteenth century in pneumatological terms and thereby increase our capacity to describe it theologically instead of secularly, that the other theological claims we make about the church's life gain coherence.

Conversion

The response of Jesus to Nicodemus' question about how one might be born again from above could hardly be more enigmatic: "The wind blows where it chooses."[74] In the Christian context conversion, in its manifold forms, is universally acknowledged as the work of the Spirit. In Romans 8 Paul adamantly differentiates new life in the Spirit from the old life of the flesh. He impresses on readers that the new birth and new life typifying conversion are the result of Divine in-breaking. The Spirit's work is disruptive on two levels, both to the nihilistic flat line of history and to individual biography. To recount history with attention to conversion as a mark of the Spirit's presence can contextualize events like the rejection of christoformity in the sixteenth century that led to the martyrdom of thousands of Anabaptists. It can do this in two ways. First, this violence is contextualized within the sweeping character of the history of the convention of conversion. Deep changes in this convention alert us to the possibility

---

73. Consider respectively John 3:1–21; Acts 10:47; 1 Cor 6:17, 12:13; Eph 4:1–5; Rom 8:23; 2 Cor 1:20–22, 5:1–5.

74. John 3:8.

that either the character of the Spirit's presence changed or the response of the Christian community has. This is the case because communities not marked by conversion are not communities where Christ's Spirit acts. Second, and perhaps more obviously, this fratricidal violence is contextualized within the dynamics of individual conversion stories. A church made up of individuals who have not experienced the Spirit's gift of new life in Christ is bound to fall short of its christoform mandate. It might be helpful to discuss this second mode of contextualization further before returning to the former.

Dietrich Bonhoeffer's famous commentary on the story of the rich young man in Matt 19:16–22 places great emphasis on the moment of decision when the human creature is confronted with the divine command. The rich man tries to hide behind an ethical conundrum, wondering which commands are to be obeyed. Bonhoeffer writes, "Only the devil has a solution to offer to ethical conflicts. It is this: keep asking questions, so that you are free from having to obey. Jesus takes aim at the young man himself instead of his problem."[75] Speaking in Kierkegaardian idiom, Bonhoeffer exhorts his readers to consider Christ's call individually. In the context of Christendom the risk is that folk religion will take the place of a genuine response to the call of Jesus.

It is widely, though certainly not universally, agreed that the notion of an individual crisis conversion is overemphasized in Evangelicalism. Yet aversion to this manipulative and individualistic model must not become an avoidance of the extent to which the Christian life is undertaken by individual persons in response to Christ. For Christian communities that practice believers' baptism the personal character of new life in Christ is essential. The communal nature of the body of Christ does not erase the need for an individual response to the gospel. This is attested to throughout the NT, with the widening of God's people at Pentecost comes a need for purposeful response. This is not to say that the biblical model of salvation is individualistic; but rather, that the individual cannot be subsumed within the community. Therefore a pneumatologically sensitive remembering of fratricidal persecution must retain the knowledge that the regimes that inflicted such suffering were made up of individuals in various states of response to Jesus' instructions to the questioner, and his blunt command: "Come follow me."

---

75. Bonhoeffer, *Discipleship*, 72.

To observe the dynamics of individual conversion requires a register according to which the judgments of memory can be made. Scripture provides this at numerous points: the apostle Paul, for example, does so through the list of the Spirit's fruit in Gal 5:22–23 and the assertion in Rom 8:17 that those who are heirs with Christ will participate in his suffering. If we are to look for the Spirit's work on the face of history we are to look for conversion and new life: to look for this we look for those who participate in Christ's suffering and whose lives demonstrate the Pauline virtues. The level of certainty provided by such a register is certainly not absolute; nevertheless, it produces a modicum of data according to which the story of the Anabaptist martyrs might be told. The *Martyrs Mirror* falls short of being pneumatologically conscious in that it largely fails to look for the church beyond the Anabaptist community according to these marks. Even if, as most Anabaptists hold, the establishment of the Petrine office and the institution of infant baptism was a mistake, the presence of these features alone is an insufficient signal to warrant the summary de-churching of communities that hold to them, for in these communities conversion continued. We should note, however, that such openness to redrawing the lines is far from a rejection of van Braght's claim that the willingness to persecute is itself an unmistakable mark of heresy. Considering conversion as a mark of the Spirit's presence coheres with the judgment that the willingness to kill the so-called "heretic" marks a lack of conversion and signals either that the Spirit has not been given voice or that the divine breath has been deliberately ignored. The temptation to historicize such events and thereby to relativize these types of judgments is an avoidance of the transcendence of Christ. What this means for our interpretation of the Spirit's presence in the *persecuting* "church" is that the absence of suffering along with the absence of the Pauline virtues at the corporate level tells us that individuals operating under the joint authority of the church and civil government may have not positively responded to the Spirit. This is no different from the NT record. Not all who encountered Jesus or the power of the Spirit responded appropriately. Nevertheless, this did not cast doubt on the Spirit's presence to the NT church, nor on God's work through Christ's body.[76]

In addition to accounting for the individual and existential character of conversion, the account that van Braght and Yoder endeavour to provide would be improved by attending to historical studies that directly consider

---

76. For an alternative, constructive account of martyrdom and Mennonite-Catholic relations specifically, see Bergen, "Problem or Promise."

the dynamics of the dominant conventions of conversion. In speaking of the conventions of conversion we concern ourselves with the features of corporate practice and by extension, churches as such. This is important because if the actions of individuals never imply the church then the church exists over and against its members.[77] If we are to consider the convention of conversion in the church in a sweeping way we encounter the necessary task of the historical inquiry. Two recent texts that both attend to the dynamics of the convention of conversion and exemplify the possibilities of the historian's role in pursuing the question of the Spirit's accompaniment of the church through time are Kilian McDonnell and George T. Montague's book *Christian Initiation and Baptism in the Holy Spirit* and Alan Kreider's *The Change of Conversion and the Origin of Christendom*.[78] What both of these studies emphasize, and the reason I cite them, is that while both are critical of certain developments within the church they maintain that these communities are still identifiable as part of the universal church. They deal substantially with the specific historical institution of Christ's body precisely by recognizing its fallibility and the material consequences of unfaithfulness. In short, these two studies model the historical and narrative style of Yoder's ecclesiology while broadening the scope of his critique. They also prompt focused pneumatological questions directly linked to liturgy—actual and lingering acts of church communities.

Both of these texts are revisions to standard forms of ecclesial memory, yet both take the church's continuity seriously enough to entertain the possibility that the standard renderings of its past may be perpetuating contemporary problems instead of helping to solve them. The concrete nature of the stories they tell about the church's past pulls the discussions surrounding contemporary division down from the realm of abstract, confessional differences to the plane of actual events and practices. The sort of history on offer here is one that opens doors for us to understand ecclesial life as a predicate of the Spirit. This is because they deal concretely with parts of the church's life directly linked to the Spirit's mission. Yet the character of this historical evaluation is such that it assumes the necessity of the actions of individuals and communities for the performance of the church.

---

77. Bergen, *Ecclesial Repentance*, 216, 220–21, extends this Rahnerian notion to argue that the contemporary practice of ecclesial repentance implies that the church itself sins and not only its members.

78. McDonnell and Montague, *Christian Initiation and Baptism*; Kreider, *Change of Conversion and the Origin of Christendom*. Also see, among Kreider's other writings in the field of Christian history and missiology, Kreider, ed., *Origins of Christendom*.

In short, it fits with the concept of ecclesial mediation developed earlier. The goal of this sort of re-narration in a post-denominational age is not to paper over difference or try to "explain away" unfaithfulness. Its benefit is the push it provides contemporary Anabaptists to consider the history of the church as a shared story of the response of Western Christians to the legacy of the early church. This, as opposed to thinking of ecclesial history as a series of oppositional genealogies—as an account of fracture, declension, and triumph.

The story that historical accounts of conversion can sensitize us to is one in which the church's marginalization of the Spirit in its worship life and its cheapening of the expectations of conversion may have had real consequences. We might contrast this with Yoder's account of the Constantinian shift, described above as a development of the traditional Anabaptist declension narrative. As useful as Yoder's account is, it is in some ways in danger of becoming a Constantinian history itself, inasmuch as it puts rulers and governments at the center of the story. The narrative of Constantinianism is useful for purposes of cultural critique, yet to the extent that its focus remains imperial it can turn our attention away from the interruption of God's presence and the response of human communities. Attending to the dynamics of conversion as an individual process and as a convention practiced by members of a tradition across time highlights the agency of congregations and individuals. This reminds us that it is possible to uphold the Spirit's work in the church without forgetting the violence of the sixteenth century. While this does preserve the divinely ordered freedom of the human creature to ignore the Spirit, the very attention paid to pneumatic work limits the temptations of anthropocentrism and prepares the scope of our ecclesial memory to understand the sixteenth-century upheaval and persecution in terms of responsiveness to the Spirit.

As we consider the church's story through the lens of conversion we are better able to construe the relationship of the church's life to that of the Spirit in dynamic terms, meaning that at any one time its expression may differ. For the church's part, it is certainly possible that this may mean a full or partial rejection of the Spirit's work. Nevertheless, this need not preclude the Spirit's faithfulness to the baptizing community as evidenced by the fact that conversions meeting the requirements of the register discussed earlier did not cease even in the dominant churches. We might also understand this violence of the sixteenth century as a form of judgment allowed by God to proceed upon the church in light of the church's limited responsiveness to the Spirit. The ecclesial reforms or new life among both radical and magisterial Protestants as well as Roman Catholics attest to the effectiveness of the Spirit's work. Thus, Anabaptists might read the sixteenth century not as evidence counter to the Spirit's presence in the church but, to the extent that it brought new life, as confirmation of it. The emergence of a community whose practice of conversion aligned more closely with the biblical register is evidence that the Spirit did not abandon the church.

These judgments are possible only under the assumption that God faithfully responds to the prayer of Jesus in John 17:21 and at some level preserves the unity of the church. The Spirit's work in renewal is God's faithfulness to the whole. The Mennonite theologian Jeremy Bergen argues that the church's holiness is found precisely in its ability to repent and to repudiate some of its past actions. Yet he says, "This holiness is not the church's 'progress' in understanding, but the way in which it subjects itself to the Spirit's action."[79] A significant problem arises, then, when reform groups like the Anabaptists disregard this expressed will of Christ and understand the Spirit's presence in their midst as vindication of their tradition alone. The irony is that the account of martyrdom that this chapter opened with, the story of George Wagner, may not, despite its inclusion in a book about Anabaptist heroes, be that of an Anabaptist at all. Wagner's connection to Anabaptism is unclear.[80] The irony of Wagner's story placed alongside those of Anabaptists is a reminder that martyred spiritual ancestors are not badges of individual denominational triumph. Rather, if they are true martyrs for the gospel, they are so on behalf of the whole church.[81]

As the Anabaptist community struggles to find new, less triumphalist ways of narrating church history that can account for the emerging recognition of shared conviction and lineage across the denominational spectrum, the voices that are worth paying attention to will be those that do not ignore the church's troubled past and are not hemmed in by the logic of disunity. By observing both the personal dynamics and the conventions associated with conversion as a marker of the Spirit's work, Anabaptist memory can more

---

79. Bergen, *Ecclesial Repentance*, 225.

80. George, *Theology of the Reformers*, 299. York, *Purple Crown*, 98, suggests that another sixteenth-century martyr commemorated in the *Martyrs Mirror*, Leonard Keyser, was not an Anabaptist either. It should be noted, however, that neither George nor York provide documentation or defend their intriguing claims.

81. Bergen writes, "If [the] early Anabaptists are truly martyrs—that is, if they truly point to Christ with their entire lives and with their deaths—then they are witnesses for the *entire* church, not just for Mennonites" ("Lutheran Repentance at Stuttgart," 335).

The Spirit and the Problem of Fratricide

coherently describe the Spirit's presence in persecuting bodies. Within this theological space the violence experienced by the early Anabaptists is the product of both a lack of conversion and of the Spirit's fresh work to bring about the form of Christ in the community bearing his name.

Unity

"There is one body and one Spirit" the writer of Ephesians tells us.[82] Throughout the NT the presence of the Spirit in the lives of believers presents itself publicly as love for others and particularly as love for other Christians.[83] From this we conclude that a second mark of the Spirit's work is the unification of believers in love. Subsequently, an appropriately penumatological telling of the story of the body of Christ must be mindful of the Spirit's historic and ongoing call to unity in Christ. Yet the record of the church's life under this heading is mixed at best. The church's story is fraught with accounts of discord and division. The classic Anabaptist response exemplified in the *Martyrs Mirror* is to search for an edenic age of the church's life and then develop a genealogical connection to the early Anabaptist groups. This effectively disqualifies those communities not found within that line. However, this approach fails to deal substantively with the problem of division. Instead, through the triumphalism of vindictive historiography it inadvertently perpetuates the very logic of disunity. Though many early Anabaptist leaders remained in a type of dialogue with the wider church, one that might be appropriately labelled "agonistic," the formalization or reification of Anabaptism as a tradition represented by the historiography of the *Martyrs Mirror* is a clear departure from this.[84]

A contrasting theology of ecclesial division can be found in the work of the Anglican theologian Ephriam Radner. I point to Radner because the catholic quality of his theology sensitizes him to these issues in ways that many from free church traditions are blind to. In his telling the issue of ecclesial unity is best understood typologically. In *The End of the Church* Radner carries this out with reference to the withdrawing of God's Spirit from divided Israel and God's abandonment of Jesus on the cross.[85] Radner

---

82. Eph 4:4.

83. Acts 4; Gal 5:13–23; 2 Tim 1:7; Col 1:8.

84. It remains to be seen whether new denominational structures provide a platform for unity or strengthen the walls of division.

85. Radner, *End of the Church*.

argues that the Spirit has withdrawn the divine presence from the divided church as a form of redemptive judgment. Given this, the divided state of the church means that ecclesial life ought to be characterized by penance. This is masked by a contemporary ecumenical mood that privileges a center-less diversity and affirms disunity. Radner's book is intentionally an exercise in pneumatological history. He surveys the divisive nature of what are traditionally understood to be marks of the Spirit's presence: the interpretation of Scripture, miracles and holiness, vocation, and, finally, the Eucharist.[86] In a divided church each of these is contested. Radner investigates historical examples through the lens of the Spirit's presence and leaves readers with the somewhat un-programmatic advice to stay within the shattered church. Faithfulness, for Radner, assumes a penitential posture in hope that God might restore the church.

Radner's typological approach to disunity reminds us that the Spirit's faithfulness could even look like abandonment. Looking through this pneumatically shaped lens, it might be the case that the killing of Christians by Christians was a form of the Spirit's judgment in response to the church's unfaithfulness. This would not be to suggest that the individuals who suffered are to blame for their suffering. Rather, it means that the suffering of the church as a corporate body at its own hands is the result of its straying from the Spirit's guidance. Since Anabaptists participate in the universal church, an Anabaptist ecclesiology that would render baptism coherent as an act of God mediated by the church must also take a penitential shape. This does not mean self-abasement, but it is a recognition that the heinous acts of the prosecution, torture, and murder of "heretics" to which the church was complicit were acts of sin. It was a sin for Christians who were church leaders, civil servants, or neighbours to participate directly or indirectly in killing George Wagner and Christina Haring. Yet as the opening verses in Ephesians 4 remind us, through unity of the Spirit Christians exist in one body. The body that sinned in the murder of Anabaptists is the body of which Anabaptists are a part. As members of that church Anabaptists respond to the inconceivable reality of Christians killing their brothers and sisters in repentance.

By attending to unity in love as a mark of the presence of the Spirit, we are led to incorporate repentance into the story Anabaptists tell about the church. The fact that Anabaptists have largely avoided killing others does not

---

86. As the reader has probably surmised, the shape of this part of the chapter is inspired by Radner's book, though the categories I use are more amenable to Anabaptism.

redirect this. A lack of charity among Anabaptists is made evident by ongoing schismatic relationships, which demonstrate a striking virility in producing new denominations. Though in some cases these various groups continue to relate as members as one family and even work in concert, this is far from always the case.[87] Too often these divisions represent disunity and a lack of charity. Therefore, the challenge for Anabaptist ecclesiology is to overcome the triumphalism of the *Martyrs Mirror* with repentance. Repentance is to be offered on behalf of mistakes made by Anabaptists, but also, as members of the larger body of Christ, on behalf of the sins of the larger church. A theological accounting, not the manufacture of excuses, for deep mistakes like the killing of fellow believers can itself be a penitential activity. Given the church's history of unfaithfulness, an ecclesiology that is not penitential identifies itself as an ecclesiology failing to listen to the Spirit.

During the trauma of the Second World War Dietrich Bonhoeffer described the necessity of the church's repentance this way: "The guilt we must acknowledge is not the occasional mistake or going astray, not the breaking of an abstract law, but falling away from Christ, from the form of the One who would take form in us and lead us to our own true form."[88] The mystery of God's grace in Bonhoeffer's view is that we who have fallen away from Christ can even know to repent. He writes, "Acknowledgement of guilt is based only on the grace of Christ, because of Christ's reaching out for those who have fallen. With this acknowledgement the process of human conformation with Christ begins."[89] For Bonhoeffer it is tautological to say that the church is the place where guilt is acknowledged. If it were any other way the church would not exist. In like manner to even sketch a response to sixteenth-century fratricide is to follow the contours of penance. If the Spirit is active in Anabaptist communities it will be observed in repentance for a lack of charity. The presence of the question of how the terror of the sixteenth century could have happened might itself be the Spirit's nudging toward the reparation of the breach that these events occasioned. Only when it is assumed that those communities complicit in these actions

---

87. The number of schisms among Anabaptist groups in which they ceased to fellowship with each other is too great to detail here. Recent examples, though, might be the creation of Alliance of Mennonite Evangelical Congregations and Biblical Mennonite Alliance. Both are conservative groups. However, the fallout from the Mennonite denominational merger in the United States demonstrates a lack of ability to nurture unity among more acculturated groups as well.

88. Bonhoeffer, *Ethics*, 135.

89. Ibid.

were and are still not Christians can such questions be avoided. Conviction to take up the posture of penitence may not be the sort of work we might wish of the Spirit, for it is always easier to hope for vindication. For the body of Christ, however, such triumphal vindication would be simultaneously the damnation of our members. As Jesus' parable about the lost son reminds us, who is one child to determine the love of the father for another?

This invocation of the parable of the lost son in this way exposes my conviction that those Christians who were complicit in the killing of other Christians committed sin. This brings us to another key aspect of the way Anabaptists might understand their relationship to the story of the larger church. In considering current divisions and ongoing violations of the commandment of love, Anabaptists must not let go of the conviction that the killing of one's enemies is wrong. Even more, that killing to preserve "orthodoxy" is deeply abhorrent. If a pneumatological rendering of the history of the church is to pay special attention to the presence or absence of fraternal charity it cannot gloss over the lack clearly evidenced by a willingness to kill. It must continue to affirm that to bear suffering by choice in witness to the gospel is to take the form of Christ while to cause such suffering is not. If the Spirit is prompting contemporary ecumenical movements the unity they produce will not only be one of official repentance and concord but it will also produce a shared ethic that identifies such life-taking as sin. A truly charitable unity then will not be a marriage of contemporary convenience but a deep recognition that those who were martyred, whether Anabaptist, Anglican, Lutheran, or Catholic, followed Jesus while those complicit in their deaths did not.

To continue to hold to the propriety of nonviolent witness and martyrdom does not in itself make the Anabaptist reading of church history triumphalist. It is certainly not a wild card that can be played in defence of the whole Anabaptist tradition. It does not invalidate baptisms performed in churches whose leaders endorsed persecution, and it by no means provides direct support for other current Anabaptist beliefs and practices. For instance, the fact that Anabaptist communities in Bolivia trace their lineage to sixteenth-century martyrs provides no excuse for the twenty-first century sins of mass rape and other abuses alleged to have been perpetrated in some of these communities.[90] Furthermore, it should also be recognized

---

90. See "Mennonites Accused of Mass Rape in Bolivia," *Reuters*, June 24, 2009, found online at http://in.reuters.com/article/idINIndia-40557220090624; also see Karla Braun, "Responses Tentative to Rapes in Bolivia," *Mennonite Weekly Review*, January 10, 2010.

that Anabaptists are not alone in their peace witness. The report on the dialogue between Mennonites and Roman Catholics rightly recognizes that throughout the Middle Ages there existed a continuous witness for peace within the Catholic Church.[91] In addition, various Pentecostal traditions such as the Assemblies of God were initially strongly pacifist.[92] Yet the Anabaptist community tells its story as a reminder that the body of Christ is most clearly found in church communities that advocate loving enemies instead of destroying them. That this is deeply controversial among Christian communities is a reminder that in a fractured church the interpretation of Scripture divides as much as it unifies.

Promise

The third marker of the Spirit's work employed to advance the goal of a more pneumatologically sensitive Anabaptist telling of the church's story focuses on the Spirit's role as a down payment or promise of the fulfillment of God's reign. Thus, we might say that to narrate the church's past rightly is to allow memory to be shaped by the future to which the Spirit's presence bears witness. Through the Spirit Christian communities anticipate the future of the world in God, and in this the unity of Christ's body. This anticipation is marked by their present life under the Lordship of Christ in the knowledge that the final consummation of redemption has yet to occur. By centering this discussion on the term "promise" I intend to indicate the mutuality of the church's patient hope in response to the Spirit's role as guarantee. The Spirit's role as a down payment for future inheritance of the saints both affirms and relativizes history within the providence of God.[93]

It is generally in this same spirit that Bergen, drawing on Radner's work cited above, explores the recent phenomena of churches publicly apologizing for wrongdoing. In his book *Ecclesial Repentance* Bergen points out that while there was a time when churches did not publicly repent, they now do.[94] He argues that despite the fact that this practice is new it is not simply the product of an increasingly irrelevant body attempting to make

---

91. "Called Together to be Peacemakers: A Report on the International Dialogue between the Catholic Church and Mennonite World Conference, 1998–2003," 43.

92. Alexander, *Peace to War*. Alexander's definition of pacifism in contradistinction to bellicism is also helpful.

93. Eph 1:13–14.

94. Bergen, *Ecclesial Repentance*, 2.

good in the eyes of the public; that is to say, it is not political correctness. The doctrine of the communion of saints is a key part of his explanation of the veracity of this form of corporate repentance. The communion of saints is affirmed in the Apostles Creed and premised on the unity of believers in Christ. Its claim is that believers are a part of one body across time, from which not even death can separate them.[95] What this means for Bergen is that there is theological rationale for contemporary churches to repent for the sins of their predecessors. They have not only a right, but even an obligation, to speak on behalf of the dead because the church speaking today and the church that carried out sinful acts in the past is one and the same body. It is thus entirely appropriate for Anabaptists to respond to the painful memories of persecution not just by seeking reconciliation, but also by bearing guilt as members of the church. The eschatological anticipation of the future community of those adopted in Christ is formative.

However, an Anabaptist understanding of the church's eschatological identity can be distinguished from that of its mainline cousins. One way to describe this is to point out that an Anabaptist typological construal of the church's story moves in a direction that Radner's does not. This important feature of Anabaptist thought is worth pursuing at some length to establish the eschatological cloth from which the Spirit's promissory role is to be cut. Not all Anabaptists would endorse the account that I do here, but what follows is certainly not idiosyncratic.[96] Yoder's development of the classic Anabaptist narrative points the way by asserting the centrality of the Constantinian problem in which the unity and mission of the church are compromised by an ill-advised marriage between church and empire. It is not surprising at all that a charitable unity among believers would be strained when concerns of imperial supremacy are involved. It is not surprising that charitable discernment on moral and doctrinal issues would be sacrificed on alters of political expediency and security. Readers of the OT have seen this before. We see it in Israel's experience with monarchy. Indeed Eusebius, Constantine's greatest apologist and chronicler, would make this same comparison, by casting Constantine as the new David.[97] The violent

---

95. See Heb 11–12; Eph 2:16–18; Rom 8:38–39.

96. Since writing this I have become aware of Barry Harvey's recent book. Harvey identifies his approach as "Catholic Baptist," and his response to Radner is similar, though more developed, than mine (*Can these Bones Live?*, 97–101).

97. The debate about Constantine's legacy is ongoing. See Leithart, *Defending Constantine*. The Oct. 2011 issue of the *Mennonite Quarterly Review* is dedicated to engaging Leithart's book and includes both pointed critiques from others and a response from the author.

Anabaptist movement that took control of Münster and declared it to be the New Jerusalem essentially trod the same Constantinian path.

Against Eusebius' glorification of the emperor and Anabaptist's misadventure in Münster stands the LORD's original response to Samuel regarding Israel's request for a king: "They have not rejected you, but they have rejected me from being king over them."[98] In both the case of Israel and the Christianization of Rome in late antiquity, the assumed divine right of the king to rule coupled with the "justified" use of violence to defend the faithful provided the rationale for the exploitation of the citizenry. It would also inevitably lead to the demand of compromise from priest and clergy. The Torah, Christian Scriptures, and the prophetic tradition became threats to the everyday order, instead of being essential to it. The result was that the people of God were asked to live without the resources of training in the ways of God and the visible expressions of being God's people. In parallel to Radner's typology this leads to a situation in which the church, like Israel, was asked to live without the full manifestation of the Spirit's presence. One effect was that the church's experience of the Spirit's promissory role was deeply troubled.

Though the contours of God's covenant faithfulness to Israel were difficult to discern, particularly during the nadir of the monarchy, it did not cease. Indeed, God's faithfulness was embodied in the monarchical line of David. However, only a few generations after David, this same line, now deeply disobedient, was implicated in the division of Israel and even its exile. Despite Israel's attempts to restore the failed monarchy through Ezra, the Maccabees, and others like them, God remained faithful, even using the institution as a medium of Divine self-revelation. The opposing factions of second temple Judaism represent the unclear nature of this faithfulness and the ambiguity of the imperial character of the people of God. As Christians understand it, however, God's faithfulness was punctuated in exclamatory fashion through Jesus of Nazareth. Yet this faithfulness to the line of Jesse and the Jewish people is not necessarily an endorsement of the imperial ambitions of Israel. In the nationalist movement of the zealots this option was available to Jesus, but he rejected it. Though the early Christians did affirm Jesus as Lord, his rule is of its own genus, and the power of his kingship without parallel. The early Christians also understood the reach of his authority to be beyond the slightness of Israel's geographic pretensions.

---

98. 1 Sam 8:7.

Israel's desire for a king whose power they could apprehend with their eyes amounted to a rejection of God's preferred way of leading them. It cost them dearly, just as Samuel told them it would. The synthesis of church and empire described by Yoder as the Constantinian shift bears similarity. The Spirit was to be the sign of God's rule and a promise of things to come. Or as Paul puts it, the Spirit was given as a "guarantee" that God will swallow up mortality in life, that humans will be enveloped in a heavenly dwelling far superior to the earthly tent from which we groan for release.[99] In light of this anticipation of God's rule Anabaptists should affirm that the theocratic character of Constantinianism is not inappropriate in a deep sense, though it is terribly impatient. Endorsers of Constantinian figures old and new are not wrong to long for God's obvious rule on earth; their timing is misguided.

If we turn our attention again to the violence of sixteenth-century Europe, the product of this typological linking of Israel and the church is such that the undoing of Christianity's imperial pretensions in that century can be understood as the Spirit's check on the church's usurpation of divine timing and dissatisfaction with the Spirit's role as the guarantee of the promised inheritance. Though traditional explanations for the upheaval of the sixteenth century point to a variety of intellectual and social factors, the sort of pneumatological reading undertaken here is necessary to coherently display the ecclesiology endorsed in this project. Thus in theological perspective the fratricide explored in this chapter can be viewed as a reaction to the outworking of the Spirit's faithfulness, as the Spirit's release of the church to suffer the consequences of its pretentiousness. In that moment parts of the church no longer possessed the skills of discernment necessary to identify the work of God's Spirit. They could not see that to voluntarily suffer on behalf of the gospel was to take the form of Christ, while to cause such suffering was to oppose Christ. Nevertheless, precisely in the midst of this twisted response were Christians on every side of the many fractures whose peaceable lives are to be understood as the result of the Spirit's ongoing re-creation of humanity in the image of Jesus and promise of a future in the family of God.

The tearing apart of the body of Christ in the sixteenth century is not the last word. It is not a chapter closed off from those either before or after. At its best contemporary ecumenical practice, by which I mean the mutual offering of forgiveness, purposeful dialogue, worship, and biblical study across denominational boundaries, is evidence that the sixteenth-century fracture

---

99. 2 Cor 5:1–5.

The Spirit and the Problem of Fratricide

is in no way final. Repentance and forgiveness are even now mending these centuries-old tears. This sort of work is an eschatologically-driven practice which recognizes the divisions that now seem so calcified soften in the light of God. There are several good examples of this type of work. A prominent one is the five-year dialogue between representatives of Mennonite and Roman Catholic traditions.[100] One of the conclusions of this process was the realization, which the official report states, that Roman Catholics and Mennonite Anabaptists share an important ecclesial conviction: "Catholics and Mennonites agree that the Church is a chosen sign of God's presence and promise of salvation for all creation . . . Here and now the Church manifests signs of its eschatological character and thus provides a foretaste of the glory yet to come."[101] For the framers of this report the act of giving and receiving forgiveness is not only about healing the wounds in the past. It is also directly connected to the fruitfulness of the witness of the church today.[102] This witness is as always eschatologically formed and embodied in the Spirit's presence in the body of Christ as a promise of salvation.

Considering the Spirit's function as a promise of the eschaton reminds Anabaptists that the state of social structures is not permanent. People who are now obviously enemies will not be so in the future. To speak metaphorically, if not directly, our children's children will be companions in the worship of God despite the apparent intransigence of our separation and despite the ways that we have and still do harm each other. Therefore the anticipation of the future given to us by the Spirit reflects into our own time and tempers our claims of irresolvable difference. The contemporary self-understanding of Anabaptism's place in the story of the universal church is best formed not just by the concreteness of history with its violence and brokenness, but also by the concreteness of humanity's future in God. Thus the claim that the Spirit accompanies the church through time must be understood through the resolution we anticipate. It is a claim made not with a myopic or idealized view of the past but within the hope of Christ—a

---

100. In addition, consider the ongoing story of Bridgefolk, which is described as a movement among sacramentally-minded Mennonites and peace-minded Catholics. More details can be found at http://www.bridgefolk.net/. Also of note is the recent process of Mennonite/Lutheran reconciliation. The formal part of this dialogue was completed in 2010 with a service of repentance and reconciliation at Stuttgart. Miller, "Lutheran Dialogue with Mennonites," 293–314.

101. "Called Together to be Peacemakers," 25.

102. Ibid., 44.

hope that we expect to be fulfilled on the grounds of God's down payment of the Spirit's presence.

In sum, the Spirit's role as a promise contributes two things to our attempt to grapple with the church's failings. First, it reminds us of the delayed character of the consummation of redemption. The Spirit's witness is to a future inheritance, not to an immediate fulfillment. Communities that practice believers' baptism must not be deluded about the stability of the extent to which the church has previously or even now takes the form of Christ. Second, as the church of the present is the skin of the Spirit's promise of salvation, this body must look to its future through the possibility of the Spirit and discard short-sighted lenses that perpetuate unfaithful division. In this hope Anabaptist communities encounter other Christian communities not as past enemies, but as future co-celebrants at the divine banquet, the culmination of history to which the Spirit now bears witness.

The theological space which the Spirit's work in the church occupies is outlined by these three focal markers of conversion, unity, and promise. Each has significant implications for the chapter's leading question, some of which we have just explored. In turn my suggestion is that a more pneumatologically sensitive understanding of the church's story should attend to the contextualizing features of the dynamics of conversion, the penitential response required by the church's unity, as well as the patience and relativization implied in the Spirit's promissory role. Each of these revises the classical Anabaptist account of the church's history. As I have endeavoured to show, each also illuminates how it could be that the Spirit could be present in the church at a time when its members were not only the persecuted but also the persecutors.

As a participating witness baptism depends on the Spirit's work of making Christ present to candidates through the church community. Given the violent history of the church, the Spirit's ongoing faithfulness seems initially quite preposterous. On the rocks of the church's history theoretical ecclesiologies break apart and the idea that Christian communities mediate God's presence seems hopelessly idealistic. And yet this chapter has provided a theological demonstration of how Anabaptists might begin to retell their history in the context of the broader church in such a way that the Spirit's presence can be affirmed in a manner less triumphalist and divisive than has previously been the case. In this context we can affirm that movements of reformation and acts of martyrdom may, like baptism and the miracles observed by the early church, manifest the Spirit's work.

A properly nuanced narrative of ecclesial decline upon which Anabaptist identity depends does not need to be a denial of God's action in baptism or the Spirit's ongoing work in a church that has committed grave sin. Such a narrative is not a rejection of theologies of baptism that emphasize God's necessary role in the practice itself.

If baptism is a product of the Spirit's work through the church, it should be assumed that this work is dynamic and not mechanical. Yes, God remains faithful even when humans are not, but this Divine faithfulness to the church retains the character of God's faithfulness to Israel. At times it might take the form of releasing the community to the ramifications of its own disobedience. Critical reforming movements are wrongheaded if they understand their existence as a mark of the invalidation of the whole. In this light Anabaptists can understand the Spirit's presence in the church to enable its sacramental life, of which baptism is an important feature, as both an affirmation and a limitation of the unique character of the ongoing Anabaptist tradition. It is affirmed inasmuch as the early Anabaptist movement can be said to be the result of the Spirit's faithfulness to the church. It is limited to the extent that this faithfulness implies Anabaptist identity is rightly dependent on the church catholic. Finally, the presence of the Spirit calls all Christians to anticipate their future union in worship of the Slain Lamb, and in anticipation of this eschatological reality, to work toward clear demonstrations of Christian love in this age during which they are to take together the form of that same One. Along with the celebration of communion, baptism is a central practice through which the Christian community is formed toward this end.

5

Baptism: A Theological and Liturgical Proposal

For in one Spirit we were all baptized into one body—Jews or Greeks, slaves or free—and we were all made to drink of one Spirit.

(1 Cor 12:13)

"Faith and baptism are two kindred and inseparable ways of salvation," writes Basil in the fourth century. "[F]aith," he says, "is perfected through baptism, baptism is established through faith . . ."[1] Generations earlier, in the second century, Ignatius urged those under his care to recognize the benefits of baptism, to see the practice as a way of putting on the protective equipment necessary for the Christian life.[2] As an act of formation and as an act of commitment baptism mattered deeply to these early church leaders; it mattered to them in a way that resonates, perhaps counterintuitively, with the short story about a young boy's baptism that opened the first chapter of this book.

In considering baptism, we encounter paradigmatically the entirety of the way of God with human creatures, a divine gift inseparable from human response. By now it is clear that I assume that the gift of baptism is not merely a social ritual or a symbolic representation of a spiritual reality. Baptism functions within the church's mediating role as an event ordained by God to tangibly enact divine grace. Through the Spirit it is a welcoming and empowering act of the church; it is also an act of apprenticeship in the way of Jesus by which candidates are formed anew through participation in his death and resurrection. It is not primarily a descriptive or symbolic

---

1. Basil, *On the Holy Spirit* 12.28 (*NPNF* 8:18).
2. Ferguson, *Baptism in the Early Church*, 209.

act, a statement about facts otherwise invisible. Instead, it accomplishes something. What should concern us is not baptism's meaning as such but its function. It is a participating witness.

It is doubtful that many of the authors or communities considered in this book would question the assertion that baptism is important, and yet I have sought to show that not all Anabaptist understandings are equally adequate. Some depend on misguided ecclesiological assumptions. In this chapter, I intend to pull the various threads of my argument together and provide a coherent account of baptism—describing it as a participating witness—that can help amend the problems in Anabaptist thought described earlier. The summation of this is a proposal for practicing baptism that seeks to make use of ancient precedent in achieving the goal of this thesis: to diagnosis the inadequate account of divine action in contemporary Anabaptist practice and to provide a construal of baptism that attends to the way in which church communities mediate the work of God in the world. If the concept of ecclesial mediation that I have argued for is the taxonomic equivalent to baptism's genus as a church practice, then participative witness is its species.

Though the concept of participative witness will be discussed further in this chapter, it is by design that this book concludes with a liturgical proposal. To conclude with only a theoretical affirmation or a conceptual scheme would fail to match the method of this study with its subject. A theological consideration of the life of the church demands that theorization be practicable. If not, the answers it represents are not answers at all, since, to speak historically and theologically, the church is a community, a body, before it is an idealized concept. Because the goal of this chapter is descriptive, it does not have a thesis other than the general one that guides this book. This chapter is meant to display conceptually and performatively a renewed practice of baptism. Toward this end I attempt to present a fairly succinct theology of baptism that follows from the work of the previous chapters and to put forward a proposal for baptismal practice ordered chronologically, beginning with inquiry and concluding with the ritual washing itself.

A THEOLOGICAL ACCOUNT

In the first two chapters of this book, I argued that the practice of believers' baptism has been distorted in significant ways. Most obviously, it has become common to baptize *children* under the guise of believers' baptism.

I argued that this signals a deep ecclesiological confusion and does not represent a positive *via media* between believers' baptism and infant baptism. It is an unproductive hybrid that is incoherent in either tradition. Beneath this problem in contemporary Anabaptist communities lies theological disarray related to the question of whether or not God acts in the life of the church and whether or not the church mediates God's active presence. Up to this point I have been developing the ingredients of a doctrinal response from a variety of angles toward a confessional and practical synthesis involving a refashioned statement of belief, renewed liturgy, and reformed practice. We are now at an appropriate point in this project to more directly distill a theology of baptism by denoting its function in the life of the individual, the church, and the redemptive work of God.

Descriptive Limitation and the Importance of Form

Though I have written much about the church and its practices already in this project, it might be just as important to highlight what has *not* been said, for in the field of Christian theology knowing when to stop talking is as important as carefully using correct vocabulary. The Orthodox theologian Alexander Schmemann provides relevant insight in his book *Of Water and the Spirit*. At the heart of Schmemann's analysis of the baptismal liturgy is his indictment of developments in sacramental theology that allowed for a separation of a sacrament's *form* from its *essence* long before the disagreements of the Protestant Reformation. He argues that in the early tradition form was important because, as he says, "its very nature and function is 'epiphanic', because it reveals the essence, truly *is* and *fulfills* it."[3] Only through its form does one encounter a sacrament's "knowledge and explanation." However, in the new approach, form was reduced to an "external sign and guarantee" of some essence, which can be comprehended apart from the form. Thus, in the new approach, Schmemann argues, the essence "can and must be known and defined apart from the form and even prior to it, for otherwise one would not know what is being 'signified' and 'guaranteed' by means of the form."[4] A specific form was required for a sacrament's validity, but it did not itself reveal what was made valid.

3. Schmemann, *Of Water and the Spirit*, 56–57 (emphasis altered).

4. Ibid. (emphasis altered). Schmemann does not attribute this development to a specific individual, but in the same context refers to it as the "'original sin' of all modern, post-patristic, western theology."

Baptism: A Theological and Liturgical Proposal

For Schmemann, the intellectual hubris involved in the separation of form and essence is a trespass against the inscrutable character of the relationship between what congregations can do, the form, and what it is that the divine Spirit is doing: its epiphanic character. I do not take the substance of this critique to mean that we are eternally bound to every detail of a particular baptismal liturgy. Anabaptists have no stake in arguing that the ongoing process of discernment, of conversation between community, Spirit, Scripture, and world needs to end in a static list of propositions. We are free to recognize the lack of uniformity in the church's liturgy across time and geography. To ignore this would be just as hubristic as divorcing form and essence; it would be to announce that the church has finally *possessed* the ordinance. The challenge of this project has been to re-construe baptism in a way that clarifies what is—and must be—said about believers' baptism, but not to push beyond the bounds of scrutability. Our goal should not be to elbow our promethean selves into the hallways of the divine life to which we have not been given invitation. The challenge is to accept baptism as a gift of the ancient church, even as a gift of Jesus himself.

The difficulty of understanding the relationship of human action and the work of God sends some theologians on a quest for ontological and metaphysical solutions to the mysterious interweaving. However, the lack of Anabaptist sacramental development frees us to affirm that it is plausible, even likely, that we simply do not have the analytical tools to carry out this job. The practice of baptism is similar to the incarnation and even the resurrection in this way. Throughout this volume I have referenced Paul's description of baptism in the sixth chapter of Romans. It is significant that in chapter eight Paul follows his theological connection of baptism to the death and resurrection of Jesus with a longer excurses on life in the Spirit. Paul writes, "If the Spirit of him who raised Jesus from the dead dwells in you, he who raised Christ from the dead will give life to your mortal bodies also through his Spirit that dwells in you."[5] If this is the theological territory we are treading then the mechanics of this relationship are indeed inscrutable.

This is not to say that we should give in to the easy solution of simply describing the practices or sacraments of the church as "mysteries" and leave it at that. The non-canonical gospel of Philip vaguely suggests that baptism, chrismation, and the eucharist are each a mystery. However, the canonical Scriptures do not describe these practices this way. The mystery in the mind of the NT authors, in a most general sense, is the character of God's

---

5. Rom 8:11.

providence. For example, in Ephesians 3, Paul invokes the word "mystery," or *mystērion*, three times. Here the divine mystery Paul refers to is that gentiles are heirs to the promise of Jesus together with Israel. Two chapters later, Paul uses the same word in relationship to Christ and the church. If we are to take the biblical witness as our guide, we must remain cautious about an academic proclivity to distil theological claims into mechanical suppositions, to reduce the transcendent to all-too transcendable. Whenever God works in the created world—though materialistic explanations abound—the process of this action is by its very nature beyond the grasp of naturalistic analysis. But this mechanical process is not the mystery, at least not in the cosmology of the NT, which retains a Jewish openness to God working in history. The language of the NT is not univocal, but generally speaking, the mystery is that God chooses to act in mercy and ultimately, kenosis.

There is another aspect of Schmemann's analysis, which is the affirmation that form is important. In his own way, Pilgrim Marpeck also makes this claim, for if baptism is a co-witness, it is by implication particular and bounded. Since baptism is not a shell for meaning, communication, or grace; and since in the doing of it something actually is happening—God's grace is actually at work through the church *visibly*—then surely how it is done matters. Therefore baptism's form is not open for endless reinvention. If that were the case the church would lose its specificity and the gospel might be just another disembodied attempt at fulfilling a set of spiritual desires. Form is important because the new humanity into which baptism ushers people has particular traits and a particular form. The virtues and practices that form this community are not infinitely plastic. Some readers may be worried by statements like these, having in mind pictures of an Anabaptist liturgical colonialism. However, my hope is that the liturgical form suggested in this chapter is such that it cannot be practiced without a deep and constant involvement in the life of Jesus. This involvement, not the policing of liturgy, is what shapes Christian communities into his form.

Though attention to form is a necessary corrective for Anabaptist groups, it is crucial that we not think of formalization as ultimately important. In some circles, narrow issues of baptism's form, or mode, have been cause for schism. This is misguided. After all, neither Jesus, nor Peter, nor Paul provides a recipe. The NT does not present baptism as a clever technique, and the working of God's saving grace is not subject to conjuring. The desirable similarity implied in the liturgy suggested later in this chapter is not intended to communicate that a particular set of physical actions imported from the first century themselves constitute baptism, the essence of Christianity, or God's grace.

This presentation of the theology and practice of baptism might seem too loose for some and too restrictive for others; nevertheless, the point is that baptism's form is of relative importance due to the fact that for a ritual washing to be baptism a certain recognizable procedure is required. The form of this practice denotes the muddy history of people uniquely involved in God's desire to create a community that expresses a new sort of kinship. This form does more than that, it also *involves* participants in this history, a storied tradition that reaches back through the turbulence of the Reformation and the intrepid ancient church to the community of disciples going out from their homes after having been transformed by the Messiah, Jesus. Through this transformation came the epiphany of being members of Jesus' own body, of which he remains the head.

Baptism as Participating Witness

In previous chapters I argued that as a constitutive element of the life of the church baptism participates in its sacramental character. Therefore, Anabaptist communities can hold that baptism need not be reduced to a public statement about an inward change, nor must they separate the effectiveness of the ordinance from its evident social and symbolic context. In a development of Marpeck's notion of co-witness I suggested that we can understand baptism as a participating witness, a responsive activity of the church through which God acts. This description can be deepened in several ways.

Amidst my argument that the faults of current baptismal practice demands a more overt emphasis on the way the church is the body of Christ, the biblical image of this community as Christ's bride remains relevant because it preserves the alterity of Jesus to the church. Though Scripture does not invoke the marital figure with direct relevance to the ordinances of the church, its basic outline is relevant because these aspects of ecclesial life are events in which the characteristics of God's relationship to the church are practically focused and publicly displayed. It is worth observing, then, that for the parties involved, marriage has both an objective and subjective character. It happens *to* them and yet without their willing "yes" it does not happen at all. This is obviously the case for the bride and groom, but it is similar for the extended families joined through the union. Each party chooses and is chosen. In the symbiosis of marriage, new members are brought into these families and a new family is created. This encounter's dual sense, or mutual character, figures the nature of humanity's relationship to God in the life of the church. Baptism allies with this figure and can be understood similarly.

By appropriating elements of Bonhoeffer's ecclesiology, I have argued for a sacramental understanding of the church and by extension, baptism. By emphasizing the NT motif of the church as the body of Christ I have been working to recover an understanding of how God acts in the lives of individuals through congregations. This implies the participative elements of my description. However, I have not suggested what might seem logical to some—that an emphasis on the church's mediating role implies the normative status of infant baptism. As with marriage, believers' baptism is rightly understood as an act simultaneously enabled by candidates and having a determinative effect on them. The description I offer seeks to acknowledge the plural character of the relevant and active agents, thereby encompassing the early Anabaptist view of baptism as the candidate's free act of commitment. However, it also ties this pledge to the church's welcoming of the candidate into the people of God. This means that on a conceptual level describing baptism as a participating witness must account for its multiple dimensions. First, on a vertical plane it must account for baptism's non-monergist and non-competitive character, in which God's free action and the human creature's free response are both real and effective, neither to the detriment of the other. Second, on a horizontal plane it must account for the multiplicity of agents involved in baptism, including God, church, and baptismal candidate. Third, it must account for baptism's apocalyptic and proleptic sense of time in which the relevant events surpass the myopia of modern historical relativity to include the life, death, and resurrection of the new adam, the baptismal process itself, and the future consummation of redemption. In construing baptism as a participating witness Anabaptists can affirm these various dimensions, acknowledging that through this rite both congregation and baptizand participate with the Spirit in witness to God's redemptive work.

As the body of Christ, the baptizing community is animated by the breath of God, the Spirit, and partakes in God's new creation. The community into which the candidate is welcomed is more than just a society that lives in reference to a historical event—the life, death, and resurrection of Jesus. This community participates in God's ongoing new creation; in and through it Christ continues to create the world anew. This welcoming is a social matter of identity and belonging, yet it is also much more. As Noah's family was saved from destruction through God's provision of the ark, which they were called and enabled to build, so the salvation of baptizands involves their participation in this initiatory practice of the Christian community. Baptizands participate in the death and resurrection of Jesus. They are washed and cleansed. Ultimately it is God who does these things, but God wills that they be carried out by his people. Baptism is a witness to the redemptive work of God, and just as there is no gospel without the witness-bearing of proclamation, so God wills that redemption not be without the participating witness of ecclesial practices.

"The true light, which enlightens everyone, was coming into the world."[6] This is how the Gospel of John describes the incarnation. The epistle to the Colossians refers to this same one as "the image of the invisible God."[7] In these texts and others like them God reveals himself as one who enters creation and thereby searches, finds, and redeems those creatures made in the divine image—the very creatures which have rejected fellowship with him by breaking the covenant.[8] The God who welcomes, renews, and empowers in baptism is the same God who initiates and affects the redemption of humanity, all the while preserving human integrity, not forcefully carrying out his salvific will but revealing his power in love and vulnerability. Particularly instructive here are the images used in the three parables of Luke 15 where God is likened to a shepherd searching for a lost sheep, a woman searching for a coin, and a father welcoming home a rebellious son. Practiced and understood as a participating witness, baptism joins in the sacramental character of the church. With its privileged status as an ecclesial rite it bears special importance as a mark of the church and participates in its formation.

The function of baptism in the economy of grace is ultimately indistinguishable from the effectual character of the gospel. Nevertheless, as a participating witness baptism is both a response and an effective act. It possesses these twin characteristics in part because there are two relevant events. The first is the original redemptive work accomplished by Christ. The practice of baptism is a witness to the candidate and the gathered community that Christ's work has occurred and that it is effective in the life

---

6. John 1:9.
7. Col 1:15.
8. Compare to Barth, *CD* 4/1.

of the new member. The second event is that of baptism itself, which as a witness is distinct from, even though it is determined by, the life, death, and resurrection of Christ. Baptism has been ordained by Christ to participate in his subsequent and ongoing work in the world. As a physical and personal event baptism mediates the accomplished redemption in Jesus; it marks and affects the appropriation of it as participation in his body.

In Romans 6 Paul says that baptism unites Christians with the death and resurrection of Christ. Paul's view of baptism as an effectual practice is paradigmatic, and it follows that baptism participates in God's redemptive work. In Acts 5 Peter and other early church leaders give rationale for not being dissuaded from proclamation by claiming that with the Spirit they are witnesses to definitive events, Jesus' death and exaltation. The apostles hoped that through their witness God would continue to refashion Israel. Throughout this book I have argued that through the life of the congregation baptism functions similarly. Though all rituals acquire significance within a community, an important distinction of baptism is that the relevant community is understood to be more than a religious association: it is the body of Christ. Therefore, we say that God acts in the work of the church. As part of the mediatory work of the church, baptism is a public witness by the Spirit to the effectiveness of God's redemption. In its welcoming function baptism participates in this redemption by including the candidate in the people of God, incorporating them into the *totus Christus*.

A brief exploration of James McClendon's description of baptism as a "performative sign" will help clarify what I mean.[9] In describing baptism this way, McClendon is relying on the linguistic philosophy of J. L. Austin. Austin argues that words, whether written or spoken, can do more than merely name or label. Words can become "performative utterances" that accomplish things. Again, marriage is a helpful and classic example. The declarative authority of the officiant and the parties involved is brought to bear to make the marriage happen in the phrases, "I do" or "I now pronounce you . . ." Given the right conditions this verbal act does something—it accomplishes. If the performative quality of language extends to non-verbal signs, baptism can also be understood as just such a performative sign.[10] McClendon sees ample precedent in his own Baptist tradition for viewing baptism this way.

---

9. McClendon, "Baptism as a Performative Sign," 403–16.
10. Ibid., 410.

The helpfulness of McClendon's description is that it allows us to see how the sign character of baptism can itself be effectual and not simply referential. This helps us move beyond the functional bifurcation implied in Marpeck's terminology of "co-witness," which is equal to the popular separation of the baptism of the Spirit from the baptism of water. When we say that God acts through the church by the Spirit, and when we say that baptism is one particular instance of this, we need not hedge from the claim that this happens through a visible sign. All this is meant by the phrase "participating witness" and corroborated by McClendon's notion of a performative sign.

However, the performative terminology, derivative as it is from the discipline of linguistic philosophy, is theologically limited. We see this through the way McClendon defends his preference of the performative sign descriptor in place of sacrament. He provides rationale for this position by citing P.T. Forsyth, who writes, "The Sacraments will never become the symbol of a united Church till the whole tissue of thought, speech, and practice in connection with a metaphysic or magic of the elements as substance has been converted and transfigured, and they are construed as acts of Christ in person through the corporate personality of the Church, embodying the gospel's action in and by sacramental souls."[11] Though McClendon refers to Forsyth's requirements to question the viability of sacramental language, the reality is that the performative concept does not measure up either. This is the case because Austin's terminology is ill-suited for the task of theological description. Without the (re)construal of an underlying metaphysic performative terminology fails to provide baptism with any substantial theological, to say nothing of christological, mooring. It can show that signs do work, as I acknowledged above, but it cannot show that a sign can do the sort of work that Christians claim baptism does. If baptism participates in the divine economy in the way that both Forsyth and McClendon surely believe it does, such mechanistic analysis is simply too provincial for its subject.

It is Austin who points out that a performative utterance requires the pre-existence of an accepted convention within which it might be effective. When someone says, "I hereby bequeath . . ." a convention of bequeathing must already exist. Austin suggests, furthermore, that performative utterances can be undermined by a number of other problems, what he calls

---

11. As quoted in ibid., 412.

"infelicities."[12] These concepts of convention and infelicity form the criteria with which to evaluate the effectiveness of performative utterances. This further shows that the application of Austin's thought to baptism remains limited, for even though baptism is certainly carried out in the context of the communal significance of the convention, its effectual power is not lodged there. It could not be, for the social dependence of a convention cannot reach across the ugly ditch that differentiates a religious association from the body of Christ. Of course baptism can "misfire," to use Austin's term, but this obscures the deeper truth that without the gracious act of God there would be no "firing" at all. From a Christian perspective the infelicities of baptism's practice themselves depend on the reality of a power deeper than even a social imaginary. Of course McClendon would not disagree with this. Yet I believe the point stands: as a participative witness baptism's function is not merely linguistic or referential, though these are requisite mechanisms of ritual. Baptism physically marks and participates in the ecclesial administration or stewarding of God's grace.[13] It renders the effects of grace perceivable, which for creatures reliant on sensual perception is of no mere secondary importance.

McClendon's argument reminds us that the language of participating witness must point to the gospel. It reminds us that baptism is an eschatological practice bearing witness to and participating in the kingdom of God. As such it is an epic practice that reaches beyond the sphere of social conventions. Believers' baptism is the sign of an individual new birth that points toward the reign of God and the renewal of all creation. Rebirth and participation in Christ's resurrection, as implied in Romans 6, are embodied in baptism in such a way that the practical outworking of such regeneration is intrinsic to the act itself. Thus the liturgy of this rite is obliged to recognize the truth that the baptism of infants clearly proclaims, which is that this practice of the church is not self-generating. It does not happen on the initiative of the individual; but instead, is a work of Christ's body. Baptismal liturgy fails to recognize the completeness and sufficiency of God's acts to set humanity aright if it does not locate the response of the individual and the community, including the linguistic and semiotic performances along with their requisite social conventions, in the prior graciousness of God.[14]

---

12. Austin, "Performative Utterances," 237–41.

13. Consider 1 Pet 4:10.

14. Here I am inclined to follow Barth in his revision of Zwingli; Barth, *Regarding Baptism*, 20.

Baptism: A Theological and Liturgical Proposal

Therefore our baptismal liturgies must both acknowledge the mediatorial role of the church and the self-giving work of redemption accomplished in the life, death, and resurrection of Jesus of Nazareth as that which ultimately makes such a practice possible.

The mode of God's revelation and reconciling work upholds the importance of the human creature's genuine response to divine initiative. In this same line of thought I have noted that Anabaptists have often referred to baptism as a pledge to highlight its voluntary and ethical character. A key text in this regard is 1 Pet 3:21, a text that Thomas Finger says was probably the one cited most often by early Anabaptists when discussing baptism.[15] It is surprising then that today few contemporary denominational statements cite it. The early Anabaptist reading of this passage highlights the word *eperōtēma* as an appeal, or request, for a good conscience. For them this clearly indicated conscious, intentional action. Balthasar Hubmaier, Michael Sattler, and other early Anabaptists argued that baptism is not a sign of inclusion in the covenant as circumcision was, since as Paul states in Rom 2:29, it is not baptism that replaces circumcision but the circumcision of the heart carried out by the Spirit.[16] By describing baptism as participative I do not intend to undo this traditional understanding; such a witness participating in conversion is not the seal of Reformed theology. Rather, the language of participation upholds baptism's divinely circumscribed nature as a free response of human creatures. With the text of 1 Peter Anabaptists claim that the ark, not circumcision, is a figure related to the function of baptism, and therefore I have argued that Anabaptist communities can claim the importance and power of the ritual without detaching the dispensation of God's grace from the ark of the gathered community. Baptism is an event of the grace of God, not in the water or the oil themselves, nor in the precise mode, but inasmuch as these elements together participate in the work of the body of Christ. Through the power of the Holy Spirit baptism enables people to live as followers of Jesus—to desire, intend, and perform this way of life. Believers' baptism, unlike the various forms of pedobaptism, affirms the necessity of genuine response and honest intention by limiting baptism to those who freely profess faith. In this way baptism encapsulates the nature of the Christian life as something neither passive nor self-generating. Baptism is a focal image of the Christian experience

---

15. Finger, *Contemporary Anabaptist Theology*, 161.
16. Finger, *Anabaptist Theology*, 161n12.

in the way it brings together the subjective and objective characteristics of this way of life.

In the opening chapter of this book I suggested that my analysis of contemporary denominational theologies of baptism is both critical and affirmative. Much of this project has focused on the critical elements of this analysis. Yet it is important to clearly state that elements of the contemporary Anabaptist characterization of baptism are affirmed in the description of baptism as participating witness. The fact that many descriptions fall short of accounting for the necessary mediatory aspects of the ordinance does not deny that the participative nature of baptism includes its function as a baptizand's pledge to endeavor to live in response to the gracious work of God. A crucial theological assumption is that through Jesus' calling of the disciples and empowering of the church, humans are made, and revealed to be, capable of bearing witness to the gospel. They are endowed with a sense of worth and dignity that comes from a source more stable than their own fleeting ability or talent. In their adoption through Jesus they are granted the august title "children of God."[17] Baptism is an opportunity for individuals to state their intention to walk worthy of this calling. In Ephesians 4 Paul urges his readers to "lead a life worthy of the calling to which you have been called . . ." In the next few verses he urges them to maintain the unity of the Spirit and reminds them of the one hope, faith, and baptism grounded in the transcended singularity of God. Baptism is the point at which the purposing of the individual encounters the manifold power of the body of Christ.

Previously I referenced the baptismal theology of Balthasar Hubmaier as an example of the rationalist temptation native to Anabaptism. I also cited Hubmaier's theology more approvingly with respect to the link he draws between baptism and accountability to the office of the keys. In a short tract ambitiously titled "Summa of the Entire Christian Life," Hubmaier describes part of the progression of this life in a way that reveals his view of baptism more clearly. It is worth quoting at length:

> After the person has now committed himself inwardly and in faith to a new life, he then professes this also outwardly and publicly before the Christian church, into whose communion he lets himself be registered and counted according to the order and institution of Christ . . . Then he lets himself be baptized with outward water in which he professes publicly his faith and his intention,

17. Consider John 1:12; Rom 8–9; Eph 5:1; Phil 2:15; and much of 1 John.

namely, that he believes he has a gracious, kind, and merciful God and Father in Heaven through Jesus Christ, with whom he is well pleased and satisfied. *He also has expressed his intention to him and committed himself already in his heart henceforth to change and amend his life. Such he testifies also publicly with the reception of water.* If he henceforth blackens or shames the faith and name of Christ with public or offensive sins, he herewith submits and surrenders to brotherly discipline according to the order of Christ (Matt 18:15ff).[18]

For Hubmaier, believers' baptism is the foundation of ecclesial discipline, or to use a more friendly word, discipleship. Baptism is the church's work, and thereby God's work, and in this it is the individual's entryway to the disciplined community. When functioning properly the discipline of spiritual siblings is not capricious. It is an act of care. Likewise, it is not authoritarian since any authority it exerts is collectively held by the community. This does not, however, make the character of the disciplined community easily palatable for modern people, for it implies that the modern regime of desire is to be countered by the regimen of body life. Yet the regimen of the christoform community is one chosen by each individual and it is one that requires the ongoing contribution of each. It is no alien authority, nor clericalist power grab. Centered outside themselves in Christ, members of the baptized community are given the mandate of inviting others to this center and subsequently into their midst.[19] Empowered by the Spirit of God and trained in the life of the community, Christians grow in their ability to exercise wise and restorative judgment.[20] This sort of Spirit-empowered communal discernment opposes individualism though it seeks to maintain space for the individual, indeed even claiming that in the context of the body of Christ—the new adam—individuals become truer persons. Put negatively, the practice of baptism is wrongheaded when carried out by a community lacking confidence the peculiar ordering of the good conferred in its participation in Christ by the Spirit.[21] In performing its central rite the baptismal community denies that humans are capable of regenerating themselves, initiating their own salvation, or even achieving their own unity, whether through a vaunted lineage or impeccable doc-

18. Hubmaier, *Theologian of Anabaptism*, 85 (emphasis added).
19. Here I am thinking of Matt 28:16–20 and Rom 6:1–14.
20. Matt 18:15–20; 2 Cor 3:6; Gal 5:16–26.
21. This parallels the idea of the church as a *polis* in its own right. See Rasmusson, *Church as Polis*, 174–374.

trine. Nevertheless, baptism's liturgy must enact the decisive participation of candidates, for without their real response and involvement believers' baptism is incoherent.

An Ancient Christian Practice

Though the legacy of the church's past is sometimes burdensome, as considered in the previous chapter, it is also a gift. I believe that much can be gained in particular by developing a contemporary proposal for the practice of baptism in conversation with the patterns set by the ancient church. The liturgical proposal presented in the subsequent section of this chapter is intended to enact the reception of this tradition as a gift by using pre-Nicene Christian accounts as key resources. In addition to being a good steward of a gift, the act of considering the practice of baptism in light of history is an acknowledgment of several important features of the Christian faith. First, it is an acknowledgement that Christian interpretation of the Bible is a communally determined process, and that the relevant community includes those of earlier ages. Second, it is an acknowledgement that Christianity is not merely a belief system, or worldview, but is a way of life passed from one generation to another. Third, approaching the question of baptism's form in this way acknowledges that living as a Christian in the contemporary world is not uniquely challenging or inherently more difficult than in previous eras. There is much we can learn from the communion of saints. Pre-Nicene history is particularly relevant here. Not, as it is sometimes claimed, because the later church was entirely compromised, but because several important features of Christianity in North America increasingly resemble the social location of pre-Nicene churches. Unlike the Christendom context of the Medieval or even the Reformation period, the Christian faith in North America now exists alongside many other religions, worldviews, and social liturgies. Though in some cases adherence to Christianity may continue to be socially advantageous, this is far from uniform. Christian communities no longer receive outright government preference. As Christians in North America continue to come to terms with this change, historical examples continue to prove their value. A second reason that I privilege pre-Nicene accounts is because many of them are less affected by the highly speculative and metaphysically driven theorization that accompanies later attempts to describe the essence of the sacrament behind its form.

Baptism: A Theological and Liturgical Proposal

One of the best sources for understanding early Christian baptism is the *Didache*. It will be helpful to consider several important aspects of this one document in light of my description of baptism as a participating witness. This will provide opportunity to further explain the concept and will also help us gain footing in the ancient field before beginning additional constructive work. The *Didache* is special because of the way its early origin in the first or second century sheds light on the early days of the Jesus movement. This document has been described as a manual of church order developed for initiating non-Jews into Christian communities. The implication is that the textual world of this document does not assume baptismal candidates were trained in the Hebrew Scriptures nor had developed the habits of a moral life associated with the culture of the synagogue. This gives a view unique from many NT documents of a similar period, but faces issues similar to the catechetical requirements of many contemporary Christian communities. It focuses on the practical matters of the way of life taken up by Jesus' followers in which baptismal candidates anticipated participation.

The *Didache* is technically an anonymous text without an original title. Its current conventional name, *Didache*, is a shortened form of an acquired moniker that simply means something like "systematic training" or "technical apprenticeship."[22] It likely had no one author, but developed through oral tradition to provide a brief of the community's way of life. The *Didache* can be divided into the following sections: (1) an outline of the community's way of life; (2) guidelines for eating, baptizing, fasting, and praying, (3) guidelines for discerning hospitality; (4) guidelines for setting aside first fruits and appointing overseers; and (5) a closing set of warnings and a declaration of hope.[23] The first two sections are the longest and the most relevant to this project.

"There are two ways," begins the *Didache*, "one of life, and the other of death."[24] The first section of the document outlines these two ways. Commentator Aaron Milavec believes that this opening section of the *Didache* is an outline of the skills and virtues in which candidates would be apprenticed under a mentor's oversight. This apprenticeship had a dual purpose: first, it copied a traditional way of learning a technical skill and applied it to learning the Christian way of life; and second, it began to meet important relational needs for candidates who likely sacrificed such ties in choosing

---

22. Milavec, "Introduction," in *Didache*, ix–x.
23. Milavec, "Brief Commentary," in ibid., 43.
24. Ibid., 3.

to join the community of Jesus followers.[25] As baptismal preparation this is instructive in that it shows how concrete communities worked with the Spirit to effect new ways of life in converts. Even in this preparatory phase the rite participates in God's redemptive work.

This first part of the *Didache* begins descriptively, saying with traditional Jewish emphasis that the way of life is first to love the creator God and second to love one's neighbor as one's self. After this comes a series of instructions, directing hearers to "pray for your enemies" and "love the ones hating you." In addition, they were to "abstain from fleshly and bodily desires," and, in the tone of the Sermon on the Mount, turn the other cheek when struck and give more than what is demanded. The *Didache* then offers a reprise of the Decalogue, enjoining hearers to avoid a whole list of activities from the likes of murder and abortion, to illicit sex, and practicing magic. Hearers are to speak truthfully and to not make any destructive plans against their neighbours. They are to avoid the evil of murder by not even becoming angry, avoid illicit sex by not lusting, avoid idolatry by not being a diviner, avoid theft by not being false, and avoid blasphemy by not being a grumbler. The text continues in detail, advocating a long list of virtues, including gentleness, mercy, goodness, and humility. It then shifts to providing instruction about the future behaviour of the candidates, who are told that they will not cause dissention but will be generous, trusting in God's provision. They will train their children well and treat their slaves courteously. They will despise hypocrisy and willingly confess their failings.[26] All these things the *Didache* opposes to the way of death, from which it is hoped candidates will be saved.[27]

It is important to observe that the ritual washing of baptism did not stand by itself as a symbol of some unseen transaction. Preparation and moral training were needed to participate in the way of Jesus. Baptism signalled the completion of an important stage of this training, but it was something that required special preparation through a very practical process facilitated by a concrete community. This is further illustrated by the fact that in the days just before the ritual washing, the *Didache* recommends both those baptizing, perhaps each mentor, as well as the baptismal candidates fast to ready themselves. Other members of the community were encouraged to do the same as an act of solidarity.

25. Milavec, "Brief Commentary," in ibid., 47–49.
26. Ibid., 3–15.
27. Ibid., 17.

As for the rite itself, we read that candidates were to be immersed "in the name of the Father, and of the Son, and of the Holy Spirit."[28] As a Christian ordinance it required a recognizably trinitarian formula. The importance of form, inseparable from function or meaning, is further pressed when the text gives specific guidelines for the type of water source used. The best case is if candidates can be immersed in flowing water. However, even these ancient Christians were flexible in the details. If this mode of baptism was not practical, it is recommended that some other water, preferable cold, be used for immersion. If neither of these was an option, pouring water on the candidates three times in the triune name is said to be sufficient.[29]

The full practice of baptism begins before the ritual washing and continues after it. Following baptism the community was to share the eucharistic meal together. This was not a meal open to all hangers-on. The *Didache* states bluntly, "Let no one eat or drink from your eucharist except those baptized in the name of the Lord."[30] To follow the meal a model prayer is suggested that begins like this: "We give you thanks, holy Father, for your holy name, which you tabernacle in our hearts, and for the knowledge and faith and immorality which you revealed to us through your servant Jesus. To you is the glory forever."[31] The model prayer concludes with an appeal for the Lord to return and to remember, save, perfect, and gather the church. The practice of the eucharistic meal in conjunction with baptism highlights the priority of participation in the church community in the function of baptism. In its hope and anticipation it also illustrates baptism's eschatological character.

Ancient examples such as the *Didache* are valuable because they link twenty-first century members of the communion of saints to those from the first and second. They demonstrate the rigour and import of this ecclesial rite. Baptism for the communities represented by the *Didache* was not a life-stage marker or an opportunity for sentimentalism. Its example is helpful because it demonstrates the potential pedagogical richness of the practice. It shows how baptism can function as the fundamental resource for new Christians, participating in God's redemptive work as it bears witness to it.

---

28. Ibid., 19.
29. Ibid.
30. Ibid., 23.
31. Ibid., 25.

Participating Witness

PERFORMING BAPTISM

The liturgical proposal that follows is effectively this book's conclusion. Even so, and even though it is meant to show the fruit of my argument, it is only that—a proposal. It is one way of imagining how Anabaptists might practice believers' baptism today. It is as much a heuristic, or a place to begin a congregational discussion, as it is a usable script. With this goal in mind, the tone of this chapter shifts, to meld practice to theory, to contemplate the performance of baptism as a participating witness in and to God's redemption of human creatures.

Inquiry

As seen in the example of the *Didache*, the formational power of baptism lies in the Spirit's working, not just in the ritual of washing, but in the events and processes that surround it. This historical truism fits well with the tradition in Believers Church circles of not automatically baptizing persons at a particular age or life stage. The arguments made in this book toward reclamation of the objective quality of believers' baptism do not compromise baptism's subjective aspects, for believers' baptism does not occur without the consent, indeed the initiative, of the candidate. It is precisely this involvement of the baptismal candidate that provides opportunity for meaningful and effective preparation for baptism. However, before considering this topic in any depth a word should be said about children. Members of communities that do baptize infants appropriately remind Anabaptists of the importance of this issue.

In continuing to affirm that children are not appropriate candidates for baptism it ought not be assumed that they have no place in the community of faith—they do. This is rightly recognized through the ceremony of infant dedication, which is regularly practiced in Anabaptist communities. Pilgram Marpeck alludes to something like this in his 1532 confession when he states:

> [I]nfants should be named before a congregation and God shall duly be praised for them; thanks and blessing shall be given to His fatherly goodness that, through Christ Jesus our Lord and Savior, He has also had mercy on the innocent creatures and that, without discrimination, He has taken them in His hands and assured them of the kingdom of God . . . We admonish the parents to cleanse

> their conscience, as much as lies in them, with respect to the child, to do whatever is needed to raise the child up to the praise and glory of God, and to commit the child to God until it is clearly seen that God is working in him [or her] for faith or unfaith.[32]

The practice of infant dedication accords well with believers' baptism as it praises God for the gift of a child and provides a setting for both congregations and parents to publicly affirm their intent to raise the child in the knowledge of Christ. The subsequent participation of children in the life of the congregation might be loosely modeled after the experience of catechumens, though it should not be confused with the formal catechetical process leading to baptism. The operative assumption must be that children are fully under the grace of God and that on account of this grace administered through the sacrament of the congregation's life they may avoid the depths of broken sinfulness to which they might otherwise attain. This parallels Marpeck's reading of Luke 18:16 where he suggests that the presentation of the children to Jesus is for the purpose of a protective blessing and not for baptism.[33] The liturgy of believers' baptism serves as a visual teacher for children in the congregation, reminding them of the possibility of their eventual full and intentional inclusion in the community. Yet its clear reservation for adults releases children from the pressure of making a premature commitment with ramifications beyond the possibility of their comprehension. It also discourages parents and their congregations from thinking that *they* can determine their children's response to God's grace.

This discussion of baptism assumes that there are persons who would like to join local Christian communities. We count this as the product of the Spirit's work and the faithful witness of Christians to the gospel. The church is most truly itself in mission, and will continue to welcome new members. It is beyond the scope of this project to suggest how, beyond baptism, churches should or should not join the Spirit's work in encouraging outsiders to participate in their worship life. However, the practice of baptism assumes that churches are characterized by a winsome hospitality. The result of this will be the need for them to carefully initiate new members in a respectful and theologically coherent way. This initiation may begin either with an invitation extended to the seeker or a statement of interest on his behalf. Either way, the next step in the initiation process is traditionally called "inquiry." This term is useful because it can imply a

---

32. Marpeck, *Writings*, 147.
33. Ibid., 241–43.

period of mutual consideration, with questions from the community directed toward the potential candidate and questions from the individual directed toward the community.

It may be the case that some who wish to join may have already been baptized. Determining how these persons should be welcomed and trained is another important practical question. In cases where the already baptized seeker has little useful training in the Christian faith the process should probably look very similar to the one outlined below with the exception of baptism itself. When considering the validity of baptisms, Anabaptist communities would do well, as alluded to in the last chapter, to acknowledge the working of God and the faithfulness of other Christians outside the Anabaptist tradition. If one seeking to join a church has already been baptized with water in the triune name, the God of the apostles, by a community affirming the Lordship of Jesus, that baptism should be recognized. This has been a contentious topic in some Anabaptist circles. It has been particularly so in instances where Anabaptist groups required new members, even those from other Anabaptist communities, to be rebaptized if their initial baptism was not done through immersion or some other specified mode.[34] Paul's statements in Ephesians 4 regarding the oneness of baptism must be understood to lead away from the schismaticism of requiring rebaptism, even of people baptized as infants.

This does not mean Anabaptist communities should consider baptizing infants. There is excellent biblical, historical, and theological warrant for not doing this. However, discontinuing the practice of rebaptism is an acknowledgement, attentive to the Spirit's eschatological guarantee of unity, that the Protestant Reformation is not normative for the church and that in North America infant baptism is not a tool of the government. Though Anabaptists rightly consider indiscriminant infant baptism a misguided practice, if it is carried out by the body of Christ it is, as Paul suggests, linked to the very oneness of God. The requirement of rebaptism implies the rejection of the community that performed the initial baptism. This only makes sense when the initial baptism was performed by a community who did not acknowledge the Lordship of Christ and therefore did not baptize. Though the recognition of infant baptisms does not imply the propriety

---

34. An example of this is the Mennonite Brethren, who until 1963 required new members from General Conference Mennonite churches to be rebaptized. The "Mennonite Brethren Confession of Faith" (Article 8: Christian Baptism) continues to require the rebaptism of potential members who received infant baptism. See Jost, "Mennonite Brethren Theology of Baptism," 21–32.

Baptism: A Theological and Liturgical Proposal

of baptizing children as "believers," when practiced with integrity and followed by confirmation, the baptism of infants can be a coherent practice. Without accepting the larger theological matrix of infant baptism, however, the baptism of children in Anabaptist communities lacks this possibility.[35]

It is sometimes the case that individuals want to be baptized a second time since they no longer consider their prior baptism meaningful. With the theological construal of baptism developed in this project in mind, it is appropriate to say that this sort of thinking only considers half the issue. God's redemptive action is not dependent on a human emotional experience. Embedding this affirmation in the liturgical life of Anabaptist communities might serve to counter the notion that the only thing we can rely on to provide meaning and direction with respect to the myriad of life's questions, from the mundane to the ultimate, is a magical coming together of sensual manipulation and emotional receptivity. Therefore, inquirers after baptism should be asked if they have already been baptized and carefully redirected if they have. The twinning of faith and discipline that this represents is pedagogical since the re-direction of already baptized candidates affirms the faithfulness of God for the benefit of the inquirer. It is never too late to live more deeply into the biographical fact of baptism.

If the potential candidate is not already baptized, what should the next step be? An important one might be a brief explanation of just what may be entailed if their quest continues. The title of an essay by Stanley Hauerwas communicates the tone of these initial conversations—"Christianity: It's Not a Religion, It's an Adventure."[36] The point is not to give a convincing sales pitch regarding the wonderful benefits of adding one's name to the church's roster; instead, it should be a compassionate, sobering description of the costs, difficulties, and relatively unknown outcomes of Christian discipleship.

There are a number of important sources in the early tradition that give us useful examples of this initial interchange, which is sometimes called the "examination." One, the *Didache*, has already been introduced. The most prominent feature of the *Didache* is the stark separation between two ways, the way of life and the way of death. It is likely that this demonstrates an important early component of baptismal preparation was for the inquirer, or potential candidate, to come to terms with the ethical demands

---

35. Reciprocally, it seems proper for communities that practice believers' baptism to insist with the *BEM* document that indiscriminant infant baptism compromises the possibility of mutual recognition (*Baptism, Eucharist and Ministry*, 7).

36. Hauerwas, "Christianity: It's Not a Religion: It's an Adventure," 522–35.

of the community they hoped to enter. This could be taken as a sign of early Christian exclusivity, but it is better understood as an act of care for the inquirer and the community. Potential candidates are made aware of the conceivable social, financial, and professional costs that might be entailed in the Christian life. The intent in recommending a recovery of this element of baptism is not to communicate that Christian ethics are more important than Christian truth claims. Instead, it is to counter a tendency in contemporary Christianity toward a conviction that belief can be disconnected from practice. Beliefs about the afterlife or the unseen realm by themselves need cause little disruption in daily life; yet, these are not the sort of beliefs that the communities of the *Didache* or Anabaptist Christians claim to hold most dear. Informing possible candidates of material—real world—costs involved in faithful Christianity places these drawbacks clearly in view. Some examples of ancient Christian baptism go so far as to delineate professions that were inappropriate for Christians. Leaving a profession in which one has invested years is no small thing. The prefacing of doctrine with ethics in the *Didache* resonates with Anabaptist thought. Craig Hovey has convincingly argued that an important aspect of early Anabaptism, Swiss Anabaptism in particular, was this sort of interdependence of doctrine and ethics. This exemplifies what might be called in Lindbeckian terms a "cultural-linguistic" understanding of doctrine in which doctrinal claims are held to intra-systemic standards. Conceiving of doctrine in this way means that claims about belief are falsifiable by inadequate performance. This is why for Anabaptists *rightly* participating in the Lord's supper is an important ethical touchstone.[37] Hovey's observation helps show that prefacing catechetical instruction with ethical disclosure is not necessarily to be legalistic. Through truthfulness regarding possible costs, the sales tactics of a consumerist culture are turned on their head.

The ethical forthrightness of the *Didache* is similar to Justin Martyr's *First Apology* when he describes the Christian views of practices like magic, the "exposure" of children, the swearing of oaths, and so on.[38] His *Second Apology* gives similar testimony to the importance of right living. Likewise, the theme is upheld in the *Apostolic Tradition*, which may be representative of the ancient church in Rome and North Africa. This ancient document gives a list of vocations prohibited for baptismal candidates: idol maker,

---

37. Hovey, "Story and Eucharist," 315–24.
38. Justin Martyr, *First Apology* 16–30 (ANF 1:168–72).

prostitute, pagan priest, brothel keeper, gladiator, and the like.[39] It is evident that for pre-Nicene Christians one of the first prerequisites for entering the catechumenate was beginning the process of breaking those ties and everyday vocational connections that might compromise the candidate's ethical and spiritual reformation.

The witness of these early Christian communities represented by the *Didache*, Justin, and the *Apostolic Tradition* destabilizes dominant contemporary understandings of religion as best fenced by the private realm. When the leaders of Anabaptist congregations give possible candidates a clear-eyed description of the cost of following through with their desire to join the Christian community, they perform two crucial services. First, they honor the individual as a person whose life and integrity are more valuable than being an additional number on the congregational roster. In rejecting the temptation to sell membership or to think of their congregations as personal scorecards, such leaders uphold the important Christian virtue of truthtelling. Second, such leaders begin the pedagogical process of transmitting the grammar of the communities they serve. The point is not just to sever obvious ties with violent, abusive, or deceptive careers and life practices to keep one's hands clean. No, the most important function of this way of initiating the catechetical process is to begin to communicate key features of the process of Christian formation: that service, humility, and compassion are virtues valued above acquisativeness, and that individual choice exists in relationship to communal discernment.

What of right belief? Was coming to believe the things that Christians held to be true not important for our early Christian exemplars? While Justin Martyr's description of entering the Christian community is limited, it does describe candidates as those who have been persuaded that what Christians *believe* is true. These individuals are instructed to fast and pray for the remission of their sins, a task existing members were encouraged to join.[40] Irenaeus describes in book IV of his *Against Heresies* the importance of having an "accurate knowledge" of the system of Christian doctrine before one undertakes the process of conversion.[41] Belief and knowledge are important, yet it seems likely that the picture Aaron Milavec draws from the *Didache* of someone entering an apprenticeship is the dominant posture of one embarking on the catechetical journey. The process of assimila-

---

39. Bradshaw, Johnson, and Philips, eds., *Apostolic Tradition*, 88–95.
40. Justin Martyr, *First Apology* 61 (*ANF* 1: 183).
41. Irenaeus, *Against Heresies* 4.pref.2 (*ANF* 1:462).

tion alluded to in this document seems to imply a mentoring relationship between the one hoping to join the community and a spiritual and ethical guide. Historian Paul Bradshaw corroborates this with the Syrian tradition, claiming that for baptismal candidates moral instruction preceded the hearing of the word.[42]

Preliminary discussions with possible candidates for baptism should center on an honest description of the subsequent moral expectations. These discussions, though, should also explore the individual's motivation for joining the community, assessing whether or not he or she possesses a basic understanding of what Christians believe, and amending where necessary. This is not the time for in-depth instruction but for honest representation. The decision of whether an individual is ready to enter catechetical training should be a process of mutual discernment between representatives of the community and the individual. The representatives would do well to assess whether or not the possible candidate should proceed. It is unlikely that individuals who are too young to be trusted to drive a car, vote, or otherwise be treated as adults should be regularly considered for such serious instruction and subsequent commitment. The assessment of possible candidates should take into account the observable signs of the individual's calling to the community, decisions and changes already evident in their lives, and should be sensitive to the Spirit's guidance.

Turning our attention back to the model of early Christian initiation, we are reminded that candidates for baptism were not alone on their journey. Their participation in the catechetical process often depended on their apprenticeship under the guidance of more mature Christians. Tertullian writes from roughly the same time period as Ireneaus and Justin. He describes the important role of sponsors. These were mentors who presented candidates to the catechetical instructor.[43] Robert Cabié says that these mentors "communicated to [candidates] their own experience of the Christian life and would attest to [candidates'] progress before the church authorities."[44] This act of presentation is given corroborating testimony by the *Apostolic Tradition*,[45] and is surely indicative of the early steps taken by those entering the catechumenate. They would leave behind old ties and take up the role of an apprentice to a mature member or members of the

---

42. Bradshaw, *Origins of Christian Worship*, 154–55.
43. Tertullian, *On Baptism* 18 (ANF 3:678).
44. Cabié, "Christian Initiation," 23.
45. Bradshaw, Johnson, and Philips, eds., *Apostolic Tradition*, 82–86.

Christian community.[46] Many of our contemporary ecclesial and civil educational models place learners in age-defined cohorts, a practice that undercuts a traditional transmission of wisdom and segregates communities by age. In contrast, the practice of involving sponsors or mentors in the catechetical process affirms the intergenerational quality of Christ's body and incorporates modeling and relational educational strategies. Catechesis certainly should involve learning doctrine, but it is most faithful to the gospel when taught as a way of life.[47] Involving mentors, or sponsors, in catechesis helps meet this objective.

To sum up the recommendations of this section: (1) Potential candidates should be given a clear description of both the joys and challenges of the Christian life. (2) As possible candidates become members of the catechumenate—actual candidates—they should be provided with a mentor or mentoring group of suitable compatibility. The mentor's responsibility is significant, for the rest of the community looks to them to guide the candidate and eventually present them before the congregation for baptism. In talking of mentors, formation, and pedagogy it is easy to forget that through these fairly commonplace processes used by the church God acts. God uses the ordinary of creation in the work of redemption—this is the participatory claim.

Catechesis

The discussion thus far has dealt with preparation for the period of formal catechesis, but has yet to touch the catechetical process itself. In many situations pedagogy precedes formal instruction. This is not unique to Christian catechesis. For example, college students already have an impression of the value of their education through the disposition of older students and the architecture of their campus long before classes begin. In the case of Christian catechesis this overlap intentionally blurs the boundaries of the learning period and communicates to those who wish to formally join the community that Christian formation, or discipleship, is ongoing and pervades every corner of the Christian life. Ongoing formation is a characteristic of the

---

46. Bradshaw, *Origins of Christian Worship*, 154–55, notes that mentors or sponsors were not universally part of the early baptismal preparation. He suggests that early Syrian practice did not include them.

47. Related here is J. K. A. Smith's critique of "worldview-based" Christian education (*Desiring the Kingdom*).

Christian life, yet a period of formal catechesis remains necessary. This aids the candidate in gaining, in a relatively short time, significant understanding of and practice in the Christian life. It also upholds the integrity of the community by passing on its language. The grammar of the Christian community's language is best learned like any language, through simultaneous immersion and formal grammar instruction. Christians are immersed in this linguistic world through worship and everyday conversations. In this light sermons are akin to grammar lessons intended to remind communities of their adopted language. Yet it is catechesis that sets out this grammar in a particularly coherent and comprehensive fashion.

One of the most vexing questions we can ask at this juncture is how long the catechetical process should take. Clement, writing from Rome near the end of the first century, describes a three-year period. This is not always taken by scholars as a literal description, yet the *Apostolic Tradition* and Cyprian of Carthage make similar claims.[48] Some scholars find such a long process plausible in light of its parallel to Josephus's description of similar initiation periods among communities of Jewish Essenes.[49] In his book *The Rites of Christian Initiation*, Maxwell Johnson presents a clouded picture. He suggests that the Armenian three-week period of catechesis represents another ancient custom characteristic of Syrian Christianity.[50] If the discrepancy between three weeks and three years is not enough to complicate matters, even other variants exist. An early Egyptian derivation of the *Apostolic Tradition* called the *Canons of Hippolytus* sets the length of the catechumenate at forty days.[51] For their part, Tertullian, Justin, and the *Didache* all confirm the existence of the catechumenate but do not explicitly describe its length. What are we to make of this variety? It is likely that this diversity in early accounts reflects an actual diversity in practice. The NT does not give direct instruction on this matter: in the absence of a canonical norm it is probable that a variety of practices flourished, reflecting, among other things, the varied background of candidates on account of Christianity's gradual distance from the Jewish faith that had formed many of its early members.

---

48. Johnson, *Christian Initiation*, 66, 96–110; Bradshaw, Johnson, and Philips, eds., *Apostolic Tradition*, 96–98.

49. Bradshaw, Johnson, and Philips, eds., *Apostolic Tradition*, 96–98.

50. Johnson, *Christian Initiation*, 60–63.

51. Ibid., 65.

Baptism: A Theological and Liturgical Proposal

Like early Christian communities, contemporary Anabaptist congregations should choose a period of catechesis that responds to their immediate situation and the makeup of their candidates. That said, contemporary social realities in North America bear enough similarity to open the door for several suggestions. First, the residual cultural awareness of Christianity demands a period of careful instruction that allows ecclesial communities to delineate for potential members the commonalities and divergences between the way they understand the Christian life and the spiritual vagaries floating about in the wider culture.[52] Christian communities would do well to help potential members understand precisely what sort of God their community worships. It is doubtful that this sort of careful parsing of cultural god-talk could be done in less than several months of weekly instruction. Additional content of catechetical training only amplifies the necessary length of this process.

Another factor that would require a longer period is the fact that the Christian calendar is an important pedagogical tool. The progression of Lent, Easter, Pentecost, and the rest tell the Christian story in the context of worship. The juxtaposition of this calendar to national and cultural ways of keeping time forms candidates' theological understandings, shapes their experience of grace, and outlines the relationship of the Christian community to the broader culture. Therefore, Anabaptist catechesis should be shaped most formally by the Christian calendar and the regular worship life of the community. These two structures outline the content of the candidate's training, while the arrangement of apprenticeship forms the primary methodology.

There are two additional important parts of the catechetical process that we must explore. First, Anabaptists understand the Christian life to be characterized by service. The grammar of Anabaptist theology can never be abstracted from this very tangible part of the Christian life. The exact outlines of this component would surely need to be determined in a case-by-case basis, yet there are some general things that can still be said. Ideally, this component of catechesis should follow the larger apprenticeship form. This means that such service should not be akin to public service components of university education in which the individual carries out some worthy task on her own. The service component of Christian formation

---

52. One example of the importance of this can be seen in the response of those in the West to the recent catastrophic tsunami in southeast Asia. Hart, *The Doors of the Sea*, 1–44, shows how popular questions of theodicy trade on leftover deist assumptions.

would do better to take place alongside other Christians in the context of the worshiping community. There may well be existing areas of church life that facilitate this. However, there are also opportunities in the settings of larger denominational networks that can facilitate this very nicely. It is no accident that many Anabaptist congregations continue to show the effects of the years of voluntary service rendered by conscientious objectors as well as those of young people choosing to defer the completion of their education for involvement in similar programs. These experiences have deeply impacted participants, assisted the communities in which they served, as well as shaped denominational cultures. These service programs doubtlessly need to be regularly revised in light of cultural changes, but they continue to properly display part of the servant character of Christian discipleship. Christian catechesis in its Anabaptist variant should help candidates reflect on their service experiences alongside the history of exemplary Christian lives and interpret them within the grammar of Anabaptist theology.

Second, Christian catechesis rightly involves formal instruction in Christian practices and the history of the church. Anabaptist catechesis should do these things as well. Here again individual circumstances affect precise implementation, but some generalities can be suggested. Much of the teaching on Christian practices would seem to occur best in response to the worship life of the congregation. Questions like, "How do Christians pray?" would logically be discussed in the context of the congregation's prayer life; "How do Christians manage their finances?" in the context of the congregation's own stewardship of tithes and offerings; "How do Christians rightly practice sexual fidelity?" in the context of the recognition of family, marriage, and singleness in the congregation; "How do Christians interpret Scripture?" should be treated again and again in response to the congregation's life in, with, and under the Bible. Likewise, it is hoped that the worship life of the congregation is appropriately historically aware so that it can be used as the basis for instruction in the church's history. This component will of course demand more formal instruction, but even this should be in response to what the congregation actually does. It is crucially important that this instruction cover the grand sweep of church history, but also particular and local aspects. The Brethren in Christ understand church history differently than do Presbyterians, and this should be sympathetically observed in a catholic spirit when new members are being trained.

Catechesis is the work of the whole congregation. Important aspects are delegated to the co-ordinating pastor and carefully chosen mentors. At bottom, though, it is the work of God to which baptism is a witness. Correct form and content alone are incapable of re-forming individuals into true persons after the form of Christ, the new adam. In summary, the period of catechesis should follow an initial phase of inquiry, ensuring that the candidate is given fair warning about the possible demands of the journey ahead. The recommendations of this section can be summarized as follows: (1) an important component of the process should be an apprentice-like relationship between the candidate and a mature sponsoring individual or group; (2) formal catechesis should ideally cover a full year, making use of the Christian calendar and participation in Christian worship as pedagogical tools; (3) Christian service is an essential component of Anabaptist formation; and (4) Christian practices and the history of the church should be taught in the context of the life of the congregation. Preparation for baptism is best carried out intentionally by the local church in a manner that is contextually sensitive, yet aware of the gravity of this part of the candidate's journey. Then if congregations are faithful, if candidates are enabled to respond appropriately, and if God through his Spirit wills it, the process of preparation will lead to baptism itself.

A Liturgy of the Ritual Washing

Christian baptism has traditionally taken place either on Easter or Pentecost. Since baptism is tied so closely to these two biblical events it is not surprising that its performance would be coupled to one of these celebrations. Strangely, many Anabaptist groups today baptize at irregular times. Some are probably trying to follow the immediacy they see in NT examples, and others are perhaps just happy to provide a service. As with inquiry and catechesis, we will see that considering the ancient practice alongside modern variations is a fruitful contrast.

In early Christianity the choice of baptismal dates seems to have diverged along East/West lines. In the East the paradigm for baptism relied heavily upon a mimetic relationship to Jesus' baptism in the Jordan and emphasized both the role of the Holy Spirit and the importance of Pentecost. For this reason these Christians preferred to baptize at this time. These same Christians placed great emphasis on the sacred anointing before the actual bath portion of the ritual. At the same time the baptismal theology of the West emphasized Pauline themes of symbolic participation in the death and resurrection of Christ as well as the necessity of renouncing

Participating Witness

evil and exorcizing it from the candidate's life. Many of these Christians included two anointings in the baptism ritual, though neither was nearly as important as the washing itself. Christians in the West preferred to hold baptisms on Easter.[53]

We have already considered examples of catechesis in several ancient sources in addition to the *Didache*. It will be helpful to do the same with respect to the washing. The ancient Syrian document called the *Acts of the Apostles* is not actually a description of the apostles' assumptions about baptism, but Johnson reminds readers that it is likely that this collection of Syrian Christian texts does accurately represent the practice of a Christian community in the late second and early third centuries. Two interesting and relevant features of baptism are evident in this source. First, the prebaptismal anointing, as noted above, appears to be the liturgical highpoint. Second, there is a formal invocation of the Trinitarian formula, a feature that was not universal at the time but would later become standard practice.[54]

Baptizing in the name of the Father, Son, and Holy Spirit is not foreign to Anabaptism. Though Anabaptists have often sought to avoid a creedalism that marginalizes Scripture, most baptize this way. This formula properly proceeds from the Great Commission and serves as an ecumenical platform for the shared recognition of baptismal validity. It firmly connects candidates to the broader Christian tradition. An anointing with oil is a less standard practice among contemporary Anabaptists. The recovery of this part of the rite might serve not only to reconnect contemporary Christians with their ancient Syrian ancestors, but would also provide a tangible link to a Jewish background often overlooked. These ancient connections are potentially helpful in developing deep, meaningful roots for detached modern people. They serve to remind North Americans in particular that their faith relies on the faithfulness of particular communities of the Fertile Crescent—an important tie to the catholic nature of the church in times of nationalism and war.

Justin Martyr and Tertullian also provide descriptions of baptism. Justin describes a straightforward, if not rather stark, pattern beginning with a profession of faith, followed by a communal prayer, immersion, partaking in the Eucharist, and finally exchanging the kiss of peace. Participation in the Eucharist and the exchange of the kiss of peace are important welcoming rituals. In these rites, those who recently were only candidates

---

53. Bradshaw, *Origins of Christian Worship*, 151.
54. Johnson, *Christian Initiation*, 55–60.

are acknowledged as full members of the community. In these rituals God works through the community to publicly affirm each and to confirm their new life. Tertullian's slightly later description includes a prayer invoking the Spirit, a renunciation of the devil, a threefold interrogatory profession of faith, a post-baptism anointing, laying on of hands, and partaking of the Eucharist as well as a special milk and honey mixture used to symbolize the candidate's entrance into the promised new life.[55] For all the specificity of Tertullian's account he displays a pragmatic flexibility regarding the physical context of this baptism. His account is similar to the *Didache* in that the precise type of water used is dependent upon availability.[56] This is useful precedent for contemporary Christians who have limited access to streams or rivers with acceptably low levels of pollution! Also of note in his description are the traditional renunciation of the devil and the less-familiar tasting of the sweet extravagance of milk and honey.

The *Apostolic Tradition* gives a fairly full description of the rite of baptism.[57] In this account the candidates are baptized naked, without jewelry or other ornamentation. Preference is given to doing this in a running stream. The newly baptized are anointed with the oil of thanksgiving, led newly-clothed into the church, anointed with the oil of exorcism, and sealed by the bishop. Then they are allowed to join the prayer of the community, are given the kiss of peace, partake in the Eucharist, and are given milk mixed with honey to drink. We see in this text a rich array of symbolism from the nakedness of new birth to the special significance of entering the church building.

Believers' baptism exists as a development of the ancient Christian tradition, and contemporary practice would do well to clearly invoke this history. But there remains a question of how best to do this. The practice of early Christians is itself developmental, an interpretation and application of biblical source material as well as oral tradition in a unique context. Following in this style, a contemporary order should be contextually appropriate, historically rooted, and biblically faithful. For Anabaptists, as for other Christians, the environment of discipleship that surrounds baptism is as important as the ritual. Therefore, church-rending debates over immersion, submersion, and effusion—though they do show an admirable respect for the practice and its form—are ultimately misguided. Flexibility

---

55. Ibid., 84–90.
56. Tertullian, *On Baptism* 4 (ANF 3:670–71).
57. Bradshaw, Johnson, and Philips, eds., *Apostolic Tradition* 21.

ought to be assumed on these finer points; yet it is hard to imagine that this cleansing ritual shouldn't at least get the candidate really wet. Stinginess in the use of water is a miserly practice, robbing candidates of the opportunity of actually feeling washed and the larger community of having a visual reminder of God's forgiveness, love, and regenerating grace. Baptism is not only an ongoing practice of the church, but a biographical event in the lives of individuals. It should be made memorable in ways that bring to mind its magnitude and avoid the kitschiness of so many modern celebrations.

Contemporary believers' baptism might be aided by considering the following outline developed from the dual precedent of ancient baptism and the Anabaptist tradition. Though this outline is specific, it is not meant to be wooden. Its specificity is intended to enhance its practicality and usefulness.

There is no reason to think that Easter and Pentecost are not still good times to baptize new members. Hopefully, I have presented a strong argument against on-the-spot revivalist baptisms that circumvent catechesis and fog the important affective elements of the Christian faith with a nebulous but pervasive emotivism. It is true that many biblical accounts of baptism seem to occur immediately after a confession of faith or the manifestation of the Spirit. Several stories in Acts can be read in this light.[58] It would seem though that the sort of catechetical teaching envisioned here is implicit in the circumstances of these biblical accounts. While it is possible that some contemporary individuals may have already gone through a catechesis-like experience, as would have been true for most first-century Jews and God-fearing Gentiles, this is probably exceptional.

Assuming discipleship-oriented catechesis as the most important preparation for baptism, the more proximate preparation should take place the evening before the baptismal service when baptismal candidates, their sponsors, church leaders, and other willing members gather for prayer. Some congregations may wish to fully observe early Christian practice and spend the night this way. Others will hold a shorter gathering. In either setting prayer should be offered on behalf of the candidates—that they would be preserved, cleansed, and welcomed—and on behalf of the congregation—that they would remember their own baptisms, welcome the new members, and uphold them in the faith. After prayer, inquiry should be made of each candidate and his or her respective sponsor(s) as to whether they believe the community should proceed with the planned baptism the next day. Here both the subjective and objective qualities of baptism are

---

58. See Acts 2, 8, 9, 16, 22.

embodied. The decision to carry on is both the choice of candidates and the address of God through the body of Christ.

On the following day the liturgy of the service and the content of the sermon would do well to take into account the important events taking place. The ordinance of baptism is undercut if it is simply tacked on to a service. Making baptism central not only accentuates the event for candidates, but also serves a pedagogical function for the congregation, those already baptized and those who may wish to inquire about it. It is not uncommon for contemporary baptismal services to include favorite music or poetry of the candidates. This sets the wrong tone. It communicates that the power of the ordinance, the power of any ritual or celebration for that matter, is entirely activated by the choice of the individual; it implies that it is somehow "their day" and that extraneous pieces are needed for Christian sacraments to be relevant. The day of baptism belongs to God and to God's gathered worshipers, of which the baptismal candidate is only one. Music and other pieces of the worship liturgy should be carefully chosen to compliment the suggested baptismal outline and to allow the congregation to fully participate in the event.

The portion of the service dedicated to baptism might begin with prayer, asking God through his Spirit to hallow the time, the space, and the materials involved. This initial prayer will be followed by the presentation of each of the candidates by their mentor or sponsor. Sponsors should address the congregation, telling them why they believe their apprentice should be baptized as a member of their community and the larger body of Christ. After this presentation the congregation is given opportunity to respond, providing their affirmation for the baptisms about to take place. This might take a variety of forms depending on context. Representative members of the congregation might stand and give their affirmation; a responsive reading, a reading from Scripture, even a song could be used with the same intent. This part of the baptismal rite is no mere formality, for it is through the voices of the gathered body of Christ that God's Spirit speaks.

The next segment of the service would sensibly proceed by focusing individually on each candidate. The officiating congregational leader would question candidates regarding their belief in a basic set of Christian claims and their rejection of evil. If the one who officiates would make note at this point of the particularly insidious forms of evil, this would help to communicate the importance of this part of the ordinance, which is often overlooked even though it is central to the Christian life.

It is assumed that each candidate has already shared the story of their coming to the faith with members of the community, perhaps even the whole congregation. Many Anabaptist groups include such an element in the baptismal service. This is not ideal since a fear of public speaking distracts many candidates from the seriousness of baptism. It also detracts from the joyful welcome each candidate should receive and needlessly sets up unnecessary comparisons between them. This is especially detrimental in this context because in the encounter with God's grace in baptism all are equal. Following the brief examination or questioning, the officiating pastor should say a brief prayer of petition and thanksgiving over the candidate. Then the candidate is washed either by pouring or submersion and the trinitarian formula invoked. This should occur as close to the congregation as possible. This location is preferable to a distant font or on a stage above the level of the community, which can communicate that baptism is a show—something performed by an expert. Proximity heightens the reality of the physical symbols for the congregation; it demonstrates that the congregation is a participant in the event and also communicates to the newly baptized that each one of them have been welcomed into a specific community by actual people.

Following the washing a brief prayer invoking the presence of the Spirit should be given over each. At the end of this prayer the officiating leader might perform the ancient custom of blowing on the candidate's forehead as a symbol of the gift of the Spirit. Then the candidate should be sealed with oil in the sign of the cross. Here exists a prime opportunity to involve someone who is not a member of the congregation but perhaps a supervising denominational leader from a different Christian tradition. Having such a person involved in the baptism demonstrates that candidates are not only baptized into the local church community but also into the Christian tradition at large.

Once all the candidates have been baptized in this way the congregation should sing a song of welcome and thanksgiving. This dually expresses the joy of Christ at the presence of new members in his flock and thanks God for the redemptive nature of the calling Spirit. During this song the newly baptized may be given the ancient honey and milk symbol of entrance into God's promised new geography. The sweetness of the honey and the richness of the milk communicate the goodness of God's care and the bounty of God's provision. Finally, the baptisms are completed by the sharing of communion among all gathered. With due attention to propriety, this would be best done using actual bread and wine, each in generous portion. Wafers and grape juice fail to properly connote an actual meal of celebration. They are not sensually rich enough to honor the goodness of God's original creation or the re-affirmation of it in the incarnation. It would be beneficial for the corporate celebration of communion to be followed by a genuine feast shared by all. In this way communion retains its link to the act of eating together and sharing resources. It may also be appropriate for members of the community to present the newly baptized with useful gifts symbolic of the support the group intends to provide the new member.

It would be negligent to consider baptism merely an initiatory rite to be done once and left behind. Baptism can serve as an ongoing formational resource in the worship life of Anabaptist communities. In the NT Paul regularly invokes baptism, not as a theoretical construct or as a boundary-guarding ritual, but as an eminently practical event. In Gal 3:27–28 he writes, "As many of you as were baptized into Christ have clothed yourselves with Christ. There is no longer Jew or Greek, there is no longer slave or free, there is no longer male and female; for all of you are one in Christ Jesus." In Eph 4:1–6 Paul "begs" his readers to live worthy of their "calling." He describes the virtues and communal character of this life and invokes a series of unifying motifs: body, Spirit, hope, Lord, faith, *baptism*, God, and Father.

Baptism remains useful in part because it is a biographical fact. Amidst the vagaries of human spirituality, baptism is a tangible marker. "Remember your baptism" has been the invitation of preachers and bishops throughout Christian history. A similar need is approached in contemporary revivalist rallies involving a call for attendees to dedicate, re-dedicate, or re-re-dedicate their lives to Jesus. There may be nothing inherently wrong with these rituals if they steer clear of emotional manipulation; however, Christian communities can do better by attending to their ancient practices such as baptism.

The invitation to "Remember your baptism" is an invitation to a renewed practice of the faith. But it is not an invitation like that of the Evangelical rally since it reminds the baptized that something happened to them in their baptisms and that the reality of the event cannot be undone by a waning of their enthusiasm. "Remember your baptism" is a reminder that part of each Christian's biography is the event that marks God's drawing them into fellowship, the event that marks their Spirit-enabled decision to live congruent with the kingdom of God. Baptism anticipates that enthusiasm will slack, that resolve will loosen its hold on the will. That is why it is done in the context of a period of formation that does not begin with the day of baptism and does not end as the service concludes. The newly baptized are immediately involved in the worship and service life of the church in appropriate capacities. This is one of the reasons why baptism should not be done in the context of non-ecclesial gatherings, such as summer camps or revival meetings. It is important that the whole congregation be reminded of their baptism regularly. The doctrine of the priesthood of all believers requires this.

One helpful way congregants can be reminded of their baptism is by sprinkling all members of the community with water when baptism takes place, perhaps even a cheerful splashing of everyone within reach if the context permits. This is of course not a rebaptism, but a tangible reminder of the event of their being welcomed into the people of God. It is certainly not a request for re-commitment, but rather a reminder to allow the fundamental commitment of baptism to continue shaping one's life. Likewise, other events in the church's worship life should be linked to baptism. The celebration of Easter and Pentecost could be related to baptism through liturgy, art, and sermon since baptism is the primary response of Christians to these two events. Christian marriage, communion, ordination, and even funerals proceed on the assumption of baptism; the dedication of newborn children anticipates and prays for it. These ceremonies mark the breadth of our lives, and each is undergirded by God's work in baptism. As an event in which candidates act out their growing faithfulness to Jesus and are acted upon by God through the church, baptism encompasses the basic structure of the Christian life. As a participating witness baptism responds to the redemptive work of Christ and participates in the ongoing realization of this in the lives of those who would follow in the way of Jesus.

If the church's life across time is like a vine, if it is in need of ongoing pruning, then theological work continues. With respect to baptism and other central ecclesial practices the work is crucial because these aspects of the Christian faith hold significant potential for sustaining the vibrant life of the church and demonstrating the charity that indelibly marks Christ's body. Baptism marks the Christian's participation in Christ's death, yes, but also in his resurrection. The sustaining potential that the cultivation of right practice holds does not come from some generic benefit of orthopraxy but from the power of God's Spirit, a power that awakens the human creature to life in God's new creation.

Bibliography

Adams, Nicholas, and Charles Elliott. "Ethnography is Dogmatics: Making Description Central to Systematic Theology." *Scottish Journal of Theology* 53/3 (2000) 339–64.

Aland, Kurt. *Did the Early Church Baptize Infants?* Translated by G.R. Beasley-Murray. London: SCM, 1963.

Alexander, Paul. *Peace to War: Shifting Allegiances in the Assemblies of God.* Telford, PA: Cascadia, 2009.

Aquinas, Thomas. *Summa Theologica.* Translated by Fathers of the English Dominican Province. New York: Benziger Brothers, 1947.

Asad, Talal. *Formations of the Secular: Christianity, Islam, Modernity.* Stanford: Stanford University Press, 2003

Augustine. *Confessions.* Translated by Garry Wills. New York: Penguin, 2006.

Austin, J. L. "Performative Utterances." In *Philosophical Papers*, 3rd ed., edited by J. O. Urmson and G. J. Warnock, 233–52. Oxford: Oxford University Press, 1979.

Barth, Karl. *The Teaching of the Church Regarding Baptism.* Translated by Ernest A Payne. London: SCM, 1948.

———. *Church Dogmatics.* 1/1: *The Doctrine of the Word of God.* 2nd ed. Translated by G. W. Bromiley. Edited by G. W. Bromiley and T. F Torrance. Edinburgh: T. & T. Clark, 1975.

———. *Church Dogmatics.* 4/1: *The Doctrine of Reconciliation.* Translated by G. W. Bromiley. Edited by G. W. Bromiley and T. F Torrance. Edinburgh: T. & T. Clark, 1956.

———. *Church Dogmatics.* 4/2: *The Doctrine of Reconciliation.* Translated by G. W. Bromiley. Edited by G. W. Bromiley and T. F Torrance. Edinburgh: T. & T. Clark, 1958.

———. *Church Dogmatics.* 4/4: *The Christian Life: Baptism as the Foundation of the Christian Life.* Translated by G. W. Bromiley. Edited by G. W. Bromiley and T. F Torrance. Edinburgh: T. & T. Clark, 1969.

Bauerschmidt, Frederick C. "Baptism in the Diaspora." In *On Baptism: Mennonite-Catholic Theological Colloquium, 2001–2002.* Edited by Gerald W. Schlabach, 16–61. Kitchener, ON: Pandora, 2004.

Beasley-Murray, G. R. *Baptism in the New Testament.* New York: St. Martin's, 1962.

Bedard, Walter M. *The Symbolism of the Baptismal Font in Early Christian Thought.* Studies in Sacred Theology 45, 2nd Series. Washington: The Catholic University of America Press, 1951.

Bedouelle, Guy. "Reflection on the Place of the Child in the Church: 'Suffer the Little Children to Come unto Me.'" *Communio* 12/4 (1985) 349–67.

Bell, Catherine. *Ritual: Perspectives and Dimensions.* New York: Oxford University Press, 1997.

Bibliography

Bellah, Robert N. *Habits of the Heart: Individualism and Commitment in American Life*. New York: Harper & Row, 1985.

Bender, Harold S. "A Brief Biography of Menno Simons." In *The Complete Writings of Menno Simons*, translated by Leonard Verduin, edited by J. C. Wenger, 4–29. Scottdale, PA: Herald, 1956.

———. "Pilgram Marpeck, Anabaptist Theologian and Civil Engineer." *Mennonite Quarterly Review* 38/3 (1964) 231–65.

Bergen, Jeremy M. "Problem or Promise? Confessional Martyrs and Mennonite–Catholic Relations." *Journal of Ecumenical Studies* 41/3–4 (2004) 367–88.

———. *Ecclesial Repentance: The Churches Confront their Sinful Pasts*. London: T. & T. Clark, 2011.

———. "Lutheran Repentance at Stuttgart and Mennonite Ecclesial Identity." *Mennonite Quarterly Review* 86/3 (2012) 315–38.

Bergestresser, P., and S. H. Bashor. *The Waynesboro Discussion on Baptism, the Lord's Supper, and Feet-Washing*. Compiled by W. W. Cotten. York, PA: Teachers Journal, 1888.

Bibby, Reginald W. and Donald C. Posterski, *The Emerging Generation: An Inside Look and Canada's Teenagers*. Toronto: Irwin, 1985.

———. *Mosaic Madness: The Poverty and Potential of Life in Canada*. Toronto: Stoddard, 1990.

Blough, Neal. "The Church as Sign or Sacrament: Trinitarian Ecclesiology, Pilgram Marpeck, Vatican II and John Milbank." *Mennonite Quarterly Review* 78/1 (2004) 29–52.

———. *Christ in Our Midst: Incarnation, Church and Discipleship in the Theology of Pilgram Marpeck*. Kitchener, ON: Pandora, 2007.

———. "Pilgram Marpeck, Martin Luther and the Humanity of Christ." *Mennonite Quarterly Review* 61/2 (1987) 203–12.

Bonhoeffer, Dietrich. *Discipleship*. Edited by Geffrey B. Kelly and John D. Godsey. Translated by Barbara Green and Reinhard Krauss. Vol. 4 of *Dietrich Bonhoeffer Works*. Minneapolis: Fortress, 2003.

———. *Ethics*. Edited by Clifford Green. Translated by Reinhard Krauss, Douglas W. Stott, and Charles C. West. Vol. 6 of *Dietrich Bonhoeffer Works*. Minneapolis: Fortress, 2005.

———. *Life Together*. Edited by Geffrey B. Kelly. Translated by Daniel W. Bloesch and James H. Burtness. Vol. 5 of *Dietrich Bonhoeffer Works*. Minneapolis: Fortress, 2005.

———. *Sanctorum Communio*. Edited by Clifford Green. Translated by Reinhard Krauss and Nancy Lukens. Vol. 1 of *Dietrich Bonhoeffer Works*. Minneapolis: Fortress, 1998.

———. *Letters and Papers from Prison*. Edited by John W. de Gruchy. Translated by Isabel Best et al. Vol. 8 of *Dietrich Bonhoeffer Works*. Minneapolis: Fortress, 2010.

Bourdieu, Pierre. *The Logic of Practice*. Translated by Richard Nice. Stanford, CA: Stanford University Press, 1990.

Boyarin, Daniel. "Judaism as a Free Church: Footnotes to John Howard Yoder's *The Jewish-Christian Schism Revisited*." *Cross Currents* 56/4 (2007) 6–21.

Boyd, Stephen B. "Anabaptism and Social Radicalism in Strasbourg, 1528–1532: Pilgram Marpeck on Christian Social Responsibility." *Mennonite Quarterly Review* 63/1 (1989) 58–76.

Bradshaw, Paul, Maxwell E. Johnson, and L. Edward Phillips, editors. *The Apostolic Tradition: A Commentary*. Hermeneia. Minneapolis: Fortress, 2002.

Bibliography

Bradshaw, Paul F. *The Search for the Origins of Christian Worship: Sources and Methods for the Study of Early Liturgy.* 2nd ed. New York: Oxford University Press, 2002.

van Braght, Thieleman. *The Martyr's Mirror.* 2nd ed. Translated by Joseph F. Sohm. Scottdale, PA: Herald, 2001.

Brooks, Oscar Stephenson. *The Drama of Decision: Baptism in the New Testament.* Peabody, MA: Hendrickson, 1987.

Brown, Dale W. "Communal Ecclesiology: The Power of the Anabaptist Vision." *Theology Today* 36/1 (1979) 22–29.

Buckley, James L. "Christian Community, Baptism, and the Lord's Supper." In *The Cambridge Companion to Karl Barth,* edited by John Webster, 195–211. Cambridge, MA: Cambridge University Press, 2000.

Bulgakov, Sergius. *A Bulgakov Anthology.* Edited by James Pain and Nicolas Zernov. Philadelphia: Westminster, 1976.

Burgess, Andrew. "A Community of Love? Jesus as the Body of God and Robert Jenson's Trinitarian Thought." *International Journal of Systematic Theology* 6/3 (2004) 289–300.

Cabié, Robert. "Christian Initiation." In *The Church at Prayer: The Sacrament,* compiled and edited by Aimé Georges Martimort, translated by Matthew J. O'Connell, 11–100. Collegeville, MN: Liturgical, 1988.

"Called Together to be Peacemakers: A Report on the International Dialogue between the Catholic Church and Mennonite World Conference, 1998–2003." August, 2003. Online: http://www.vatican.va/roman_curia/pontifical_councils/chrstuni/mennonite-conference-docs/rc_pc_chrstuni_doc_20110324_mennonite_en.html.

Calvin, John. *The Institutes of the Christian Religion.* 2 vols. Edited by John T. McNeill. Translated by Ford Lewis Battles. Library of Christian Classics 21. Philadelphia, Westminster: 1960.

Camp, Lee. *Mere Discipleship: Radical Christianity in a Rebellious World.* 2nd ed. Grand Rapids: Brazos, 2008.

Caputo, John D. "The End of Ethics." In *The Blackwell Guide to Ethical Theory,* edited by Hugh LaFollette, 111–28. Malden, MA: Blackwell, 2000.

Carter, Craig. *Rethinking Christ and Culture: A Post-Christendom Perspective.* Grand Rapids: Brazos, 2006.

Cavanaugh, William T. *Theopolitical Imagination: Discovering the Liturgy as a Political Act in an Age of Global Consumerism.* London: T. & T. Clark, 2002.

———. *Torture and Eucharist: Theology, Politics, and the Body of Christ.* Oxford: Blackwell, 1998.

Clowney, Edmund P. *The Church.* Downers Grove, IL: IVP, 1995.

Colwell, John E. *Promise & Presence: An Exploration of Sacramental Theology.* Milton Keynes, UK: Paternoster, 2005.

———. "A Radical Church: A Reappraisal of Anabaptist Ecclesiology." *Tyndale Bulletin* 38 (1987) 119–41.

Congar, Yves. *The Mystery of the Temple.* Westminster, MD: Newman, 1958.

Connolly, William A. *Why I Am Not a Secularist.* Minneapolis: University of Minnesota Press, 1999.

———. *Capitalism and Christianity, American Style.* Durham, NC: Duke University Press, 2008.

Covington, Sarah. "Paratextual Strategies in Thieleman van Braght's Martyr's Mirror." *Book History* 9 (2006) 1–29.

Bibliography

Crisp, Oliver D. "Robert Jenson on the Pre-Existence of Christ." *Modern Theology* 23/1 (2007) 27–45.
Cullmann, Oscar. *Baptism in the New Testament*. Translated by J. K. S. Reid. Philadelphia: Westminster, 1950.
Cyril of Jerusalem. *The Catechetical Lectures of St. Cyril*. Oxford: Parker, 1872.
Dalton, Andrea M. "A Sacramental Believers Church: Pilgram Marpeck and the (Un)mediated Presence of God." In *New Perspectives in Believers Church Ecclesiology*, edited by Abe Dueck, Helmut Harder, and Karl Koop, 223–36. Winnipeg: CMU Press, 2010.
Davies, J. G. *The Architectural Setting of Baptism*. London: Barrie & Rockliff, 1962.
Demson, David E. "'Church Practices': Sacraments or Invocations? Hütter's Proposal in Light of Barth's." *Toronto Journal of Theology* 18/1 (2002) 79–99.
Dintaman, Stephen. "The Spiritual Poverty of the Anabaptist Vision." *Conrad Grebel Review* 10/2 (1992) 205–8.
Doerksen, V. "Writings of Pilgram Marpeck." *Mennonite Quarterly Review* 53/1 (1979) 84–85.
Doyle, Dennis M. "The Contribution of a Lifetime: George Lindbeck's *The Church in a Postliberal Age*." *Modern Theology* 21/1 (2005) 157–62.
Duesing, Jason G. "Pilgrim Marpeck's Christian Baptism." *Faith and Mission* 23/3 (2006) 3–15.
Dujarier, Michael. *A History of the Catechumenate: The First Six Centuries*. Chicago: Sadlier, 1979.
Dulles, Avery. *Models of the Church*. Rev. ed. New York: Doubleday, 1991.
Dunn, James D.G. *Unity and Diversity in the New Testament*. Philadelphia: SCM, 1990.
Durnbaugh, Donald F. "Free Churches, Baptists, and Ecumenism: Origins and Implications." *Journal of Ecumenical Studies* 17/2 (1980) 3–20.
Durnbaugh, Donald F. *The Believers' Church: The History and Character of Radical Protestantism*. New York: MacMillan, 1968.
Dyck, C. J. "Anabaptist Baptism: A Representative Study." *Church History* 37/2 (1968) 216–17.
Eckerstorfer, Bernhard A. "The One Church in the Postmodern World: Reflections on the Life and Thought of George Lindbeck." *Pro Ecclesia* 13/4 (2004) 399–423.
Enns, Fernando. *The Peace Church and the Ecumenical Community: Ecclesiology and the Ethics of Nonviolence*. Kitchener, ON: Pandora, 2007.
———. "Believers Church Ecclesiology: A Trinitarian Foundation and Its Implications." In *New Perspectives in Believers Church Ecclesiology*, edited by Abe Dueck, Helmut Harder, and Karl Koop, 107–24. Winnipeg: CMU Press, 2010.
———. "Believers Church Ecclesiology: A Vital Alternative within the Ecumenical Family." In *New Perspectives in Believers Church Ecclesiology*, edited by Abe Dueck, Helmut Harder, and Karl Koop, 107–24. Winnipeg: CMU Press, 2010.
Erickson, Millard. *Christian Theology*. 2nd ed. Grand Rapids: Baker, 1998.
Fahey, Michael. "Sacraments." In *The Oxford Handbook of Systematic Theology*, edited by John Webster, Kathryn Tanner, and Ian Torrance, 267–84. Oxford: Oxford University Press, 2007.
Farrow, Douglas. *Ascension and Ecclesia: On the Significance of the Doctrine of the Ascension for Ecclesiology and Christian Cosmology*. Grand Rapids: Eerdmans, 1999.
Fast Dueck, Irma. "(Re)learning to Swim in Baptismal Waters: Contemporary Challenges in the Believers Church Tradition." In *New Perspectives in Believers*

Church Ecclesiology, Edited by Abe Dueck, Helmut Harder, and Karl Koop, 237–55. Winnipeg: CMU Press, 2010.

Ferguson, Everett. "Inscriptions and the Origin of Infant Baptism." *Journal of Theological Studies* 30/1 (1979) 37–46.

———. *Baptism in the Early Church: History, Theology, and Liturgy in the First Five Centuries*. Grand Rapids: Eerdmans, 2009.

Fiddes, Paul S. *Reflections on the Water: Understanding God and the World Through the Baptism of Believers*. Macon, GA: Smyth & Helwys, 1996.

———. *Participating in God: A Pastoral Doctrine of the Trinity*. London: Darton, Longman & Todd, 2000.

Finger, Thomas N. "Pilgram Marpeck and the Christus Victor Motif." *Mennonite Quarterly Review* 78/1 (2004) 53–77.

Finger, Thomas N. *Christian Theology*. Vol. 2. Scottdale, PA: Herald, 1989.

———. "Christus Victor and the Creeds: Some Historical Considerations." *Mennonite Quarterly Review* 72/1 (1998) 31–51.

———. *A Contemporary Anabaptist Theology: Biblical, Historical, Constructive*. Downers Grove, IL: InterVarsity, 2004.

Initial Mennonite Response"Initial Mennonite Response." In *On Baptism: Mennonite-Catholic Theological Colloquium, 2001–2002*. Edited by Gerald W. Schlabach, 63–79. Kitchener, ON: Pandora, 2004.

Finn, Thomas. *Early Christian Baptism and the Catechumenate*. 2 vols. Message of the Fathers of the Church 5–6. Collegeville, MN: Liturgical, 1992.

Friedmann, Robert. "Ecumenical Dialogue between Anabaptists and Catholics." *Mennonite Quarterly Review* 40/4 (1966) 260–265.

Friesen, Dwayne K. *Artists, Citizens, Philosophers: Seeking the Peace of the City: An Anabaptist Theology of Culture*. Scottdale, PA: Herald, 2000.

Funk, Joseph. *The Reviewer Reviewed or, Thoughts and Meditations on the Sacrifices, Offerings, Emblems, Figures, and Types, of the Old Testament, Compared, in Their Fulfillment with the Antitypes in the New Testament*. Mountain Valley, VA: Funk & Sons, 1857.

Ganoczy, Alexander. *Becoming Christian: A Theology of Baptism as the Sacrament of Human History*. Translated by John G. Lunch. Toronto: Paulist, 1976.

Garrett Jr., James Leo. "Baptists Concerning Baptism: Review and Preview." *Southwestern Journal of Theology* 43/2 (2001) 52–67.

Gavin, Frank S.B. *The Jewish Antecedents of the Christian Sacraments*. New York: Ktav, 1969.

Gelpi, Donald. "Adult Conversion and Initiation." In *Adult Conversion and Initiation*. Vol. 1 of *Committed Worship: A Sacramental Theology for Converting Adult Christians*. Collegeville, MN: Liturgical, 1993.

George, Timothy. "The Southern Baptists." In *Baptism and Church: A Believers' Church Vision*, edited by Merle D. Strege, 39–51. Grand Rapids: Sagamore, 1986.

George, Timothy. *Theology of the Reformers*. Nashville: Broadman & Holman, 1988.

Green, Clifford. "Editor's Introduction to the English Edition." In Dietrich Bonhoeffer, *Ethics*, edited by Clifford Green, translated by Reinhard Krauss, Douglas W. Stott, and Charles C. West, 1–44. Vol. 6 of *Dietrich Bonhoeffer Works*. Minneapolis: Fortress, 2005.

Grenz, Stanley. *Theology for the Community of God*. Grand Rapids: Eerdmans, 1994.

Grimes, Ronald L. *Beginnings in Ritual Studies*. Lanham, MD: University Press of America, 1982.

Bibliography

Groarke, Louis. "What is Freedom? Why Christianity and Theoretical Liberalism Cannot be Reconciled." *Heythrop Journal* 47/2 (2006) 257–74.

Harder, Helmut. "Review Essay: Fernando Enns on Mennonite Ecumenism." *Mennonite Quarterly Review* 79/2 (2005) 251–59.

Harper, Brad and Paul Louis Metzger. *Exploring Ecclesiology: An Evangelical and Ecumenical Introduction.* Grand Rapids: Brazos, 2009.

Hart, David Bentley. *The Doors of the Sea: Where Was God in the Tsunami?* Grand Rapids: Eerdmans, 2005.

Harvey, Barry. *Can These Bones Live? A Catholic Baptist Engagement with Ecclesiology, Hermeneutics, and Social Theory.* Grand Rapids: Brazos, 2008.

Hauerwas, Stanley, and James Fodor. "Remaining in Babylon: Oliver O'Donovan's Defense of Christendom." In *Wilderness Wanderings: Probing Twentieth-Century Theology and Philosophy,* 199–224. Boulder, CO: Westview, 1997.

Hauerwas, Stanley. *A Community of Character: Toward a Constructive Christian Social Ethic.* Notre Dame, IN: University of Notre Dame Press, 1981.

———. *The Peaceable Kingdom.* Notre Dame: University of Notre Dame Press, 1983.

———. *Sanctify Them in the Truth.* London: T. & T. Clark, 1998.

———. "Christianity: It's Not a Religion: It's an Adventure." In *The Hauerwas Reader,* edited by John Berkman and Michael Cartwright, 522–35. Durham, NC: Duke University Press, 2001.

———. *With the Grain of the Universe: The Church's Witness and Natural Theology.* Grand Rapids: Brazos, 2001.

Haymes, Brian. "Baptism: A Question of Belief and Age?" *Perspectives in Religious Studies* 27/1 (2000) 125–30.

Healy, Nicholas. *Church, World and the Christian Life: A Practical-Prophetic Ecclesiology.* Cambridge, UK: Cambridge University Press, 2000.

———. "Practices and the New Ecclesiology: Misplaced Concreteness?" *International Journal of Systematic Theology* 5/3 (2003) 287–308.

Holm, Jacob. "G.W.F. Hegel's Impact on Dietrich Bonhoeffer's Early Theology." *Studia Theologica* 54/1 (2002) 68–72.

Hostetler, John A. *Amish Society.* 4th ed. Baltimore: Johns Hopkins University Press, 1980.

Hovey, Craig. "Story and Eucharist: Postliberal Reflections on Anabaptist Nachfolge." *Mennonite Quarterly Review* 75/3 (2001) 315–24.

Hubmaier, Balthasar. *Balthasar Hubmaier: Theologian of Anabaptism.* Translated and edited by H. Wayne Pipkin and John H. Yoder. Scottdale, PA: Herald, 1989.

Hütter, Reinhard. *Suffering Divine Things: Theology as Church Practice.* Grand Rapids: Eerdmans, 2000.

Jenson, Robert. *Systematic Theology.* New York: Oxford University Press, 1997–1999.

———. *Visible Words: The Interpretation and Practice of Christian Sacraments.* Philadelphia: Fortress, 1978.

———. "The Bride of Christ." In *Critical Issues in Ecclesiology: Essays in Honor of Carl E. Braaten,* edited by Alberta L. García and Susan K. Wood, 1–5. Grand Rapids: Eerdmans, 2011.

Jeremias, Joachim. *Infant Baptism in the First Four Centuries.* Translated by David Cairns. Philadelphia: Westminster, 1960.

———. *The Origins of Infant Baptism.* London: SCM, 1963.

Jeschke, Marlin. *Believers Baptism for Children of the Church.* Scottdale, PA: Herald, 1983.

Bibliography

Johnson, Maxwell E. *The Rites of Christian Initiation: Their Evolution and Interpretation.* Rev. ed. Collegeville, MN: Liturgical, 2007.

Jones, Joe. *A Grammar of Christian Faith.* Vol. 2. New York: Rowman & Littlefield, 2002.

Jost, Lynn. "Mennonite Brethren Theology of Baptism." *Direction* 33/1 (2004) 21–32.

Juhnke, James C. "Gemeindechristentum and Bible Doctrine: Two Mennonite Visions of the Early Twentieth Century." *Mennonite Quarterly Review* 57/3 (1983) 206–21.

———. Review of *Mennonite Tent Revivals, Howard Hammer and Myron Augsburger, 1952–1962* by James O. Lehmann. *Mennonite Quarterly Review* 77/3 (2003) 484–85.

Kanagy, Conrad L. *Road Signs for the Journey: A Profile of Mennonite Church USA.* Scottdale, PA: Herald, 2007.

Kärkkäinen, Veli-Matti. *An Introduction to Ecclesiology: Ecumenical, Historical and Global Perspectives.* Downers Grove, IL: IVP Academic, 2002.

Kauffman, J. Howard and Leland Harder. *Anabaptists Four Centuries Later: A Profile of Five Mennonite and Brethren in Christ Denominations.* Scottdale, PA: Herald, 1975.

Kavanagh, Aidan, et al. *Initiation Theology: Ecumenical Insights.* Edited by James Schmeiser. Toronto: Anglican Book Centre, 1978.

Kavanagh, Aidan. "Life-Cycle Events and Civil Ritual." In *Christian Initiation: Ecumenical Insights*, edited by James Schmeiser, 9–22. Toronto: Anglican Book Centre, 1978.

Keim, Albert N. *Harold S. Bender 1897–1962.* Scottdale, PA: Harold, 1998.

Kelly, Geffrey B. *"Editor's Introduction."* In *Life Together: Prayerbook of the Bible*, edited by Geffrey B. Kelly, translated by Daniel W. Bloesch and James H. Burtness, 3–23. Vol. 5 of *Dietrich Bonhoeffer Works*. Minneapolis: Fortress, 2005.

Kenneson, Phillip D. *Beyond Sectarianism: Re-Imagining Church and World.* Harrisburg, PA: Trinity, 1999.

Klaassen, Walter and William Klassen. *Marpeck: A Life of Dissent and Conformity.* Waterloo, ON: Herald, 2008.

Klaassen, Walter. "Church Discipline and the Spirit in Pilgram Marpeck." In *Geest in het geding*, 169–80. Alphen aan den Rijn: Willink, 1978.

———. *Anabaptism: Neither Catholic nor Protestant.* Kitchener, ON: Pandora, 2001.

Klassen, William. "Pilgram Marpeck: Liberty Without Coercion." In *Profiles of Radical Reformers*, 168–77. Kitchener, ON: Herald, 1982.

———. "The Limits of Political Authority as Seen by Pilgram Marpeck." *Mennonite Quarterly Review* 56/4 (1982) 342–64.

———. "Pilgram Marpeck and Our Use of Power." *Conrad Grebel Review* 17/1 (1999) 42–50.

———. "The Legacy of the Marpeck Community in Anabaptist Scholarship." *Mennonite Quarterly Review* 78/1 (2004) 7–28.

Koelpin, Arnold J. "On Baptism, the Challenge of Anabaptist Baptism and the Lutheran Confession." In *No Other Gospel*, 255–77. Milwaukee: Northwestern, 1980.

Koop, Karl *Anabaptist-Mennonite Confessions of Faith: The Development of a Tradition.* Kitchener, ON: Pandora, 2004.

Kraus, C. Norman. *God our Savior: Theology in a Christological Mode.* Scottdale, PA: Herald, 1991.

Kraybill, Donald B. *The Riddle of Amish Culture.* Rev. ed. Baltimore: Johns Hopkins University Press, 2001.

———. *Concise Encyclopedia of Amish, Brethren, Hutterites and Mennonites.* Baltimore, Johns Hopkins Press, 2010.

Bibliography

Kreider, Alan. *The Change of Conversion and the Origin of Christendom*. Harrisburg, PA: Trinity, 1999.

———— editor. *The Origins of Christendom in the West*. London: T. & T. Clark, 2001.

Kroeker, Travis. "Why O'Donovan's Christendom is not Constantinian and Yoder's Voluntaritey is not Hobbessian: A Debate in Theological Politics Re-Defined." *The Annual of the Society of Christian Ethics* (2000) 41–64.

Leithart, Peter. "Infant Baptism in History: An Unfinished Tragi-Comedy." In *The Case for Covenantal Infant Baptism*, edited by Gregg Strawbridge, 246–62. Phillipsburg, NJ: P. & R., 2003.

————. *Defending Constantine: The Twilight of and Empire and the Dawn of Christendom*. Downers Grove, IL: InterVarsity, 2010.

Lindbeck, George. "Ecumenism and the Future of Belief." In *The Church in a Postliberal Age*, edited by James J. Buckley, 91–105. Grand Rapids: Eerdmans, 2002.

Lossky, Vladimir. *The Mystical Theology of the Eastern Church*. Crestwood, NY: St. Vladimir's Seminary Press, 1976.

Lumpkin, William Latane. *A History of Immersion*. Nashville: Broadman, 1962.

Luther, Martin. *The Babylonian Captivity of the Church*. Translated by A. T. W. Steinhauser, Frederick C. Ahrens, and Abdel Ross Wentz. Vol. 36 of *Luther's Works*. Philadelphia: Fortress, 1959.

————. *Lectures on Romans: Glosses and Scholia*. Edited by Hilton C. Oswald. Vol. 25 of *Luther's Works*. Saint Louis: Concordia, 1972.

MacIntyre, Alasdair. *After Virtue: A Study in Moral Theory*. Notre Dame: University of Notre Dame Press, 1984.

————. *Whose Justice? Which Rationality?* Notre Dame: University of Notre Dame Press, 1988.

Mangina, Joseph. "Bearing the Marks of Jesus: The Church in the Economy of Salvation in Barth and Hauerwas." *Scottish Journal of Theology* 52/3 (1999) 269–305.

————. *Karl Barth: Theologian of Christian Witness* Louisville: Westminster John Knox, 2004.

Marpeck, Pilgram. *The Writings of Pilgram Marpeck*. Translated and edited by William Klassen and Walter Klaassen. Scottdale, PA: Herald, 1978.

————. *Later Writings by Pilgram Marpeck and His Circle*. Translated and edited by Walter Klassen, Werner O. Packull, and John Rempel. Kitchener, ON: Pandora, 1999.

Marsh, Charles. "Bonhoeffer on Heidegger and Togetherness." *Modern Theology* 8/3 (1992) 263–83.

Marsh, Charles. "Human Community and Divine Presence: Dietrich Bonhoeffer's Theological Critique of Hegel." *Scottish Journal of Theology* 45/4 (1992) 427–48.

Martens, Paul. "The Problematic Development of the Sacraments in the Thought of John Howard Yoder." *Conrad Grebel Review* 24/3 (2006) 65–77.

————."Universal History and a Not-Particularly Christian Particularity: Jeremiah and John Howard Yoder's Social Gospel." In *Power and Practices: Engaging the Work of John Howard Yoder*, edited by Jeremy M. Bergen and Anthony G. Siegrist, 131–46. Scottdale, PA: Herald, 2009.

Martimort, Aime Georges. *The Church at Prayer: An Introduction to the Liturgy*. Collegeville, MN: Liturgical, 1988.

Mattes, Mark C. "An Analysis and Assessment of Robert Jenson's Systematic Theology." *Lutheran Quarterly* 14 (2000) 463–94.

McClendon, James. "Baptism as a Performative Sign." *Theology Today* 23/3 (1966) 403–16.

———. *Doctrine*. Vol. 2 of *Systematic Theology*. Nashville: Abingdon, 1994.
———. *Ethics*. Vol. 1 of *Systematic Theology*. Nashville: Abingdon, 2002.
McDonnell, Killian, and George T. Montague. *Christian Initiation and Baptism in the Holy Spirit: Evidence from the First Eight Centuries*. Collegeville, MN: Liturgical, 1991.
McFarland, Ian A. "The Body of Christ: Rethinking a Classic Theological Model." *International Journal of Systematic Theology* 7/3 (2005) 225–46.
Mennonite General Conference, "The Nurture and Evangelism of Children: The Position of the Mennonite Church as Adopted by Mennonite General Conference at Hesston, Kansas, Aug. 26 1955," Mennonite General Conference Archive, 1898–1971, box 6, file 12, MC USA Archives, Goshen, IN.
Metaxas, Eric. *Bonhoeffer: Pastor, Martyr, Prophet and Spy*. Nashville: Nelson, 2010.
Migliore, Daniel L. *Faith Seeking Understanding: An Introduction to Christian Theology*. 2nd ed. Grand Rapids: Eerdmans, 2004.
Milavec, Aaron, translator. *The Didache: Text, Translation, Analysis and Commentary*. Collegeville, MN: Liturgical, 2004.
Milbank, John. *Theology and Social Theory: Beyond Secular Reason*. 2nd ed. Malden, MA: Blackwell, 2006.
Miller, Larry. "The Lutheran Dialogue with Mennonites: An Example of a dialogue with a Free Church (With a Postscript on Visions of Unity)." *Mennonite Quarterly Review* 86/3 (2012) 293–314.
Miller, Marlin E. "The Mennonites." In *Baptism and Church: A Believers' Church Vision*, edited by Merle D. Strege, 15–28. Grand Rapids: Sagamore, 1986.
Miller, Mary, editor and translator. *Our Heritage, Hope, and Faith*. Sugar Creek, OH: Carlisle, 2000.
Minear, Paul S. *Images of the Church in the New Testament*. 1960. Reprint, Louisville: Westminster John Knox, 2004.
Moody, Dale. *Baptism: Foundation for Christian Unity*. Philadelphia: Westminster, 1967.
Moore, John H. *Trine Immersion Traced to the Apostles*. 4th ed. Lanark, IL: Brethren at Work, 1877.
Newbigin, Lesslie. *The Household of God*. New York: Friendship, 1954.
Niebuhr, H. Richard. *Christ and Culture*. New York: Harper & Row, 1951.
Niederwimmer, Kurt, and Linda A. Maloney, translators, Harold W. Attridge, editor. *The Didache: A Commentary on the Didache*. Minneapolis: Fortress, 1998.
Nienkirchen, Charles. "Reviewing the Case for a Non-Separatist Ecclesiology in Early Swiss Anabaptism." *Mennonite Quarterly Review* 56/3 (1982) 227–41.
Noll, Mark A. *A History of Christianity in the United States and Canada*. Grand Rapids: Eerdmans, 1992.
Nolt, Steven M. *A History of the Amish*. Intercourse, PA: Good, 2003.
Nussbaum, Martha C. *Aristotle's De Motu Animalium*. Princeton: Princeton University Press, 1978.
O'Connor, Flannery. "The River." In *Flannery O'Connor: The Complete Stories*. New York: Farrar, Straus & Giroux, 1971.
———. *The Violent Bear it Away*. In *Three by Flannery O'Connor*. New York: Signet Classic, 1983.
Oden, Thomas, C. *After Modernity . . . What?* Grand Rapids: Zondervan, 1990.
Ollenburger, Ben C. "Mennonite Theology: A Conversation around the Creeds." *Mennonite Quarterly Review* 66/1 (1992) 57–89.
1001 Questions and Answers on the Christian Life. Aylmer, ON: Pathway, 1992.

Bibliography

Packull, Werner O. "Pilgram Marpeck: Uncovering of the Babylonian Whore and Other Anonymous Anabaptist Tracts." *Mennonite Quarterly Review* 67/3 (1993) 351–55.
Pipkin, H. Wayne, "The Baptismal Theology of Balthasar Hubmaier." *Mennonite Quarterly Review* 65/1 (1991) 34–53.
Putnam, Robert D. *Bowling Alone*. New York: Simon & Shuster, 2000.
Quinter, James and N. A. M'Conmell. *A Debate on Trine Immersion, the Lord's Supper and Feet-Washing*. Compiled by J. L. M'Creery. Cincinnati: Bosworth, 1867.
Quinter, James. *A Vindication of Trine Immersion as the Apostolic Form of Christian Baptism*. Elgin, IL: Brethren, 1900.
Radner, Ephraim. *The End of the Church: A Pneumatology of Christian Division in the West*. Grand Rapids: Eerdmans, 1998.
Rahner, Karl. *The Church and the Sacraments*. New York: Herder & Herder, 1963.
Rasmusson, Arne. *The Church as* Polis. Notre Dame, IN: University of Notre Dame Press, 1995.
Reimer, A. James. *Mennonites and Classical Theology: Dogmatic Foundations for Christian Ethics*. Kitchener, ON: Pandora, 2001.
Rempel, John D. *The Lord's Supper in Anabaptism: A Study in the Christology of Balthasar Hubmaier, Pilgram Marpeck, and Dirk Philips*. Scottdale, PA: Herald, 1993.
———. *Minister's Manual*. Scottdale, PA: Herald, 1998.
Rorty, Richard. *Philosophy and Social Hope*. New York: Penguin, 1999.
Rothkegel, Martin. "Pilgram Marpeck and the Fellows of the Covenant: The Short and Fragmentary History of the Rise and Decline of an Anabaptist Denominational Network," *Mennonite Quarterly Review* 85/1 (2011) 7–36.
Sattler, Michael. "Schleitheim Brotherly Union." In *The Legacy of Michael Sattler*, edited and translated by John Howard Yoder, 36 - 43. Scottdale PA: Herald, 1973.
Sawatsky, Rodney J. "History and Ideology: American Mennonite Identity Definition through History." PhD diss., Princeton University, 1977.
Scharen, Christian Batalden. "'Judicious Narratives', or Ethnography as Ecclesiology." *Scottish Journal of Theology* 58/2 (2005) 125–42.
Schillebeeckx, Edward. *Christ the Sacrament of the Encounter with God*. New York: Sheed & Ward, 1963.
Schlabach, Gerald W., editor. *On Baptism: Mennonite-Catholic Theological Colloquim, 2001–2002*, The Bridgefolk Series. Kitchener, ON: Pandora, 2004.
Schlabach, Theron F. "Mennonites, Revivalism, Modernity—1683–1850." *Church History* 48/4 (1979) 398–415
Schmemann, Alexander. *Of Water and the Spirit*. London: SPCK, 1974.
Second Vatican Council, *Lumen Gentium: Dogmatic Constitution of the Church* (1964). Online: http://www.vatican.va/archive/hist_councils/ii_ vatican_council/documents/vat-ii_const_19641121_lumen-gentium_en.html.
Shilbrack, Kevin, ed. *Thinking Through Rituals: Philosophical Perspectives*. New York: Routledge, 2004.
Siebert, Steven. "Reading Marpeck for the First Time." *Mennonite Quarterly Review* 78/1 (2004) 79–107.
Siegrist, Anthony G. "Baptismal Robes or Camel's Hair? A Theological Response to the 'Politics of Becoming.'" *Conrad Grebel Review* 26/3 (2008) 27–41.
Simons, Menno *The Complete Writings of Menno Simon*. Translated by Leonard Verduin. Edited by J. C. Wenger. Scottdale, PA: Herald, 1956.

Smith, Christian. *Soul Searching: The Religious and Spiritual Lives of American Teenagers.* New York: Oxford University Press, 2005.

Smith, James K. A. *Desiring the Kingdom: Worship, Worldview, and Cultural Formation.* Grand Rapids: Baker Academic, 2009.

Snyder, C. Arnold. "The Monastic Origins of Swiss Anabaptist Sectarianism." *Mennonite Quarterly Review* 57/1 (1983) 5–26.

———. *The Life and Thought of Michael Sattler.* Scottdale, PA: Herald, 1984.

———. "An Anabaptist Vision for Peace: Spirituality and Peace in Pilgrim Marpeck." *Conrad Grebel Review* 10 (1992) 187–203.

———. *Anabaptist History and Theology: An Introduction.* Kitchener, ON: Pandora, 1995.

———. *Following in the Footsteps of Christ: The Anabaptist Tradition.* Maryknoll, NY: Orbis, 2004.

Stephens, W. P. *The Theology of Huldrych Zwingli.* Oxford: Oxford University Press, 1988.

Stout, Tracey Mark. "Free and Faithful Witness: Karl Barth on Believers' Baptism and the Church's Relation to the State." *Perspectives in Religious Studies* 33/2 (2006) 173–86.

Taylor, Charles. *Sources of the Self: The Making of the Modern Identity.* Cambridge, MA: Harvard University Press, 1989.

The Book of Common Prayer. New York: The Church Hymnal Corporation, 1979.

Toews, Miriam. *A Complicated Kindness.* New York: Counterpoint, 2004.

Vander Zee, Leonard J. *Recovering the Sacraments for Evangelical Worship: Christ, Baptism and the Lord's Supper.* Downers Grove, IL: 2004.

Volf, Miroslav. *After Our Likeness: The Church as the Image of the Trinity.* Grand Rapids: Eerdmans, 1998.

Ware, Timothy (Kallistos). *The Orthodox Church.* New York: Penguin, 1963.

Weaver, Alain Epp. "After Politics: John Howard Yoder, Body Politics, and the Witnessing Church." *The Review of Politics* 61/4 (1999) 637–73.

Weaver, J. Denny. "Christus Victor, Ecclesiology and Christology." *Mennonite Quarterly Review* 68/3 (1994) 277–90.

———. "Some Theological Implications of Christus Victor." *Mennonite Quarterly Review* 69/4 (1994) 483–99.

———. "Violence in Christian Theology." *CrossCurrents* 51/2 (2001) 150–76.

———. "How My Mind Has Changed." *Mennonite Life* 60/2 (2005). Online: http://www.bethelks.edu/mennonitelife/2005June/weaver.php.

Webster, John. *Barth's Moral Theology: Human Action in Barth's Thought.* Grand Rapids: Eerdmans, 1998.

Weibe, Dallas. "Can a Mennonite be an Atheist?" *Conrad Grebel Review* 16/3 (1998) 122–32.

Wenger Shenk, Sarah. *Anabaptist Ways of Knowing: A Conversation about Tradition-Based Critical Education.* Telford, PA: Cascadia, 2003.

Wenger, John C. "The Theology of Pilgram Marpeck." *Mennonite Quarterly Review* 12/4 (1938) 205–56.

Wiebe, Rudy. *Peace Shall Destroy Many.* Toronto: Vintage, 2001.

Wood, Ralph C. *Flannery O'Connor and the Christ-Haunted South.* Grand Rapids: Eerdmans, 2004.

Wright, David. "How Controversial Was the Development of Infant Baptism in the Early Church?" In *Church, Word, and Spirit: Essays in Honor of Geoffrey W. Bromiley*, edited by J.E. Bradley and R. A. Muller, 46–53. Grand Rapids: Eerdmans, 1987.

Bibliography

———. "The Origins of Infant Baptism—Child Believers' Baptism?" *Scottish Journal of Theology* 40/ 1 (1987) 1–23.

———. "At What Ages Were People Baptized in the Early Centuries?" In *Biblica et Apocrypha, Ascetica, Liturgica*, edited by Elizabeth A. Livingstone, 389–94. Studia Patristica 30. Louvain: Peeters, 1997.

———. "Did the Apostolic Church Baptise Babies? A Seismological Approach." *Tyndale Bulletin* 55/1 (2004) 109–30.

———. *What Has Infant Baptism Done to Baptism? An Enquiry at the End of Christendom*. Milton Keynes, UK: Paternoster, 2005.

Yeago, David. "Apostolic Faith." Part 2. Unpublished manuscript, 2007.

Yocum, John. *Ecclesial Mediation in Karl Barth*. Burlington, VT: Ashgate, 2004.

Yoder, John Howard, "Reinhold Niebuhr and Christian Pacifism." *Mennonite Quarterly Review* 29/2 (1955) 101–17.

———. "Sacrament as Social Process: Christ the Transformer of Culture." *Theology Today* 48/1 (1991) 33–44.

———. *The Royal Priesthood: Essays Ecclesiological and Ecumenical*. Edited by Michael G. Cartwright. Scottdale, PA: Herald, 1998.

———. *Body Politics: Five Practices of the Christian Community before the Watching World*. Scottdale, PA: Herald, 2001.

———. *Preface to Theology: Christology and Theological Method*. Grand Rapids: Brazos, 2002.

———. *Anabaptism and Reformation in Switzerland*. Translated by David Carl Stassen and C. Arnold Snyder. Kitchener, ON: Pandora, 2004.

———. *The Jewish-Christian Schism Revisited*. Edited by Michael G. Cartwright and Peter Ochs. Scottdale, PA: Herald, 2008.

———. *Christian Attitudes to War, Peace, and Revolution*. Edited by Theodore J. Koontz and Andy Alexis-Baker. Grand Rapids: Brazos, 2009.

York, Tripp. *The Purple Crown: The Politics of Martyrdom*. Scottdale, PA: Herald, 2007.

Zimmerman, Earl. *Practicing the Politics of Jesus: The Origin and Significance of John Howard Yoder's Social Ethics*. Telford, PA: Cascadia, 2007.

Zizioulas, John D. *Being as Communion*. Crestwood, NY: St. Vladimir's Seminary Press, 1985.

www.ingramcontent.com/pod-product-compliance
Lightning Source LLC
Chambersburg PA
CBHW070318230426
43663CB00011B/2172